AIRCRAFT
HANDBOOK

ENLARGED 4th EDITION

Standard

AIRCRAFT
HANDBOOK

ENLARGED 4th EDITION

EDITED BY LARRY REITHMAIER;
ORIGINALLY COMPILED AND EDITED BY
STUART LEAVELL AND STANLEY BUNGAY

AERO
An imprint of TAB BOOKS
Blue Ridge Summit, PA

FOURTH EDITION
SIXTH PRINTING

© 1952, 1958, 1980, and 1986 by **AERO PUBLISHERS, INC.**
Published by TAB BOOKS
TAB BOOKS is a division of McGraw-Hill, Inc.

Printed in the United States of America. All rights reserved. The publisher takes no responsibility for the use of any of the materials or methods described in this book, nor for the products thereof.

Library of Congress Cataloging-in-Publication Data

Reithmaier, L. W. (Larrence W.), 1921-
    Standard aircraft handbook.

    Includes index.
    1. Airplanes—Design and construction.
I. Leavell, Stuart. II. Bungay, Stanley. III. Title.
TL671.28.R45 1986   629.134′2   86-6017
ISBN 0-8306-8812-9 (soft)

TAB BOOKS offers software for sale. For information and a catalog, please contact TAB Software Department, Blue Ridge Summit, PA 17294-0850.

Questions regarding the content of this book should be addressed to:

Reader Inquiry Branch
TAB BOOKS
Blue Ridge Summit, PA 17294-0850

Contents

Introduction

In keeping with the policy of maintaining the *Standard Aircraft Handbook* up-to-date, this fourth edition has been prepared. Like the third edition, all chapters have been revised to some extent.

The chapter on riveting has been revised to eliminate some outdated material, and the section on blind rivets has been expanded consistent with the more extensive use of blind rivets and their advanced installation procedures. Also, the section on hi-shear rivets has been expanded.

Due to the wide use of titanium and high-strength fasteners in the assembly of high performance aircraft, the bolts and fasteners chapter has been revised extensively. The "standard" AN bolts and nuts are seldom used on present-day jet aircraft.

The chapter on tools and their proper use has been expanded to include general purpose hand tools and metal fabricating shop equipment.

The assembly and installation methods chapter has been expanded to include updated aircraft control cable data and additional aircraft plumbing material. Electrical wiring and installation has been expanded and is now a separate chapter.

The chapter on materials and fabricating was extensively revised in the third edition. Additional clarifying information only is included in this fourth edition.

The loft and template chapter was eliminated since it was essentially outdated based on present-day practices. Appropriate material from this chapter was incorporated into the aircraft drawings chapter.

Additional standard parts are included in this chapter to account for the many patented but "standardized" fasteners used in the assembly of high-performance aircraft.

The *Standard Aircraft Handbook* is presented in shop terms for the aviation mechanic engaged in building, maintaining, overhauling, or repairing all-metal aircraft. It is also an excellent guide for the student mechanic.

Basic shop techniques and procedures such as drilling and riveting are described with emphasis on the requirements of specialized fasteners as used on high-performance aircraft. Although simple rivets and standard AN hex head bolts are still to be found, a myriad of fasteners is now available for high-strength and/or high-temperature applications. Many of these fasteners are patented and referred to by their trade names such as "Cherrylock®," "Hi-Shear® ," and "Hi-Lok® ," to name a few. Titanium rivets and bolts are increasingly used on jet aircraft because of their high strength at high temperatures combined with low weight.

The chapters on aircraft plumbing, electrical wiring, materials and fabrication, and aircraft drawings are more general in nature inasmuch as complete books could be written on each subject. These chapters emphasize the installation of plumbing and wiring, for example, rather than their fabrication.

A chapter on standard parts is provided with an explanation of the various AN, MS, and NAS standards the mechanic is confronted with. In the recent past, these parts—often called "hardware"—were generic in nature, not proprietary designs, and therefore manufactured according to standard specifications by many manufacturers. Today, many items, particularly fasteners, are patented even though a "standard," such as NAS, has been assigned.

The procedures and practices covered in this handbook are general and applicable to any aircraft. It is not intended, however, to replace the manufacturer's instructions, specifications, and approved practices.

It is assumed that readers of this handbook already have a general knowledge of aircraft and their construction.

Sources of data for this manual were obtained from the following manufacturers of aircraft, tools, and supplies:

AIMSCO
Van Dusen Aircraft Supplies
Hi-shear Corporation
Snap-on Tools Corporation
L.S. Starrett Company
SPS Aerospace Products Division
Standard Pressed Steel Company
Townsend Textron (boots, cherry fasteners)
Dzus Fastener Company, Inc.
The Aluminum Association
Chicago Pneumatic Tool Division
Aeroquip Corporation
Phillips Screw Company
Bild Industries, Inc.
Lufkin Rule Company
Lockheed-California Company
U.S. Industrial Tool and Supply Company

Also used was material from various FAA publications.

Chapter 1
Riveting

METHODS OF RIVETING

One of the most important phases of the airplane assembly is the proper riveting of the various parts into a tight and efficient joint. The driving of the rivets is accomplished by any one of several methods, and the use of various tools to upset the rivet.

Pneumatic squeezers and pneumatic riveting hammers are the most common riveting tools an individual may use when working on the structure proper. The pneumatic squeezer is illustrated here in Fig. 1-1. This is a portable type and is used primarily to join stiffeners or brackets near the edge of a structure or around an opening, since its use is limited by the length of the jaws. The squeezer applies its force to the rivet by air pressure, acting on the large cylinder, which forces the jaws together with sufficient pressure to upset the rivet shank. One of the jaws is equipped with the proper sets to fit the rivet head while the other is flat to form the upset end.

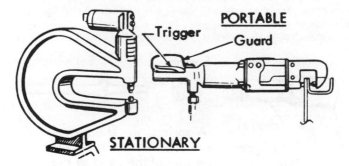

Fig. 1-1. Stationary and portable pneumatic rivet squeezers.

The pneumatic riveting hammer is illustrated in Fig. 1-2. It has the greatest use of all riveting methods due to its flexibility. Its driving action is obtained by air pressure driving a piston repeatedly against the rivet set which in turn applies its force to the head of the rivet. The rivet is upset by a bucking bar held solidly against the shank end of the rivet while the pneumatic hammer is operated.

RIVETING PRACTICES

Riveting with the pneumatic hammer generally requires partners; one driving the rivet and the other using a bucking bar which upsets the shank end.

The extensive use of this method of riveting requires skilled riveters in order to develop speed and efficiency in driving the many rivets used to join various structural parts and surfaces.

Of equal importance to the speed of riveting is, of course, to do this riveting in a manner which prevents damage to the airplane itself. This requires the constant attention and personal desire of the riveters to do good work.

The damage that may be done with the riveting hammer can readily be understood when you consider that the power of the riveting hammer is sufficient to upset the end of a rivet and could exert this same pressure against the surface of the airplane unless the driving action is confined to the rivet alone. Such damages occur when the rivet set slips from the head of the rivet or when the bucking bar is not held solidly in place while the hammer is being operated. Damage of this sort, even though only occasional can cause uncountable hours of rework or replacement of parts if not avoided.

Primary instructions to partners are illustrated in Fig. 1-3, which shows a condition where the riveter and bucker may not communicate directly and must rely on signals to each other.

Although there are several steps necessary to upset each rivet, they are

Gun	Spring	Set
Barrel Trigger Air Regulator Air Hose Connection	A spring screws over the end of the gun to hold the set.	The rivet set fits into the end of the gun.

SAFETY   A rivet gun is dangerous – never use one without a retainer spring.

Fig. 1-2. Pneumatic rivet hammer.

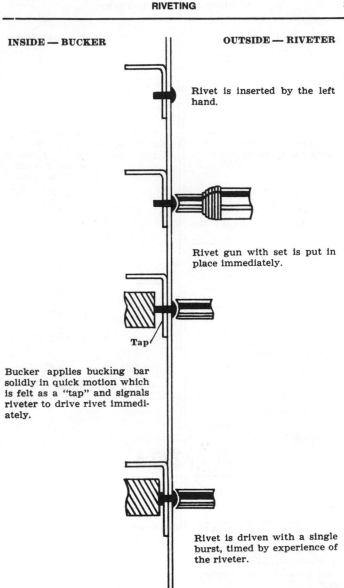

INSIDE — BUCKER   OUTSIDE — RIVETER

Rivet is inserted by the left hand.

Rivet gun with set is put in place immediately.

Tap

Bucker applies bucking bar solidly in quick motion which is felt as a "tap" and signals riveter to drive rivet immediately.

Rivet is driven with a single burst, timed by experience of the riveter.

Fig. 1-3. Operations of partners in driving rivets.

INSIDE — BUCKER

OUTSIDE — RIVETER

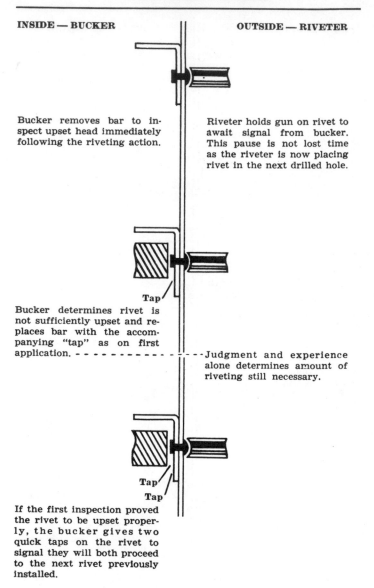

Bucker removes bar to inspect upset head immediately following the riveting action.

Riveter holds gun on rivet to await signal from bucker. This pause is not lost time as the riveter is now placing rivet in the next drilled hole.

Tap

Bucker determines rivet is not sufficiently upset and replaces bar with the accompanying "tap" as on first application. - - - - - - - - - - - - - - - -Judgment and experience alone determines amount of riveting still necessary.

Tap
Tap

If the first inspection proved the rivet to be upset properly, the bucker gives two quick taps on the rivet to signal they will both proceed to the next rivet previously installed.

done in such rapid succession by experienced riveters that they may be accomplished as fast as the riveter can insert the rivets with one hand while driving with the other. It is easy to see possible mistakes, causing damage, during this speed of riveting. Figure 1-4 shows common errors.

INSIDE — BUCKER   **OUTSIDE — RIVETER**

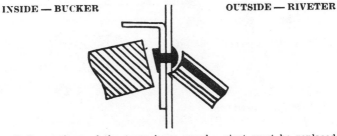

Both members of the team have erred — rivet must be replaced because of improper upset. The riveter has damaged the surface of the airplane with the edge of rivet set. Rework necessary here may necessitate special permission to use the part as is, or completely remove this section of the surface.

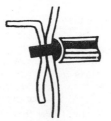

Any misunderstood signals may cause riveter to drive against rivet without the bar in place, thus dimpling the surface and bending sub-structure. Damage may be as great as above.

Rivet timing wrong — remove rivet.

Fig. 1-4.

Proper Driven Rivet. Regardless of the upsetting or driving method, the resultant article should be consistently uniform. Figure 1-5A shows several specimens of driven rivets. Figure 1-5B shows standards for judging a good rivet.

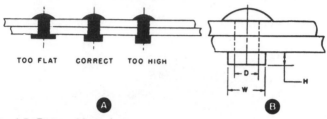

Fig. 1-5. Proper driven rivet.

The width W should equal 1 1/2 times the original diameter D, and the height H should equal one-half the original diameter.

Correct Rivet Length. To calculate the correct rivet length for a certain job, to the grip length or thickness of material through which the rivet must pass, add as follows:

Rivet dia., in.	Grip, in.	Add
1/4 or less	1/2 or less	1 1/2 diameter of rivet
1/4 or less	Over 1/2	1 1/2 diameter + 1/16 in. for every 1/2 in. of grip
5/16 or more	1 or less	1 1/2 diameter of rivet
5/16 or more	Over 1	1 1/2 diameter + 1/16 in. for every 1 in. of grip

The total is the proper length of rivet to use.

Remove Bad Rivets. Occasionally a rivet is ruined and has to be replaced. To remove it, a hole is drilled through its head, with the same size drill used for the rivet hole, just deep enough to sever the rivet head from the shank (Fig. 1-6A). The head is snapped off, then the shank is tapped from the hole with a pin punch, as shown in Fig. 1-6B. If the head is carefully drilled, the shank may be pushed out with the drill.

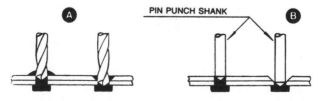

Fig. 1-6. Removal of bad rivets.

Drill Size For Rivets. The most used rivet sizes with the recommended drill size for each are as follows:

Rivet Dia., In.	Drill Size	Rivet Dia., In.	Drill Size
1/16	No. 51	5/32	No. 21
3/32	No. 40	3/16	No. 10 or 11
1/8	No. 30	1/4	1/4-in

RIVET TYPES AND IDENTIFICATION

Rivets differ and are identified by: (1) style of head, (2) material (aluminum alloy principally), and (3) size (diameter and length). To obtain a specific rivet, these three identifying terms must be called out by their proper names or by their proper identifying numbers as used on drawings. Rivets are identified by their MS (Military Standard) number which superseded the old AN (Army-Navy) number. Both designations are still is use however (Figs. 1-7 through 1-9).

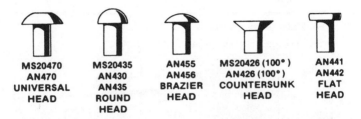

MS20470	MS20435	AN455	MS20426 (100°)	AN441
AN470	AN430	AN456	AN426 (100°)	AN442
UNIVERSAL	AN435	BRAZIER	COUNTERSUNK	FLAT
HEAD	ROUND	HEAD	HEAD	HEAD
	HEAD			

NOTE: When replacement is necessary for protruding head rivets—roundhead, flathead, or brazier head—they can usually be replaced by universal head rivets.

Fig. 1-7. Style of head and identifying number.

HEAT TREATED RIVETS

From the rivet identification (Figs. 1-8 and 1-9), you will note the several aluminum alloys used for aircraft rivets. Some of these require special heat-treat processes up to and during the time of their use, and others are ready for use as received from the manufacturer. Therefore, it is important to be able to recognize the alloy from the MS or AN code and from the markings on the head of the rivet itself.

The rivets, ready for use, are from alloys 2117, 1100 and 5056. The alloy 2117 is actually a heat-treatable alloy but is fully heat-treated before use and requires no special attention by the riveter.

The rivets from alloys 2017 and 2024, if fully heat-treated, will be too hard

YOU CAN TELL THE MATERIAL BY THE HEAD MARKING

Rivet	Material Code	Head Marking	Material
◯ ⊏	A	PLAIN (Dyed Red)	1100
⊙ ⊏	AD	DIMPLED	2117
⊕ ⊏	DD	TWO RAISED DASHES	2024
✦ ⊏	B	RAISED CROSS (Dyed Brown)	5056
⊙ ⊏	M	TWO DOTS	Monel

Fig. 1-8. Material identification.

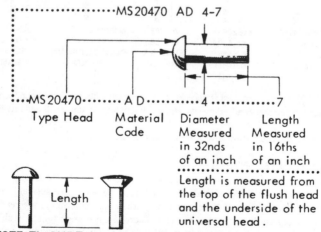

············MS 20470 AD 4-7

···MS 20470···· A D ···········4 ·············7
Type Head   Material   Diameter   Length
            Code   Measured   Measured
                       in 32nds   in 16ths
                       of an inch of an inch
··
Length is measured from
the top of the flush head
and the underside of the
universal head.

Length

NOTE: The 2117-T rivet, known as the field rivet is used more than any other for riveting aluminum alloy structures. The field rivet is in wide demand because it is ready for use as received and needs no further heat-treating or annealing. It also has a high resistance to corrosion.

Fig. 1-9. Code breakdown.

and will crack upon driving unless used in a manner to complete the heat-treat process after driving. In order to do this it is desirable to understand a little of the heat-treat process. Read about the heat-treatment of aluminum alloys and the heat-treatment of rivets in Chapter 6 where it will be noted that these rivets must be stored in refrigerators until the time of their actual use. This cold storage prevents the completion of their heat-treatment, which will proceed when the rivets are removed from cold storage and their temperature rises to room temperature. This is an aging process which hardens the alloy after a certain amount of time at room temperature. This is automatic and the riveter must use the rivet within approximately thirty minutes after removal from the refrigerator. Be aware of the process, and understand that after this time the rivets are too hard for use. Rivets that have become hard before use will not be restored to their soft condition by replacing in the refrigerator, these must be returned for full heat-treat re-processing.

FLUSH RIVETING

Preparation of a surface for flush rivets is done by one of several methods: . . .by countersinking, by dimpling, or by a combination of dimpling and countersinking. Regardless of the method of preparing the surface, the requirements are that the rivet be let into the surface until the rivet is either flush with, or slightly above the surface.

The rivet set used for flush riveting has a large, slightly contoured and highly polished surface to strike the rivet head. See Fig. 1-10.

Countersinking for flush rivets is the most direct method of preparing the surface. The hole is first drilled to suit the diameter of the rivet shank, then beveled with the countersinking tool to suit the above mentioned requirements and the rivet is ready to be driven. (See the section on tools for the description of the countersinking tools).

Figure 1-10 shows a riveted joint completed in a countersunk surface.

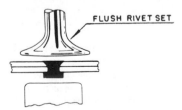
FLUSH RIVET SET

Fig. 1-10. Completed flush riveted joint.

Dimpled surfaces are prepared by the use of forming dies which actually dimple the material inward around the drilled hole until the flush rivet may be let into the surface and fulfill the requirements of flush riveting as above.

This formed section of the outer surface has a corresponding reverse dimple on the under side of the surface which is in turn nested into either a "dimpled" or a "countersunk" sub-surface. Figure 1-11 shows riveted joints in dimpled surfaces.

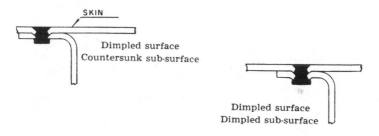

Fig. 1-11. Examples of flush rivet joints using dimpled surfaces.

The dimpling dies for the above dimpling are used with both the squeezers and the pneumatic riveting gun and are designed especially for surface and sub-surface work (Fig. 1-12).

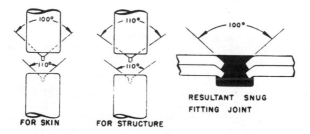

Fig. 1-12. Examples of dimpling dies.

The dimpling procedures will vary also according to individual practice; however, in general the surfaces are first fitted together and drilled to fit the rivet shank (or pre-drilled to a smaller size and reamed to full size after dimpling). They must then be disassembled for the dimpling operation on the outer surface and the dimpling or countersinking of the sub-surface.

On some applications the sub-surface only is dimpled or countersunk when disassembled and then the outer surface is replaced and dimpled into the sub-surface. The sub-surface must be backed up by a draw bar and a bucking bar while the surface is dimpled with the form tool (Fig. 1-13).

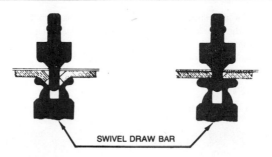

Fig. 1-13. Dimple form tools.

RIVET MILLING (SHAVING)

A driven flush rivet, as stated above, will be flush with or slightly above the surface. The amount the rivet may be above the surface depends on the various manufacturers' practice; up to .015 of an inch is allowed for some use. However, on the wing leading edge and the front section of the fuselage, as well as on all surfaces of modern, supersonic aircraft, a near perfect flush surface is desired. This is accomplished by driving the flush rivet to suit the above requirements and then milling that portion of the rivet head which protrudes above the surface. Rivet milling is a hand operation as shown in Fig. 1-14 and

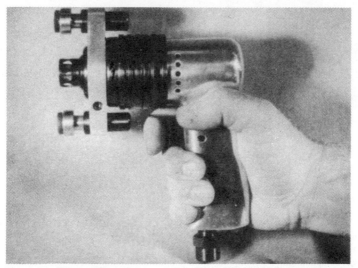

Fig. 1-14. Rivet milling tool.

is done with a high speed motor driving a milling cutter. The tool is placed directly over the rivet and is plunged straight downward to cut the excess rivet head off. Adjustable stops are provided on the tool which are set to prevent the cutter from going deeper than the surface proper.

BLIND RIVETS

There are many places on an aircraft where access to both sides of a riveted

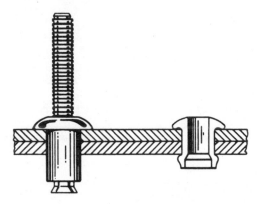

Before installation   After installation

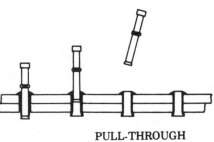

PULL-THROUGH
HOLLOW

Fig. 1-15. Pull-through rivets (hollow).

structure or structural part is impossible, or where limited space will not permit the use of a bucking bar.

"Blind" rivets are rivets designed to be installed from one side of the work where access to the opposite side cannot be made to install conventional rivets. While this was the basic reason for the development of blind rivets, they are sometimes used in applications that are not "blind." This is done to save time, money, man-hours, and weight in the attachment of many nonstructural parts such as aircraft interior furnishings, flooring, deicing boots, and the like, where the full strength of solid shank rivets is not necessary. These rivets are produced by several manufacturers and have unique characteristics that require special installation tools, special installation procedures, and special removal procedures.

Basically, nearly all blind rivets depend upon the principle of drawing a stem or mandrel through a sleeve to accomplish the forming of the bucked (upset) head.

Although many variations of blind rivets exist, depending on the manufacturer, there are essentially three types:

☐ Hollow, pull-through rivets, (Fig. 1-15) used mainly for non-structural applications.

☐ Self-plugging, friction lock rivets (Fig. 1-16), whereby the stem is retained in the rivet by friction. Although strength of these rivets approach that of conventional solid shank rivets, there is no positive mechanical lock to retain the stem.

☐ Mechanical locked stem self-plugging rivets (Fig. 1-17), whereby a locking collar mechanically retains the stem in the rivet. This positive lock resists vibration that could cause the friction lock rivets to loosen and possibly fall out. Self-plugging mechanical lock rivets display all the strength characteristics of solid shank rivets and in almost all cases can be substituted rivet for rivet.

Mechanical Locked Stem Self-Plugging Rivets. Mechanical locked stem self-plugging rivets are manufactured by Olympic, Huck, and Cherry Fasteners. The bulbed Cherrylock® (Fig. 1-17) is used as an example of a typical blind rivet which is virtually interchangeable, structurally, with solid rivets.

The installation of all mechanical locked stem self-plugging rivets require hand or pneumatic pull guns with appropriate pulling heads. Many types are available from the rivet manufacturers; examples of hand and pneumatic-operated pull guns are shown in Fig. 1-18.

The sequence of events in forming the bulbed Cherrylock® rivet is shown in Fig. 1-19.

Identification of Bulbed Cherrylock® Rivets. Figure 1-20 illustrates the numbering system for bulbed Cherrylock® rivets.

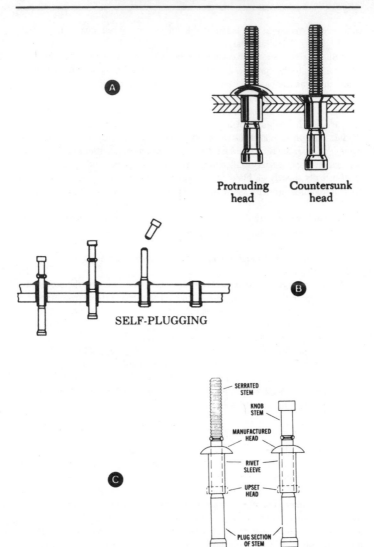

Fig. 1-16. Self-plugging (friction lock) rivets. Two different types of pulling heads are available for friction lock rivets.

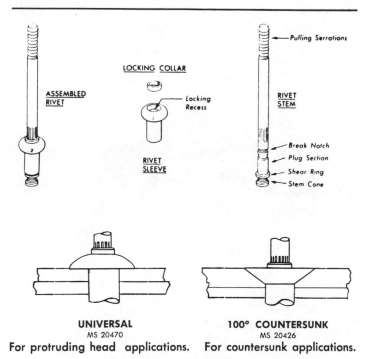

LOCKING COLLAR

ASSEMBLED
RIVET

Locking
Recess

RIVET
SLEEVE

Pulling Serrations

RIVET
STEM

Break Notch
Plug Section
Shear Ring
Stem Cone

UNIVERSAL
MS 20470
For protruding head applications.

100° COUNTERSUNK
MS 20426
For countersunk applications.

Fig. 1-17. The bulbed Cherrylock® rivet includes a locking collar to firmly retain the portion of the stem in the rivet sleeve.

Hole Preparation. The bulbed Cherrylock® rivets are designed to function within a specified hole size range and countersink dimensions as listed in Fig. 1-21.

Grip Length. Grip length refers to the maximum total sheet thickness to be riveted, and is measured in 16ths of an inch. This is identified by the second dash number. All Cherrylock® Rivets have their grip length (maximum grip) marked on the rivet head, and have a total grip range of 1/16 of an inch (example: – 4 grip rivet has a grip range of .188″ to .250″). See Fig. 1-22. To determine the proper grip rivet to use, measure the material thickness with a Cherry selector gauge as shown in Fig. 1-23. Always read to the next higher number. To find the rivet grip number without using a selector gauge, determine the total thickness of the material to be fastened; locate between minimum and maximum columns on material thickness chart (Fig. 1-24). Read directly across to right to find grip number.

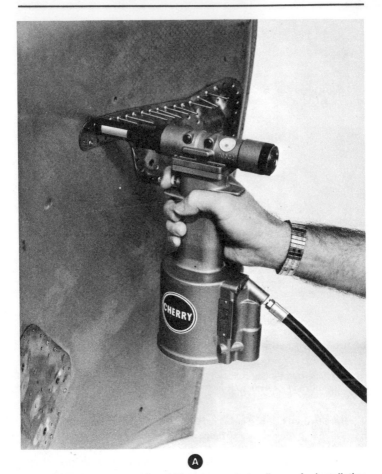

A

Fig. 1-18. Typical pneumatic and hand-operated pull guns for installation of blind rivets.

Further data on bulbed Cherrylock® rivets including materials available is included in Chapter 8, Standard Parts.

Complete installation manuals and pulling tool catalogs are available from the rivet manufacturers.

PIN (HI-SHEAR) RIVETS

Pin rivets are commonly called hi-shear rivets, although "hi-shear" is ac-

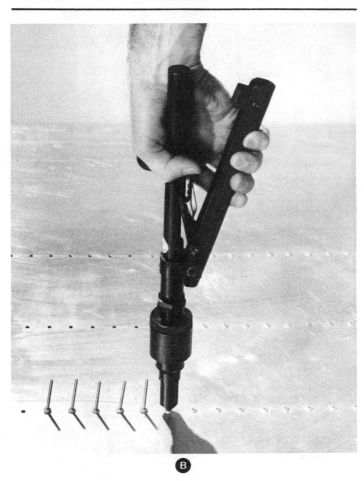

B

tually the name of the Hi-Shear Corporation, which manufacturers pin rivets as well as other products.

Hi-Shear rivets were designed primarily to replace bolts in high shear strength applications. They are probably the oldest type of high-strength rivet-type fastener used in the aircraft industry. High strength, ease and speed of installation, and weight savings over bolt and nut combinations make them attractive from a design standpoint.

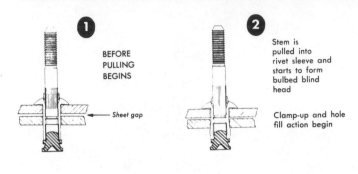

①

BEFORE
PULLING
BEGINS

← Sheet gap

②

Stem is
pulled into
rivet sleeve and
starts to form
bulbed blind
head

Clamp-up and hole
fill action begin

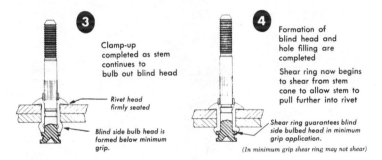

③

Clamp-up
completed as stem
continues to
bulb out blind head

Rivet head
firmly seated

Blind side bulb head is
formed below minimum
grip.

④

Formation of
blind head and
hole filling are
completed

Shear ring now begins
to shear from stem
cone to allow stem to
pull further into rivet

Shear ring guarantees blind
side bulbed head in minimum
grip application.

(In minimum grip shear ring may not shear)

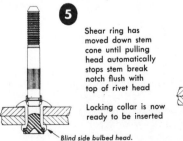

⑤

Shear ring has
moved down stem
cone until pulling
head automatically
stops stem break
notch flush with
top of rivet head

Locking collar is now
ready to be inserted

Blind side bulbed head.

⑥

**COMPLETELY INSTALLED
BULBED CHERRYLOCK**

Pulling head has
inserted locking
collar and stem
has fractured flush
with rivet head

(MAXIMUM GRIP
ILLUSTRATED)

Fig. 1-19. Steps in the formation of the bulbed Cherrylock® rivet.

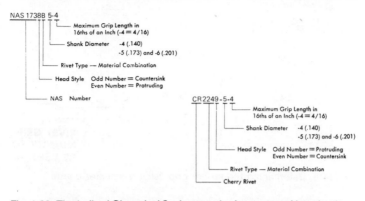

NAS 1738B 5-4
└── Maximum Grip Length in
      16ths of an Inch (-4 = 4/16)
└── Shank Diameter   -4 (.140)
                             -5 (.173) and -6 (.201)
└── Rivet Type — Material Combination
└── Head Style   Odd Number = Countersink
                       Even Number = Protruding
└── NAS   Number

CR2249-5-4
└── Maximum Grip Length in
      16ths of an Inch (-4 = 4/16)
└── Shank Diameter   -4 (.140)
                             -5 (.173) and -6 (.201)
└── Head Style   Odd Number = Protruding
                       Even Number = Countersink
└── Rivet Type — Material Combination
└── Cherry Rivet

Fig. 1-20. The bulbed Cherrylock® rivet numbering system. Note the three diameters available. The bulbed Cherrylock® rivet sleeve is 1/64 inch over nominal size. For example, the – 4 rivet is a nominal 1/8 inch rivet; however, its diameter is 1/64 inch greater.

BULBED CHERRYLOCK

Rivet Diam.	Drill Size	Minimum	Maximum
1/8	#27	.143	.146
5/32	#16	.176	.180
3/16	#5	.205	.209

Do not deburr blind side of hole.

COUNTERSINKING DIMENSIONS

|←— C —→| .010 R. Min.

Rivet Diam.	100° MS20426 HEAD		100° NAS1097 HEAD	
	C Max.	C Min.	C Max.	C Min.
3/32	.182	.176	—	—
1/8	.228	.222	.195	.189
5/32	.289	.283	.246	.240
3/16	.356	.350	.302	.296
1/4	.479	.473	.395	.389

Fig. 1-21. Recommended drill sizes, hole size, and countersunk diameter limits.

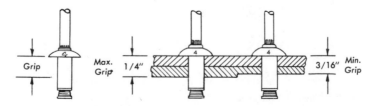

Grip   Max. Grip   1/4″   3/16″   Min. Grip

Fig. 1-22. Illustration of grip length.

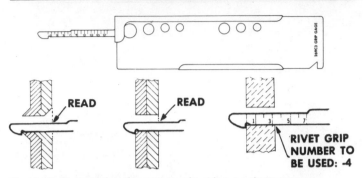

Fig. 1-23. Determining the proper grip using a selector gauge.

MATERIAL THICKNESS RANGE		RIVET GRIP NO.
MINIMUM	MAXIMUM	
See Stds. Pages	1/16"	1
See Stds. Pages	1/8"	2
1/8"	3/16"	3
3/16"	1/4"	4
1/4"	5/16"	5
5/16"	3/8"	6
3/8"	7/16"	7
7/16"	1/2"	8
1/2"	9/16"	9
9/16"	5/8"	10
5/8"	11/16"	11
11/16"	3/4"	12
3/4"	13/16"	13
13/16"	7/8"	14
7/8"	15/16"	15
15/16"	1"	16

Note: For double dimpled sheets, add countersunk rivet head height to material thickness } CSK BULBED CHERRYLOCK
RIVET HEAD HEIGHT
1/8   .035
5/32   .047
3/16   .063

Fig. 1-24. Determination of rivet grip length without a selector gauge.

Most hi-shear pins are made of heat-treated alloy steel. Some pins, however, are 7075-T6 aluminum alloy, stainless steel or titanium. Most collars are 2117 or 2024-T4 aluminum alloy. Some are mild steel, stainless steel, or monel. See Fig. 1-25. The table in Chapter 8, Standard Parts, provides head mark-

Fig. 1-25. The hi-shear rivet, pin and collar.

ings, part numbers, and other relative data. When driven with a hi-shear set, the work is tightly drawn together and the collar is forced into the pin groove, locking the pin securely into the structure as in Fig. 1-26.

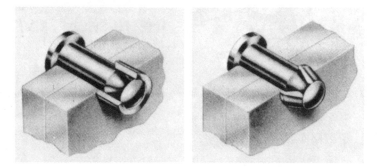

Fig. 1-26. The hi-shear rivet before and after driving.

Hi-Shear rivets are used where the loads are high and the structure correspondingly thick (Fig. 1-27), whereas rivets are used where the loads are comparatively low and the structure thin. *Hi-Shear rivets will not strengthen a thin structure connection* because the load required to "shear" a hi-shear rivet would cause the structure hole to tear in a "bearing" failure.

Hi-Shear rivets are driven with standard rivet guns or squeezers with a hi-shear rivet set adapter as shown in Fig. 1-28.

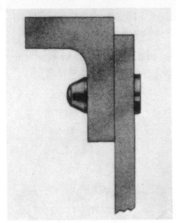

Fig. 1-27. Typical hi-shear structural connection.

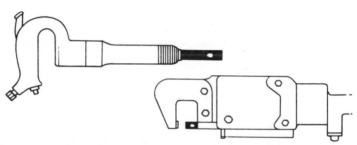

Fig. 1-28. Standard riveting tools with a hi-shear rivet set adapter.

The set forms the collar to the pin and at the same time cuts off and ejects the excess collar material through the discharge port as shown in Fig. 1-29.

How the Hi-Shear Works. See Fig. 1-30.

Selecting Hi-Shear Rivets. Figure 1-31 shows the hi-shear rivet pins

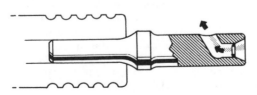

Fig. 1-29. The hi-shear rivet set adapter.

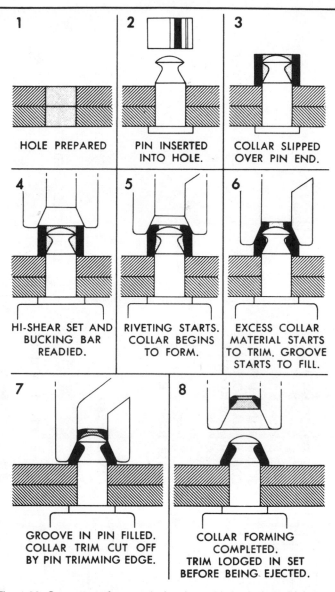

1 HOLE PREPARED

2 PIN INSERTED INTO HOLE.

3 COLLAR SLIPPED OVER PIN END.

4 HI-SHEAR SET AND BUCKING BAR READIED.

5 RIVETING STARTS. COLLAR BEGINS TO FORM.

6 EXCESS COLLAR MATERIAL STARTS TO TRIM. GROOVE STARTS TO FILL.

7 GROOVE IN PIN FILLED. COLLAR TRIM CUT OFF BY PIN TRIMMING EDGE.

8 COLLAR FORMING COMPLETED. TRIM LODGED IN SET BEFORE BEING EJECTED.

Fig. 1-30. Sequence of events in forming a hi-shear riveted joint.

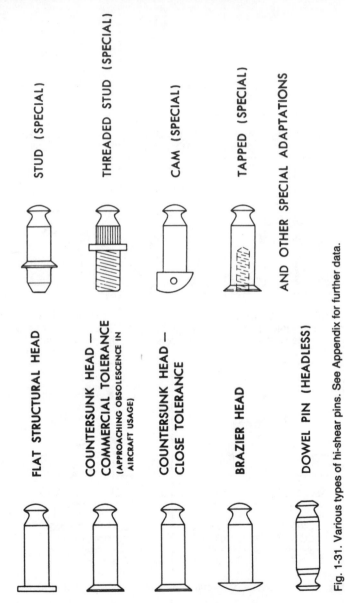

FLAT STRUCTURAL HEAD

STUD (SPECIAL)

COUNTERSUNK HEAD —
COMMERCIAL TOLERANCE
(APPROACHING OBSOLESCENCE IN
AIRCRAFT USAGE)

THREADED STUD (SPECIAL)

COUNTERSUNK HEAD —
CLOSE TOLERANCE

CAM (SPECIAL)

BRAZIER HEAD

TAPPED (SPECIAL)

DOWEL PIN (HEADLESS)

AND OTHER SPECIAL ADAPTATIONS

Fig. 1-31. Various types of hi-shear pins. See Appendix for further data.

available. Additional data is included in Chapter 8, Standard Parts.

Part numbers for pin rivets can be interpreted to give the diameter and grip length of the individual rivets. A typical part number breakdown would be as shown in Fig. 1-32.

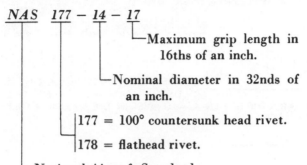

$$NAS \quad 177 - 14 - 17$$

Maximum grip length in 16ths of an inch.

Nominal diameter in 32nds of an inch.

177 = 100° countersunk head rivet.

178 = flathead rivet.

National Aircraft Standard.

Fig. 1-32. Pin rivet part number designation.

Determining Grip Length. A special scale, Fig. 1-33, is available for determination of grip length.

Hole Preparation. Hi-Shear rivets, like bolts, require careful hole preparation. First the hole must be drilled perpendicular to the manufactured head side of the work. Second, the hole must be sized within proper limits of diameter and roundness. Hi-Shear rivets do not expand during installation; therefore, they must fit the hole into which they are installed.

To obtain accurate holes, machine sharpened drills should be used. Drill motors should have chucks and spindles in good repair. Lubricants should be used on the drill wherever possible. When available, the best precaution of all is to drill through a bushed template or fixture. Where closer tolerances are required, the holes should be reamed. Hole sizes and tolerances are normally specified by engineering and called out on the drawing (blueprint).

NOTE: When countersinking for Hi-Shear rivets, the countersunk hole should not be too deep. When the head is below flush, the head backs up to the bar when it is driven and leaves a gap under the rivet head, resulting in a loose rivet (Fig. 1-34).

Installation. Generally, hi-shear riveting is the same as conventional riveting. By changing the standard set to a hi-shear set, the rivet gun is ready to shoot hi-shear rivets. Typical rivet sets are shown in Fig. 1-35.

The hi-shear rivet should be driven quickly. A heavy enough gun should be used. The bucking bar should weigh 1 1/3 times or more than the gun for maximum efficiency.

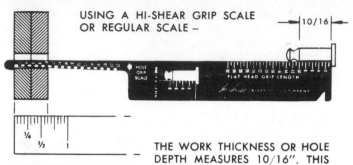

USING A HI-SHEAR GRIP SCALE
OR REGULAR SCALE –

THE WORK THICKNESS OR HOLE
DEPTH MEASURES 10/16″. THIS
INDICATES THE USE OF A –10 RIVET IN THE MAXIMUM GRIP.

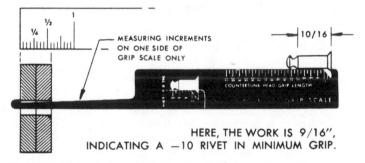

MEASURING INCREMENTS
ON ONE SIDE OF
GRIP SCALE ONLY

HERE, THE WORK IS 9/16″,
INDICATING A –10 RIVET IN MINIMUM GRIP.

Fig. 1-33. A grip length scale simplifies determination of grip length.

Riveting with Squeezers. Riveting with squeezers is preferred wherever the work permits as shown in Fig. 1-36.

Reverse Riveting. Reversed riveting, Figs. 1-37 and 1-38, with hi-shear rivets is used where there is no room for a rivet gun.

Reverse riveting requires a heavier wallop. The gun should be opened up or a heavier one should be used.

Inspection of Hi-Shear Rivets. If the rivets and collars look good on the outside, they are good on the inside. No gauges or special tools are required.

Hi-Shear Rivet Removal. This method of removal involves using a Hi-Shear rivet cutter to mill off the collar. The pin is removed with punch and hammer as shown in Fig. 1-39.

This method, using a cape chisel (Fig. 1-40), is the most commonly used. The collar is split on both sides with a chisel. The pin is removed with a punch and hammer.

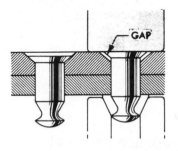

Fig. 1-34. A too-deep countersunk hole results in a loose rivet.

IN OPEN AREAS

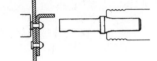

STRAIGHT SET

IN CORNER AREAS

OFFSET SET

IN AREAS OF FRAME RETURN FLANGES

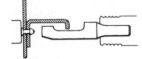

FULL-NOTCHED SET

IN CHANNEL AREAS

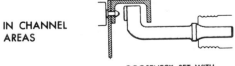

GOOSENECK SET WITH HI-SHEAR INSERT SET

Fig. 1-35. Hi-shear rivets are driven with standard rivet guns and bucking bars.

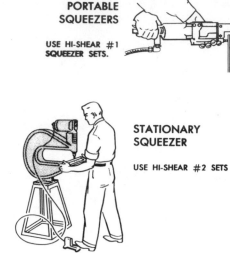

PORTABLE SQUEEZERS

USE HI-SHEAR #1 SQUEEZER SETS.

STATIONARY SQUEEZER

USE HI-SHEAR #2 SETS

HYDRAULIC SQUEEZER

USE HI-SHEAR #2 SETS & SPECIAL HEAVY DUTY SQUEEZER SETS

Fig. 1-36. Riveting hi-shear with squeezers is the preferred method when practical.

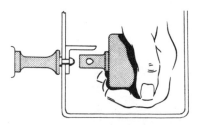

Fig. 1-37. A short straight hi-shear set inserted in a hi-shear No. 1 or No. 2 bucking bar is used against the collar end. The rivet gun fitted with a flush set supplies the impact to the hi-shear head.

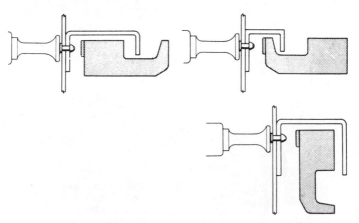

Fig. 1-38. Hi-shear No. 3 or No. 4 bucking bars, with a hi-shear insert set, are adaptable to a variety of close quarter work.

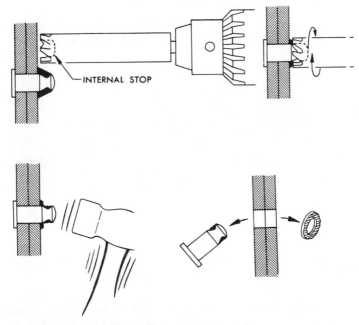

INTERNAL STOP

Fig. 1-39. Using a hollow mill to remove the collar.

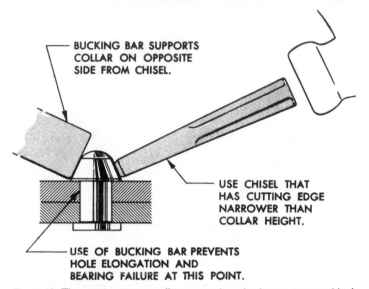

BUCKING BAR SUPPORTS
COLLAR ON OPPOSITE
SIDE FROM CHISEL.

USE CHISEL THAT
HAS CUTTING EDGE
NARROWER THAN
COLLAR HEIGHT.

USE OF BUCKING BAR PREVENTS
HOLE ELONGATION AND
BEARING FAILURE AT THIS POINT.

Fig. 1-40. The most common collar removal method uses a cape chisel.

Chapter 2

Bolts and Fasteners

Various types of fastening devices allow quick dismantling or replacement of aircraft parts that must be taken apart and put back together at frequent intervals. Bolts and screws are two types of fastening devices that give the required security of attachment and rigidity. Generally, bolts are used where great strength is required, and screws are used where strength is not the deciding factor.

The threaded end of a bolt usually has a nut screwed onto it to complete the assembly. The threaded end of a screw may fit into a female receptacle, or it may fit directly into the material being secured. A bolt has a fairly short threaded section and a comparatively long grip length or unthreaded portion, whereas a screw has a longer threaded section and may have no clearly defined grip length. A bolt assembly is generally tightened by turning the nut on the bolt; the head of the bolt may or may not be designed for turning. A screw is always tightened by turning its head.

The modern high-performance jet aircraft, however, uses very few "standard" hex head bolts and nuts in its assembly. Also, the "standard" slotted and Phillips head screws are in the minority. Some of these advanced fasteners will be described later in this chapter.

In many cases, a bolt may be indistinguishable from a screw, thus the term "threaded fastener." Also, many threaded fasteners such as the Hi-Lok® and Hi-Lok/Hi-Tigue® fasteners are essentially permanent installations like a rivet.

Aircraft threaded fasteners are fabricated from alloy steel, corrosion-resistant (stainless) steel, aluminum alloys and titanium. Most bolts used in aircraft are either alloy steel, cadmium plated, general purpose AN bolts, NAS close-tolerance, or MS bolts. Aluminum alloy bolts are seldom used in primary structure. In certain cases, aircraft manufacturers make threaded fasteners of different dimensions or greater strength than the standard types. Such threaded fasteners are made for a particular application, and it is of extreme importance to use like fasteners in replacement.

AIRCRAFT BOLTS (THREADED FASTENERS)

Most, but not all, aircraft bolts are designed and fabricated in accordance with Government standards and specifications as follows:

☐ AN, Air Force/Navy

☐ NAS, National Aerospace Standards
☐ MS, Military Standards

See Chapter 8, Standard Parts, for a discussion of Government Standards.

General-Purpose Bolts

The hex-head aircraft bolt (AN-3 through AN-20) is an all-purpose structural bolt used for general applications involving tension or shear loads where a light-drive fit is permissible (.006-inch clearance for a 5/8-inch hole, and other sizes in proportion). They are fabricated from SAE 2330 nickel steel and cadmium plated.

Alloy steel bolts smaller than No. 10-32 (3/16-inch diameter, AN-3) and aluminum alloy bolts smaller than 1/4-inch diameter are not used in primary structures. Aluminum alloy bolts and nuts are not used where they will be repeatedly removed for purposes of maintenance and inspection.

The AN73-AN81 (MS20073-MS20074) drilled-head bolt is similar to the standard hex-bolt, but has a deeper head that is drilled to receive wire for safetying. The AN-3, AN-20 and the AN-73, AN-81 series bolts are interchangeable, for all practical purposes, from the standpoint of tension and shear strengths. See Chapter 8, Standard Parts.

Identification and Coding

Threaded fasteners are manufactured in many shapes and varieties. A clear-cut method of classification is difficult. Threaded fasteners can be identified by the shape of the head, method of securing, material used in fabrication, or the expected usage. Figure 2-1 shows the basic head styles and wrenching recesses.

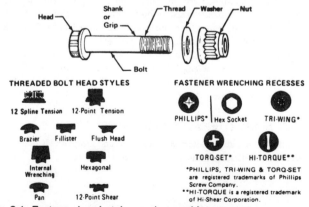

Fig. 2-1. Fastener head styles and wrenching recesses.

AN-type aircraft bolts can be identified by the code markings on the bolt-heads. The markings generally denote the bolt manufacturer, the material of which the bolt is made, and whether the bolt is a standard AN-type or a special-purpose bolt. AN standard steel bolts are marked with either a raised dash or asterisk (see Fig. 2-2); corrosion-resistant steel is indicated by a single raised dash; and AN aluminum alloy bolts are marked with two raised dashes. Additional information such as bolt diameter, bolt length, and grip length may be obtained from the bolt part number. See Chapter 8, Standard Parts.

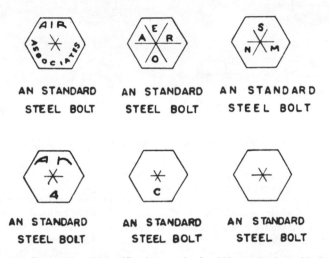

Fig. 2-2. Typical head identification marks for AN standard steel bolts.

AIRCRAFT NUTS

Aircraft nuts are made in a variety of shapes and sizes. They are made of alloy steel, stainless steel, aluminum alloy, brass, or titanium. No identifying marking or lettering appear on nuts. They can be identified only by the characteristic metallic luster or color of the aluminum, brass, or the insert when the nut is of the self-locking type. They can be further identified by their construction.

Like aircraft bolts, most aircraft nuts are designed and fabricated in accordance with AN, NAS, and MS standards and specifications.

Aircraft nuts can be divided into two general groups: Non-self-locking and self-locking nuts. Non-self-locking nuts (Fig. 2-3) are those that must be safetied by external locking devices, such as cotter pins, safety wire, or locknuts. Self-locking nuts (Figs. 2-4, 2-5) contain the locking feature as an integral part.

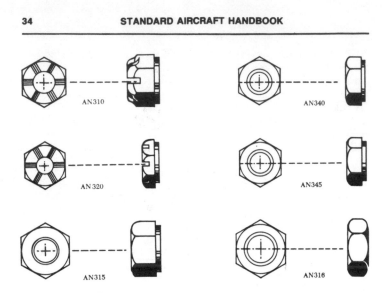

Fig. 2-3. Non-self-locking, castellated and plain nuts.

Self-locking nuts can be further sub-divided into low temperature (250 °F or less) and high temperature (over 250 °F).

Most of the familiar types of nuts including the plain nut, the castle nut, the castellated shear nut, the plain hex nut, the light hex nut, and the plain check nut are the non-self-locking type (Fig. 2-3).

The castle nut, AN310, is used with drilled-shank AN hex head bolts, clevis bolts, eyebolts, drilled head bolts, or studs. It is fairly rugged and can withstand large tension loads. Slots (called *castellations*) in the nut are designed to accommodate a cotter pin or lock wire for safety. The AN310 castellated, cadmium-plated steel nut is by far the most commonly used airframe nut. See Chapter 8, Standard Parts.

The castellated shear nut, AN320, is designed for use with devices (such as drilled clevis bolts and threaded taper pins) which are normally subjected to shearing stress only. Like the castle nut, it is castellated for safetying. Note,

FLEXLOC® Hex
Self-Locking
Regular Height

Hexagon
Self-Locking
Castellated Nut

12 Point
Self-Locking
Tension Nut

12 Point
Self-Locking
Shear Nut

12 Spline
Self-Locking
Tension Nut

12 Spline
Self-Locking
Shear Nut

Fig. 2-4. High temperature (over 250°F) self-locking nuts.

however, that the nut is not as deep or as strong as the castle nut; also that the castellations are not as deep as those in the castle nut.

Self-Locking Nuts to 250°F

The elastic stop nut is essentially a standard hex nut incorporating a fiber or nylon insert (see Fig. 2-5). The inside diameter of the red insert is deliberately smaller than the major diameter of the matching bolt. The nut spins freely on the bolt until the bolt threads enter the locking insert, where they impress but do not cut mating threads in the insert. This compression forces a metal-to-metal contact between the top flanks of the nut threads and the bottom flanks of the bolt threads. This friction hold plus the compression hold of the insert essentially "locks" the nut anywhere on the bolt.

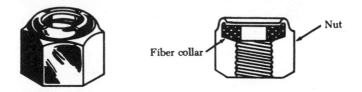

Fig. 2-5. Low temperature (250°F or less) self-locking nut (elastic stop nut, AN365, MS20365).

After the nut has been tightened, the rounded or chamfered end bolts, studs, or screws should extend at least the full round or chamfer through the nut. Flat end bolts, studs, or screws should extend at least 1/32 inch through the nut. When fiber-type self-locking nuts are reused, the fiber should be carefully checked to make sure it has not lost its locking friction or become brittle. Locknuts should not be reused if they can be run up finger-tight. Bolts 5/16-inch diameter and over with cotter pin holes may be used with self-locking nuts, but only if free from burrs around the holes. Bolts with damaged threads and rough ends are not acceptable.

Self-locking nuts should not be used at joints that subject either the nut or bolt to rotation. They may be used with antifriction bearings and control pulleys, provided the inner race of the bearing is clamped to the supporting structure by the nut and bolt.

High Temperature Self-Locking Nuts

All-metal locknuts are constructed with either the threads in the locking insert out-of-phase with the load-carrying section (Fig. 2-6), or with a saw-cut insert with a pinched-in thread in the locking section. The locking action of the all-metal nut depends upon the resiliency of the metal when the locking section and load-carrying section are engaged by screw threads.

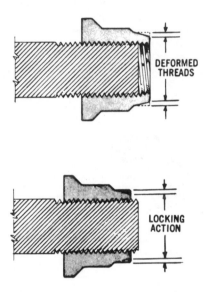

Fig. 2-6. The Boots self-locking all-metal nut.

Miscellaneous Nut Types

Self-locking nut bases are made in a number of forms and materials for riveting and welding to aircraft structure or parts (Fig. 2-7). Certain applications require the installation of self-locking nuts in channels, an arrangement which permits the attachment of many nuts with only a few rivets. These channels are track-like bases with regularly spaced nuts that are either removable or nonremovable. The removable type carries a floating nut, which can be snapped in or out of the channel, thus making possible the easy removal of damaged nuts. Nuts such as the clinch-type and spline-type, which depend on friction for their anchorage, are not acceptable for use in aircraft structures.

Various types of anchor nuts (Fig. 2-8) are available for riveting to structure for such application as removable panels.

Sheet spring nuts, sometimes called *speed nuts*, are used with standard and sheet-metal self-tapping screws in nonstructural locations. They find various

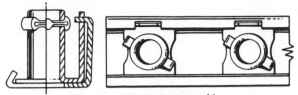

Boots aircraft channel assembly

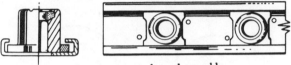

Elastic stop nut channel assembly

Fig. 2-7. Self-locking nut bases.

Fig. 2-8. Examples of anchor nuts.

uses in supporting line clamps, conduit clamps, electrical equipment access doors, and the like, and are available in several types. Speed nuts are made from spring steel and are arched prior to tightening. This arched spring lock prevents the screw from working loose. These nuts should be used only where originally used in fabrication of the aircraft (Fig. 2-9).

Fig. 2-9. Sheet spring nuts are used with self-tapping screws in non-structural locations.

AIRCRAFT WASHERS

Aircraft washers used in airframe repair are either plain, lock, or special type washers.

Plain Washers

The plain washer, AN960, Fig. 2-10, is used under hex nuts. It provides a smooth bearing surface and acts as a shim in obtaining correct grip length for a bolt and nut assembly. It is used to adjust the position of castellated nuts in respect to drilled cotter pin holes in bolts. Plain washers should be used under lock washers to prevent damage to the surface material.

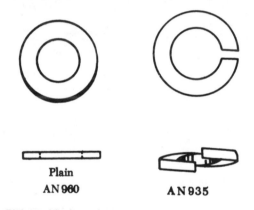

Plain
AN 960

AN 935

Fig. 2-10. Plain and lock washers.

Lock Washers

Lock washers (AN-935 and AN-936) may be used with machine screws or bolts whenever the self-locking or castellated type of nut is not applicable. They are not to be used as fastenings to primary or secondary structures, or where subject to frequent removal or corrosive conditions.

INSTALLATION OF NUTS AND BOLTS

Boltholes must be normal to the surface involved to provide full bearing surface for the bolthead and nut and must not be oversized or elongated. A bolt in such a hole will carry none of its shear load until parts have yielded or deformed enough to allow the bearing surface of the oversized hole to contact the bolt.

In cases of oversized or elongated holes in critical members, obtain advice from the aircraft or engine manufacturer before drilling or reaming the hole to take the next larger bolt. Usually, such factors as edge distance, clearance, or load factor must be considered. Oversized or elongated holes in noncritical members can usually be drilled or reamed to the next larger size.

Many boltholes, particularly those in primary connecting elements, have close tolerances. Generally, it is permissible to use the first lettered drill size larger than the normal bolt diameter, except where the AN hexagon bolts are used in light-drive fit (reamed) applications and where NAS close-tolerance bolts or AN clevis bolts are used.

Light-drive fits for bolts (specified on the repair drawings as .0015-inch maximum clearance between bolt and hole) are required in places where bolts are used in repair, or where they are placed in the original structure.

The fit of holes and bolts is defined in terms of the friction between bolt and hole when sliding the bolt into place. A tight-drive fit, for example, is one in which a sharp blow of a 12- or 14-ounce hammer is required to move the bolt. A bolt that requires a hard blow and sounds tight is considered to fit too tightly. A light-drive fit is one in which a bolt will move when a hammer handle is held against its head and pressed by the weight of the body.

Examine the markings on the bolthead to determine that each bolt is of the correct material. It is of extreme importance to use like bolts in replacement. In every case, refer to the applicable Maintenance Instruction Manual and Illustrated Parts Breakdown.

Be sure that washers are used under both the heads of bolts and nuts unless their omission is specified. A washer guards against mechanical damage to the material being bolted and prevents corrosion of the structural members.

Be certain that the bolt grip length is correct. Grip length is the length of the unthreaded portion of the bolt shank (Fig. 2-11). Generally speaking, the grip length should equal the thickness of the material being bolted together. However, bolts of slightly greater grip length may be used if washers are placed under the nut or the bolthead. In the case of plate nuts, add shims under the plate.

A nut is not run to the bottom of the threads on the bolt (Fig. 2-12B). A nut so installed cannot be pulled tight on the structure and probably will be

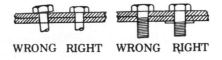

WRONG   RIGHT   WRONG   RIGHT

Fig. 2-11. Bolt installation.

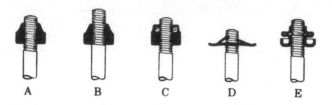

Fig. 2-12. Various grip lengths.

twisted off while being tightened. A washer will keep the nut in the proper position on the bolt.

In the case of self-locking "stop" nuts, if from one to three threads of the bolt extend through the nut, it is considered satisfactory.

Palnuts (AN356) should be tightened securely but not excessively. Finger-tight plus one to two turns is good practice, two turns being more generally used.

Torque Tables

The standard torque table (Fig. 2-13) should be used as a guide in tightening nuts, studs, bolts, and screws whenever specific torque values are not called out in maintenance procedures.

Cotter Pin Hole Line-Up

When tightening castellated nuts on bolts, the cotter pin holes may not line up with the slots in the nuts for the range of recommended values. Except in cases of highly stressed engine parts, the nut may be over tightened to permit lining up the next slot with the cotter pin hole. The torque loads specified may be used for all unlubricated cadmium-plated steel nuts of the fine or coarse-thread series which have approximately equal number of threads and equal face bearing areas. These values do not apply where special torque requirements are specified in the maintenance manual.

If the head end, rather than the nut, must be turned in the tightening operation, maximum torque values may be increased by an amount equal to shank friction, provided the latter is first measured by a torque wrench.

Safetying of Nuts, Bolts and Screws

It is very important that all bolts or nuts, except the self-locking type, be safetied after installation. This prevents them from loosening in flight due to vibration.

Safety wiring is the most positive and satisfactory method of safetying cap-screws, studs, nuts, boltheads, and turnbuckle barrels which cannot be safe-

FINE THREAD SERIES

BOLT SIZE	STANDARD TYPE NUTS (MS20365, AN310, AN315)	SHEAR TYPE NUTS (MS20364, AN320, AN316, AN23 THRU AN31)
10-32	20-25	12-15
1/4-28	50-70	30-40
5/16-24	100-140	60-85
3/8-24	160-190	95-110
7/16-20	450-500	270-300
1/2-20	480-690	290-410
9/16-18	800-1,000	480-600
5/8-18	1,100-1,300	660-740
3/4-16	2,300-2,500	1,300-1,500

COARSE THREAD SERIES

BOLT SIZE	STANDARD TYPE NUTS (MS20365, AN310, AN315)	SHEAR TYPE NUTS (MS20364, AN320, AN316, AN23 THRU AN31)
8-32	12-15	7-9
10-24	20-25	12-15
1/4-20	40-50	25-30
5/16-18	80-90	48-55
3/8-16	160-185	95-110
7/16-14	235-255	140-155
1/2-13	400-480	240-290
9/16-12	500-700	300-420
5/8-11	700-900	420-540
3/4-10	1,150-1,600	700-950

Fig. 2-13. Standard torque tables.

tied by any other practical means. It is a method of wiring together two or more units in such a manner that any tendency of one to loosen is counteracted by the tightening of the wire (Fig. 2-14).

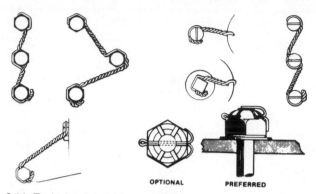

Fig. 2-14. Typical safety wiring methods.

COTTER PIN SAFETYING

Cotter pin installation is shown in Fig. 2-14. Castellated nuts are used with bolts that have been drilled for cotter pins. The cotter pin should fit neatly into the hole, with very little sideplay.

MISCELLANEOUS THREADED FASTENERS

As stated earlier in this chapter, "standard" hex, slotted, and Phillips head threaded fasteners are seldom used for structural applications on high-performance aircraft. For example, most threaded fasteners on the L-1011 jet transport aircraft are "Tri-Wing" developed by the Phillips Screw Company.

Recess No.	SCREW SIZE	
	Tension Head	Shear Head
0	0-80	
1	2-56	4-40
2	4-40	6-32
3	6-32	8-32
4	8-32	10-32
5	10-32	¼-28

Numbers must agree.

Fig. 2-15. Tri-Wing heads are numbered for easy identification, and must be fitted with a like-numbered bit for effective driving.

Other types in general use are: "Torq-Set" and "Hi-Torque.". All of these patented fasteners require special driving bits which fit into standard holders and screwdriver handles.

The Tri-Wing is shown in Fig. 2-15. Other fastener wrenching recesses are shown in Fig. 2-1. Various fasteners are illustrated in Chapter 8, Standard Parts.

Machine Screws

Machine screw threads usually run to the head and thus leave no grip for shear bearing. Machine screws, therefore, are used in tension with no concern for the threads extending into the hole.

A number of different types of heads are available on machine screws to satisfy the particular installation.

For any type of screw there is a correct screwdriver. If the screw has a slotted head, the screwdriver should fit the slot snugly (Fig. 2-16). The sides of the screwdriver should, as nearly as possible, be parallel to the screw slot sides. sides.

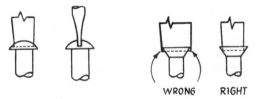

WRONG   RIGHT

Fig. 2-16. A correct size screwdriver must be used.

Reed and Prince or Phillips heads require a special driver made for the particular screw. The drivers for the two are not interchangeable (Fig. 2-17). The Phillips head has rounded shoulders in the recess while the Reed and Prince has sharp square shoulders. The use of the wrong screwdriver on these screws may result in ruining the screw head. The use of power (electric and pneumatic) screwdrivers has speeded up many installations, such as inspection doors and fillets, where the tool may be used in rapid succession on a row of screws.

PHILLIPS   REED & PRINCE

Fig. 2-17. A Phillips screw is different from a Reed & Prince screw.

Instead of a nut, threads are often tapped into the bolted structure. In this case, the bolts or screws are safetied with a wire through a hole drilled in the head (Fig. 2-14). Whenever possible, the wire should be so strung that tension is held on the bolt or screw toward tightening it. Always keep in mind the fact that the wire should tend to tighten the screws.

Machine screws (Fig. 2-18) are usually of the flathead (countersunk), roundhead, or washer-head types. These screws are general-purpose screws and are available in low-carbon steel, brass, corrosion-resistant steel, and aluminum alloy.

Roundhead screws, AN515 and AN520, have either slotted or recessed heads. The AN515 screw has coarse threads and the AN520 has fine threads.

Countersunk machine screws are listed as AN505 and AN510 for 82 degrees, and AN507 for 100 degrees. The AN505 and AN510 correspond to the AN515 and AN520 roundhead in material and usage.

The fillister-head screw, AN500 through AN503, is a general-purpose screw and is used as a capscrew in light mechanisms. This could include attachments of cast aluminum parts such as gearbox cover plates.

The AN500 and AN501 screws are available in low-carbon steel, corrosion-resistant steel, and brass. The AN500 has coarse threads while the AN501 has fine threads. They have no clearly defined grip length. Screws larger than No. 6 have a hole drilled through the head for safetying purposes.

The AN502 and AN503 fillister-head screws are made of heat-treated alloy steel, have a small grip, and are available in fine and coarse threads. These screws are used as capscrews where great strength is required. The coarse-threaded screws are commonly used as capscrews in tapped aluminum alloy and magnesium castings because of the softness of the metal.

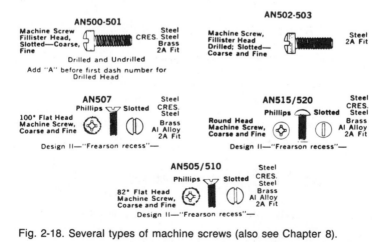

Fig. 2-18. Several types of machine screws (also see Chapter 8).

Dzus Fasteners

Although not a threaded fastener, the Dzus fastener is an example of a quick-disconnect fastener such as used for aircraft cowlings.

The Dzus turnlock fastener consists of a stud, grommet, and receptacle. Figure 2-19 illustrates an installed Dzus fastener and the various parts.

The grommet is made of aluminum or aluminum alloy material. It acts as a holding device for the stud. Grommets can be fabricated from 1100 alumi-

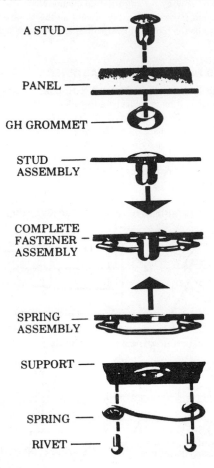

A STUD

PANEL

GH GROMMET

STUD
ASSEMBLY

COMPLETE
FASTENER
ASSEMBLY

SPRING
ASSEMBLY

SUPPORT

SPRING

RIVET

Fig. 2-19. The Dzus fastener.

num tubing, if none are available from normal sources.

The spring is made of steel, cadmium-plated to prevent corrosion. The spring supplies the force that locks or secures the stud in place when two assemblies are joined.

The studs are fabricated from steel and are cadmium-plated. They are available in three head styles: wing, flush, and oval.

A quarter of a turn of the stud (clockwise) locks the fastener. The fastener may be unlocked only by turning the stud counterclockwise. A Dzus key or a specially ground screwdriver locks or unlocks the fastener.

Special installation tools and instructions are available from the manufacturers.

HI-LOK® AND HI-LOK/HI-TIGUE® FASTENERS

The patented, high strength Hi-Lok® or Hi-Lok/Hi-Tigue® originated by the Hi-Shear Corporation is basically a threaded fastener that combines the best features of a rivet and bolt (Fig. 2-20). It consists of two parts, a threaded pin and a threaded collar. The Hi-Tigue® fastener is an updated Hi-Lok® fastener. Three primary design advantages are:

☐ A controlled preload or clamp-up consistent within ± 10 percent designed into the fastener.

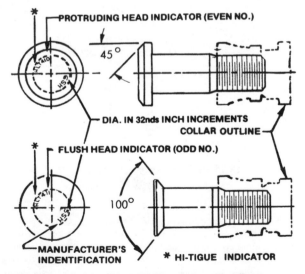

Fig. 2-20. The Hi-Lok®, Hi-Lok/Hi-Tigue® pin and collar.

☐ Minimum size and weight.

☐ Simple, quiet, and rapid installation, done from one side of the work by one worker.

Because of the collar's break-off at design preload, torque inspection after installation is eliminated, along with the problems of torque wrench use and calibration.

The threaded end of the Hi-Lok® pin contains a hexagonal-shaped recess. The hex wrench tip of the Hi-Lok® driving tool engages the recess to prevent rotation of the pin while the collar is being installed. The pin recess also offers a secondary benefit, weight savings.

The pin is designed in two basic head styles. For shear applications the pin is made in the lightweight, "Hi-Shear" countersunk style, and in a compact protruding head style. For tension applications, the MS24694 (AN509) flush and protruding head styles are available.

The self-locking, threaded Hi-Lok® collar has an internal counterbore at the base to accommodate variations in material thickness. At the opposite end of the collar is a wrenching device that is torqued by the driving tool until it shears off during installation; this shear-off point occurs when a predetermined preload or clamp-up is attained in the fastener during installation. Removal of the collar wrenching surfaces after installation saves additional weight.

The basic part number indicates the assembly of the pin and the collar part numbers (Fig. 2-21).

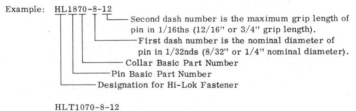

Example: HL1870-8-12
                        └── Second dash number is the maximum grip length of
                             pin in 1/16ths (12/16" or 3/4" grip length).
                        ──── First dash number is the nominal diameter of
                             pin in 1/32nds (8/32" or 1/4" nominal diameter).
                        ──── Collar Basic Part Number
                        ──── Pin Basic Part Number
                        ──── Designation for Hi-Lok Fastener

HLT1070-8-12
    └──────── Designation for Hi-Tigue Type
              Hi-Lok Fastener

Fig. 2-21. Hi-Lok/Hi-Tigue® basic part number.

See tables in Chapter 8, Standard Parts, for representative standard fastener assemblies.

The Hi-Lok/Hi-Tigue® type interference-fit pin provides improved fatigue benefits to the airframe structure. The Hi-Tigue feature on the end of the pin shank makes it possible to use a straight shank interference-fit fastener in a standard straight drilled hole to obtain the maximum fatigue life of the struture.

The Hi-Tigue® pin can be considered a combination of a standard precision pin with a slightly oversize precision ball positioned between the threads

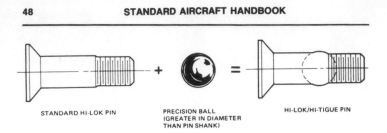

STANDARD HI-LOK PIN

PRECISION BALL
(GREATER IN DIAMETER
THAN PIN SHANK)

HI-LOK/HI-TIGUE PIN

Fig. 2-22. The Hi-Lok® /Hi-Tigue® fastener concept.

and the shank of the pin as shown in Fig. 2-22. Figure 2-23 shows the Hi-Tigue® bead area in exaggerated views.

The Hi-Lok/Hi-Tigue® pin is a straight shank, precision, threaded pin featuring a subtly shaped bead at the thread end of the shank (Fig. 2-23). The pin is installed in a straight-walled hole drilled normally at 0.002 to 0.004 inch diametral interference. The pin is available in 70° and 100° flush heads as well as protruding head styles for shear and tension applications. Pins are manufactured from all commonly used fastener alloys, including titaniums, alloy steels, and corrosion resistant steels.

The Hi-Lok/Hi-Tigue® collar is identical to the self-locking, standard controlled torque Hi-Lok® collar with the exception of the internal counterbore.

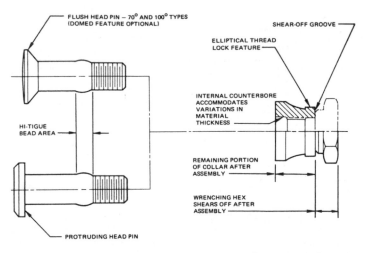

FLUSH HEAD PIN – 70° AND 100° TYPES
(DOMED FEATURE OPTIONAL)

SHEAR-OFF GROOVE

ELLIPTICAL THREAD
LOCK FEATURE

INTERNAL COUNTERBORE
ACCOMMODATES
VARIATIONS IN
MATERIAL
THICKNESS

HI-TIGUE
BEAD AREA

REMAINING PORTION
OF COLLAR AFTER
ASSEMBLY

WRENCHING HEX
SHEARS OFF AFTER
ASSEMBLY

PROTRUDING HEAD PIN

THE HI-LOK/HI-TIGUE PIN

THE HI-LOK/HI-TIGUE COLLAR

Fig. 2-23. The Hi-Lok® /Hi-Tigue® fastening system.

In the Hi-Tigue® version, the counterbore is dimensioned to accommodate the pin's Hi-Tigue® bead during assembly. Hi-Tigue® collars are available for shear, tension, and temperature applications. Collar materials include 2024-T6 aluminum alloy, A-286 alloy, 17-4PH, Type 303 stainless steel and titanium alloy.

A self-sealing torque-controlled collar containing a Teflon sealing insert within its internal counterbore is available to provide fuel-tight joints without the need for sealants.

During assembly of the collar to the pin, using standard Hi-Lok installation tools, the pin is seated into its final position and the structure pieces are drawn tightly together. Because of the collar's wrenching hex shear-off at design preload, torque inspection after installation is eliminated together with the inherent problems of torque wrench use and calibration. Inspection is visual only; no mechanical torque check is required.

Versatile pneumatic Hi-Lok® installation tools assemble both the standard and Hi-Tigue® versions of the Hi-Lok® fastener. Basic Hi-Lok® tooling is available in straight, offset, extended, and 90° right angle types to provide accessibility into a variety of open or congested structures. Automatic collar-driving tools permit assembly of Hi-Loks® up to 40 per minute. Tape-controlled automatic machines have been developed to completely automate the installation of Hi-Lok/Hi-Tigues® : drill, countersink, select the proper grip length, insert the pin and drive the collar.

INSTALLATION OF HI-LOK® AND HI-LOK/HI-TIGUE® FASTENERS

Hole Preparation

Hi-Lok® pins require reamed and chamfered holes and, in some cases, an interference-fit. For standard Hi-Lok® pins, it is generally recommended that the maximum interference-fit shall not exceed 0.002 inch. The Hi-Tigue® type Hi-Lok® pin is normally installed in a hole at 0.002 to 0.004 inch diametral interference.

The Hi-Lok® pin has a slight radius under its head (Fig. 2-24). After drilling, deburr the edge of the hole. This permits the head to fully seat in the hole.

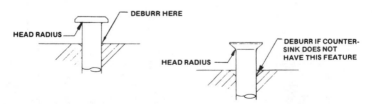

Fig. 2-24. The Hi-Lok® and Hi-Lok/Hi-Tigue® pins have a slight radius under their heads.

See appropriate Hi-Lok® Standards for head radius dimensions. For example, the 3/16 protruding head has a .015/.025 radius while the 3/16 flush head has a .025/.030 radius.

Pin Grip Length

Standard pin lengths are graduated in 1/16 inch increments. The material thickness can vary 1/16 inch without changing pin lengths. Adjustment for variations in material thickness in between the pin 1/16 inch graduations is automatically made by the counterbore in the collar (Fig. 2-25).

Grip length is determined as shown in Fig. 2-26.

Installation Tools

Hi-Lok® fasteners are rapidly installed by one person working from one side of the work using standard power or hand tools and Hi-Lok® adaptor tools.

Hi-Lok® adaptor tools are fitted to high-speed pistol grip and ratchet wrench drives in straight, 90 degree, offset extension, and automatic collar-feed configurations. Figure 2-27 shows a few of the hand and power tools available for

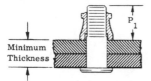

MINIMUM GRIP
(Maximum Protrusion)

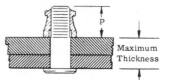

MAXIMUM GRIP
(Minimum Protrusion)

Standard Hi-Lok Pin		Minimum Protrusion P	Maximum Protrusion P_1
First Dash Number	Nominal Diameter		
-5	5/32	.302	.384
-6	3/16	.315	.397
-8	1/4	.385	.467
-10	5/16	.490	.572
-12	3/8	.535	.617
-14	7/16	.625	.707
-16	1/2	.675	.757
-18	9/16	.760	.842
-20	5/8	.815	.897
-24	3/4	1.040	1.122
-28	7/8	1.200	1.282
-32	1	1.380	1.462

Fig. 2-25. Table showing installed Hi-Lok® Pin protrusion limits.

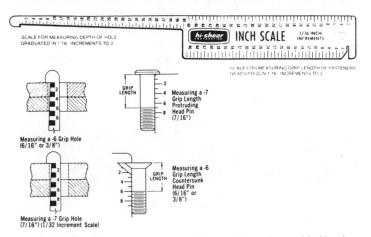

Fig. 2-26. Determining grip length using a special scale provided by the Hi-Shear Corporation.

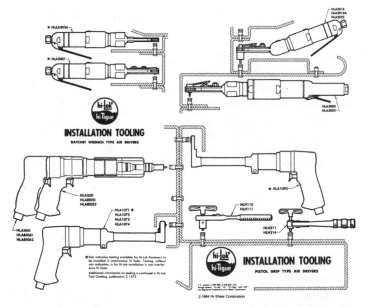

Fig. 2-27. A few of the hand and power tools available for installing Hi-Lok® and Hi-Lok/Hi-Tigue® fasteners.

installing Hi-Lok® and Hi-Lok/Hi-Tigue® fasteners.

The basic consideration in determining the correct hand tool is to match the socket-hex tip dimensions of the tool with the Hi-Lok/Hi-Tigue® pin hex recess and collar driving hex of the particular pin-collar combination to be installed. Figure 2-28 indicates the hex dimensions that must match.

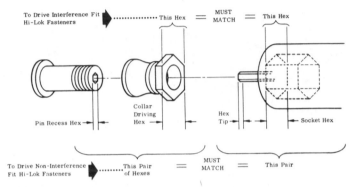

Fig. 2-28. Determining the correct hand tool by matching hex dimensions.

Installation Steps in Non-Interference-Fit Hole

Figure 2-29 shows the installation steps in a non-interference fit hole.

Installation Steps in Interference-Fit Hole

When Hi-Lok/Hi-Tigues® are installed in an interference-fit, the pins should be driven in using a standard rivet gun and Hi-Tigue® pin driver as shown in Fig. 2-30. The structure must be supported with a draw bar as shown.

When Hi-Lok/Hi-Tigue® pins are pressed or tapped into holes, the fit is sufficiently tight to grip the pin to prevent it from rotating. Hi-Lok® driver tools are available that use a finder pin instead of the hex wrench tip to locate the tool on the collar and pin (Fig. 2-31). Otherwise, installation steps for interference-fit holes are the same as for standard Hi-Lok® fasteners.

For field service all sizes of Hi-Lok® fasteners may be installed with hand tools (standard Allen hex keys and open-end or ratchet type wrenches.)

Inspection after Installation

Hi-Lok® and Hi-Lok/Hi-Tigue® fasteners are visually inspected. No torque wrenches are required.

The Hi-Lok® Protrusion Gauges offer a convenient method to check Hi-

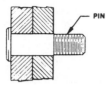

a. Insert the pin into the prepared non-interference fit hole.

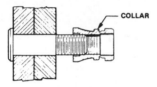

b. Manually thread the collar onto the pin.

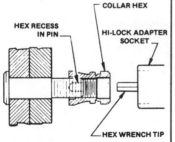

c. Insert the hex wrench tip of the power driver into the pin's hex recess, and the socket over the collar hex. This prevents rotation of the pin while the collar is being installed.

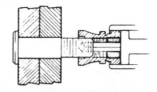

d. Firmly press the power driver against the collar, operate the power driver until the collar's wrenching device has been torqued off.

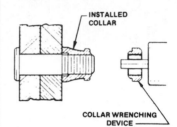

e. This completes the installation of the Hi-Lok Fastener Assembly.

NOTE:

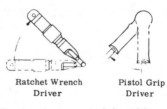

Ratchet Wrench Driver

Pistol Grip Driver

To ease the removal of the driving tool's hex wrench tip from the hex recess of the pin after the collar's wrenching device has sheared off, simply rotate the entire driver tool in a slight clockwise motion.

Fig. 2-29. Installation steps in non-interference fit hole.

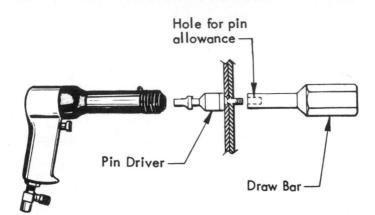

Fig. 2-30. Installing an interference fit Hi-Tigue® pin using a rivet gun.

Lok® pin protrusion limits after the Hi-Lok® pin has been inserted in the hole and before or after collar installation (Fig. 2-32). Individual gauges accommodate Hi-Lok® pin diameter sizes 5/32, 3/16, 1/4, 5/16, and 3/8. Gauges are made of .012 stainless steel and are assembled as a set on a key chain.

Removal of Installed Fastener

Removal of fasteners is accomplished with standard hand tools in a manner similar to removing a nut from a bolt. By holding the pin with a standard Allen wrench, the collar can be removed with pliers. Hollow mill-type cutters

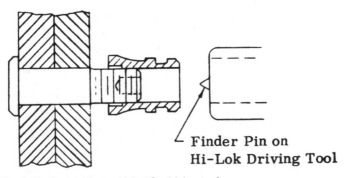

Finder Pin on
Hi-Lok Driving Tool

Fig. 2-31. Finder pin on Hi-Lok® driving tool.

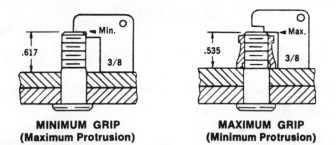

MINIMUM GRIP
(Maximum Protrusion)

MAXIMUM GRIP
(Minimum Protrusion)

Fig. 2-32. Protrusion limits for standard Hi-Lok® pins; 3/8 gauge shown as an example.

attached to power tools can also remove the collars without damage to the pin, and the pins can be reused if undamaged. Special hand and power removal tools are also available.

Chapter 3

Tools and Their Proper Use

SAFETY CONSIDERATIONS

Before commencing work on an aircraft, one's personal safety must become habit. Putting on safety glasses must be as much a part of the act of drilling a hole as picking up the drill motor.

The responsibility for this attitude lies with the mechanic, but this responsibility goes further than that. A mechanic's family needs him whole, with both eyes intact, both hands with all fingers intact, and above all, in good health.

Safety glasses or face shields must be worn during all of the following operations:

- ☐ Drilling
- ☐ Reaming
- ☐ Countersinking
- ☐ Driving rivets
- ☐ Bucking rivets
- ☐ Operating rivet squeezer
- ☐ Operating any power tool
- ☐ Near flying chips or around moving machinery

Ear plugs should be used as protection against the harsh noises of the rivet gun and general factory din. If higher noise levels than the rivet gun are experienced, a full ear coverage "earmuff" should be used since it is a highly absorbent type device.

For people who wear long hair, a snood-type cap that keeps the hair from entangling with turning drills should be worn. Shirt sleeves should be short, or long sleeves rolled up at least to the elbow. Closed-toe, low-heel shoes should be worn. Open-toed shoes, sandals, ballet slippers, moccasins, and canvas-type shoes offer little or no protection for the foot and should not be worn in the shop or factory. Safety shoes are recommended.

Compressed air should not be used for cleaning clothes or equipment.

DRILLS AND DRILLING

Drilling. The drill is a tool for originating and enlarging holes in metal or other substances. The twist drill, usually employed for general drilling purposes, has the following parts (Fig. 3-1).

- ☐ *Point*—The cone-shaped surface on the cutting end.
- ☐ *Shank*—The part of the drill that fits into the drill-press spindle or drill chuck.
- ☐ *Body*—The part from the point to the shank.
- ☐ *Dead Center*—The extreme end of the drill point.
- ☐ *Heel*—That portion of the drill point back of the tips or cutting edges.
- ☐ *Flutes*—Two spiral grooves cut in the body of the drill to permit free-cutting lips and the removal of the chips from the hole.
- ☐ *Lips*—The cutting edges of the drill point.
- ☐ *Tang*—The small end of a tapered shank drill. (Note the *margin* that gives body clearance.)
- ☐ *Web*—The supporting section of the body of the drill lying between the flutes.

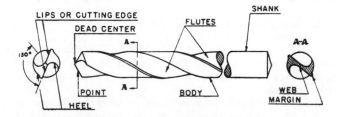

Fig. 3-1. The twist drill.

Drill sizes are designated by letters (from A to Z), by fractions giving the diameter, and by numbers giving wire drill size. See the table on page 224 for a list of drill sizes and their decimal equivalents.

Drill Grinding. It is judged that fully 95 percent of the difficulties encountered in drilling are caused by faulty grinding. A few pointers on the process follow:

1. The lengths of the cutting edges should be equal, otherwise the drill will cut an oversize hole and is liable to break.

2. The angle between the cutting edges should be approximately 118 or 59 degrees from the drill axis (Fig. 3-2). A smaller (to 90 degrees) included angle (Fig. 3-3A) should be used for soft materials such as aluminum, Bakelite, lead, or wood and a larger (to 150 degrees) included angle (Fig. 3-3B) for hard materials such as steels—stainless, manganese, or heat-treated. For brass, the lips of a blunt or wide-angle point are ground straight with the drill axis

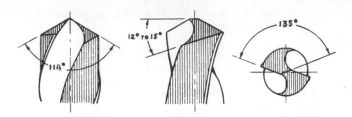

Fig. 3-2. "Standard" drill point.

as shown in (Fig. 3-3C). This is to prevent "hogging in" as the standard drill point will do.

    3. The correct lip clearance should be as illustrated in order that the heel will not drag and thus prevent the cutting edge from feeding properly. (Fig. 3-2B).

    4. The dead center of the web should meet the cutting edges correctly as shown in Fig. 3-1.

Drilling. The handling of a drill motor, though simple, should be carefully done as illustrated in Fig. 3-4A.

The drill motor is held securely by both hands. The thumb and fingers of one hand are extended to contact the work in order to steady the drill in starting as well as act as a safety stop to prevent the drill from damaging anything back of the skin.

Figure 3-4B shows what can happen if control of the drill is not kept at all times. The stringer is certain to be damaged and may have to be replaced. It is well to investigate, before drilling, where the drill point is and what it is apt to hit. When in doubt, stop and look.

In addition to the conventional electric drill motor, the pneumatic drill motor or "air drill" is becoming extremely popular, because the operator can vary the speed from high to slow to suit the particular situation.

When drilling above the eye level goggles are used to protect the eyes against chips.

The workman who knows his drills, sharpens them correctly, and uses them

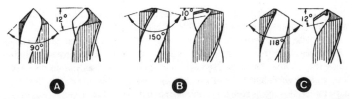

Fig. 3-3. Drill points for soft material (A), hard material (B) and brass (C).

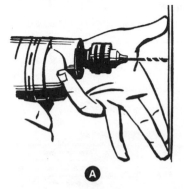

Fig. 3-4.

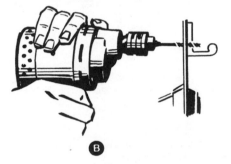

carefully with the correct feed, speed, and lubricant, finds drilling a pleasant task.

Drill speeds are, of course, dependent upon many factors, but particularly upon the material being drilled. The following information is considered good practice and is for reference in case of doubt. The speed and feed combination is very important and, although the suggestions listed below are a helpful guide, the good mechanic watches his drill point and chips to judge a job. If the outer corners of the point wear away rapidly or burn, too much speed is indicated; if the drill chips along the cutting edge, too much feed is indicated. In the case of a power feed, .007 to .015 inch per revolution (the smaller the drill, the smaller the feed) is good; in the case of a hand feed or a hand-held drill motor, sufficient pressure should be exerted to keep a steady uniform chip coming. To figure drill speeds by the following tables, check the recommended cutting speed for the given material in the Cutting Speeds table (Fig. 3-5) , then check this speed along the top of the Drill Speeds table (Fig. 3-6) against the drill size in the left-hand column.

CUTTING SPEEDS*

Material	Feet per minute	Material	Feet per minute
Aluminum	150-300	Tool steel	60-70
Brass	70-100	Stainless steel	30-40
Cast iron	70-100		

*These speeds for high-speed drills should be cut in half for carbon drills.

Fig. 3-5. Suggested cutting speeds for various materials.

DRILL SPEEDS

Drill size, in.	Feet per minute				Drill size, in.	Feet per minute			
	30	70	100	150		30	70	100	150
	Revolutions per minute					Revolutions per minute			
1/16	1,833	4,278	6,111		7/16	262	611	873	1,310
1/8	917	2,139	3,056	4,584	1/2	229	535	764	1,146
3/16	611	1,426	2,037	3,056	5/8	183	428	611	917
1/4	458	1,070	1,528	2,292	3/4	153	357	509	764
5/16	367	856	1,222	1,833	7/8	131	306	437	655
3/8	306	713	1,019	1,528	1	115	267	382	573

Fig. 3-6. Drill speeds vs. cutting speeds.

Lubricant. Drilling efficiency is greatly increased by the use of the proper drill lubricant, which serves as a coolant as well. The table in Fig. 3-7 is suggested as good practice.

LUBRICANT

Metal	Drilling	Reaming	Tapping Threading
Steels:			
Machinery	1	2	1 or 2
Carbon tool	1 or 2	2	2 or 4
High speed	1 or 2	2	2 or 4
Forgings	1 or 2	2	2 or 4
Stainless	2	2	2
Monel	2	2	2
Iron:			
Malleable	1	1	1
Cast	6	6	6
Aluminum	2, 3, or 6	2, 3, or 6	1 or 3
Brass	2 or 3	1	1 or 2
Copper	1	1	1 or 2
Bronze	1 or 6	1 or 6	1 or 2

DRILL LUBRICANTS

1. Soluble oil.	4. Sulphur-base oil.
2. Lard oil.	5. Turpentine.
3. Kerosene.	6. Dry (no lubricant recommended).

NOTE: The Cleveland Twist Drill Company publishes the most authoritative information on drilling in its "Handbook for Drillers."

Fig. 3-7. Recommended lubricants for drilling.

Countersinking and counterboring, or spot-facing, are closely related to drilling operations in that each is applied to a drilled hole.

A rivet or screw hole is countersunk to allow the rivet- or screwhead to lie flush with the surface. The countersink (Fig. 3-8) may be operated by a hand drill, by a portable electric drill motor, or by a drill press.

Fig. 3-8. A standard countersink (A) and a stop countersink (B).

When the conventional type of countersink (Fig. 3-8A) is used, it is necessary to try each hole with a rivet or screw as a precaution against getting it sunk too deep. When it is desirable to use a power tool, the stop countersink (Fig. 3-8B) is best because the depth of countersink can be controlled. In either case, the countersink shaft should be held perpendicularly to the surface of the work (Fig. 3-9C). Otherwise an unsatisfactory off-center hole will result and leave the edge of the hole exposed on one side and the screw edge rising on the other, as in Fig. 3-9B. In Fig. 3-9A the hole and the screwhead are concentric.

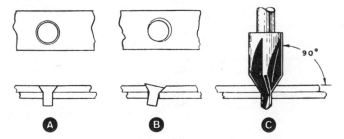

Fig. 3-9. A properly countersunk hole (A); in (B) the axis of countersink was not 90° to surface as required (C).

A counterboring tool is like a bottoming drill with a pilot and is used to sink a hole concentric with another to allow the bolt or screwhead to be sunk below the surface (Fig. 3-10). Since the action of this tool simulates that of a milling machine cutter, extreme care should be taken to have a snugly fitting pilot and a steadily held power supply.

The spot-facer is a counterboring tool generally used in small drill presses and hand drill motors. Its application in aircraft structure is principally to provide a surface for a bolt or screwhead when the hole is necessarily drilled off perpendicular to the natural surface of the casting, forging, or extrusion (Fig. 3-10C).

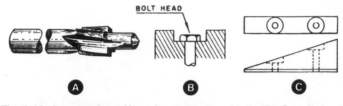

Fig. 3-10. A counterbore (A) and a counterbored hole (B). Spot-facing is at (C).

FILES AND FILING

Files are classified in three ways: by name, according to shape or style; by type, according to the type cut; and by grade, according to the grade of the cut.

The names and shapes of a few of the most popular files are as shown in Fig. 3-11.

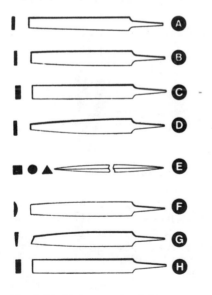

Hand—taper width, parallel thickness (Fig. 3-11A).

Mill—taper width, parallel thickness (Fig. 3-11B).

Pillar—taper thickness, parallel width (Fig. 3-11C).

Warding—much taper width, parallel thickness (Fig. 3-11D).

Square, round and *three square*—taper (Fig. 3-11E).

Half round—taper (Fig. 3-11F).

Knife—taper (Fig. 3-11G).

Vixen—parallel edges and sides (Fig. 3-11H).

Fig. 3-11. Various types of files.

American Swiss and Vixen (Fig. 3-12C, D) have special cuts and are intended for special work. The Swiss type is very find double cut at 45-degree angle, making it very fast cutting. The Vixen, as illustrated, uses a single, knife-like, curved scraper cut which cleans well as it cuts. Swiss files also come in many special shapes for die sinking, etc.

The types of general-purpose files are single cut, with a single row of parallel teeth running across the face, and double cut with two rows of parallel teeth crossing at an angle (Fig. 3-12A, B).

The principal grades are as follows:

No. 000 cut........Coarse cut	No. 2 and 3 cuts...Smooth cut
No. 00 cut........Bastard cut	No. 4 and 5 cuts.Dead smooth cut
No. 0 and 1 cuts...Second cut	

Swiss files use only the numerical expression of the cut. Vixen files use only three grades: regular, fine, and smooth. The length of a file does not include the tang. Some files, such as the hand and the pillar, have one or two safe (smooth) edges.

The important points in filing are as follows: use a straight, forward motion with steady firm pressure; prevent the file from "rocking" over the work; avoid dragging the file back across the work, as this will soon knock the edge off the file; keep the file clean by tapping it against the bench or by brushing it with a file card or wire brush.

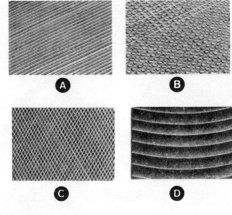

Fig. 3-12. File cuts.

Fig. 3-13. Flexible steel rule. (courtesy Lufkin Rule Co.)

MEASURING TOOLS

Rules are graduated measuring instruments usually made of metal or wood. Flexible steel rules are the most commonly used in aircraft work. Figure 3-13 shows the common 6-in. flexible steel rule graduated in 10ths and 100ths on one side and 32nds and 64ths on the opposite.

Scales, although similar to rules in appearance, are graduated to indicate proportional rather than actual measurements, as, for example, in laying out work one quarter size. Rules and scales have straight edges and may be used as a straightedge although it is considered better practice to use a straightedge designed for that purpose if one is available.

The combination square, so called because it is a combination of a rule and various angle heads, is probably the most popular all-round measuring tool (Fig. 3-14).

Calipers, the most popular precision measuring tools, are used for comparing or measuring distances. The types shown in Fig. 3-15 are outside calipers and inside calipers and are used for comparing or transferring measurements.

Micrometer calipers are calipers graduated for precision measuring down to .001 or .0001 inch. There are three types of micrometers: inside, outside,

Fig. 3-14. Combination square.

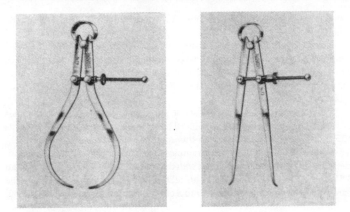

Fig. 3-15. Calipers.

and depth. A thread micrometer is a special type of outside instrument for measuring the pitch diameter of threads.

In general aircraft work, the 1-in. outside micrometer is the most common and is therefore used as the example here. It is composed of the major parts as shown in Fig. 3-16. It actually records the endwise travel of a screw during a whole turn or any part of a turn. The screw of a micrometer has a pitch of 40 threads to the inch; in other words, if the screw is turned 40 times, it will move the spindle exactly 1 in. either toward or away from the anvil. Therefore, a single turn of the screw moves the spindle 1/40 in. or 25 thousandths of an inch.

The graduated inch on the barrel is divided into 40 parts, each representing one turn of the thimble, or 25 thousandths of an inch. Each fourth division

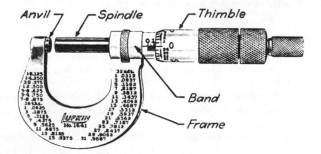

Fig. 3-16. Micrometer.

is numbered 1 through 10, representing 100 thousandths, 200 thousandths, etc. (Fig. 3-16).

Now if the spindle moves 25 thousandths for every revolution of the thimble, then 1/25 of a revolution must move the spindle one thousandth of an inch. Note then, the numbers 0 to 25 running around the thimble (Fig. 3-16), each representing one thousandth of the inch. Read the one aligning with the horizontal line on the barrel.

The micrometer reading consists of the total of the 25 thousandths lines visible plus the reading on the thimble. Thus the micrometer in Fig. 3-16 reads 125 thousandths (5 lines times 25 thousandths).

Figure 3-17 illustrates three examples of readings. First read the micrometer illustration yourself, then check with the reading following the figure. Figure 3-17A reads .304. Figure 3-17B reads .226. Figure 3-17C reads .224. Note the handy decimal equivalents on the frame of the Lufkin micrometer in Fig. 3-16.

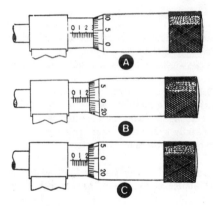

Fig. 3-17. Three different micrometer readings.

TAPS AND DIES

Taps are tools used for cutting inside or female threads in holes in metal, fiber, or other material. The two standard types are standard hand taps and machine screw taps.

Standard hand taps are made for cutting threads from 1/4 in. in diameter and larger, while machine screw tap sizes are from 0 to 10. Both are designated by the screw size and threads.

Taps are in three forms: taper tap for starting; plug tap for use when the bottom of the hole is closed; bottoming tap for cutting threads clear to the bottom of the hole (Fig. 3-18).

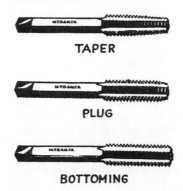

TAPER

PLUG

BOTTOMING

Fig. 3-18. Taper, plug and bottoming taps.

It is very important to start the tap straight and keep it so throughout the work, because taps, especially small ones, are easily broken if strained. Use a lubricant as previously listed in this chapter. Start the tap with steady even pressure. As soon as the tap is started, it will feed itself though. Turn the tap a half turn clockwise, then back up a quarter turn to allow it to clean.

Dies are used for cutting outside or male threads. Start the large side of the die on the work and press down firmly. As soon as the die starts, it will feed itself. Use the same motion as for taps, one half turn forward and reverse one quarter turn. Use the proper lubricant for the material.

REAMERS

Reamers are tools for enlarging drilled holes to an exact diameter while finishing them round, straight, and smooth. The two types in general use are straight reamers and taper reamers.

There are three types of straight reamers: the solid reamer, one solid piece of steel; the expansion reamer, slotted with a tapered screw to expand or contract it a few thousandths of an inch; the adjustable reamer with blade separate from the body, which is tapered with lock nuts to move the blades to larger or smaller size. The solid reamer, being ground to size and therefore more accurate, is used mostly in production; the other two are used chiefly for service and repair.

Taper reamers, as the name implies, are used to ream holes for taper pins or bolts. They are of standard taper either 1/4 or 1/2 in. per foot. Be sure that the reamer is started straight with the hole and that the hole is the right size. Turn the reamer clockwise (never counterclockwise, even when removing) with just enough pressure to keep it feeding. A reamer should be kept absolutely clean to do good work. Never allow it to strike other tools or lie against them. Always keep the blades covered with a thin film of oil to prevent rust.

GENERAL-PURPOSE HAND TOOLS

Hammers

Hammers include ball-peen and soft hammers (Fig. 3-19). The ball-peen hammer is used with a punch, with a chisel, or as a peening (bending, indenting, or cutting) tool. Where there is danger of scratching or marring the work, a soft hammer (for example, brass, plastic, or rubber) is used. Most accidents with hammers occur when the hammerhead loosens. The hammer handle must fit the head tightly. A sweaty palm or an oily or greasy handle may let the hammer slip. Oil or grease on the hammer face may cause the head to slip off the work and cause a painful bruise. Striking a hardened steel surface sharply with a ball-peen hammer is a safety hazard. Small pieces of sharp, hardened steel can break from the hammer and also from the hardened steel. The result may be an eye injury or damage to the work or the hammer. An appropriate soft hammer should be used to strike hardened steel. If the soft hammer is not available, a piece of copper, brass, fiber, or wood material should be placed on the hardened steel and struck with the hammer, not the hardened steel.

Fig. 3-19. Ball-peen and soft face hammers.

Screwdrivers

The screwdriver is a tool for driving or removing screws. Types of screwdrivers that are frequently used are the common, crosspoint, and offset. Also in use are screwdriver bits of various types. These are designed to fit screws having special-type heads. These special screwdrivers are discussed in Chapter 2.

A common screwdriver must fill at least 75 percent of the screw slot (Fig. 3-20). If the screwdriver is the wrong size, it cuts and burrs the screw slot, making it worthless. A screwdriver with the wrong size blade may slip and damage adjacent parts of the structures. The common screwdriver is used only where slotted head screws or fasteners are found on aircraft.

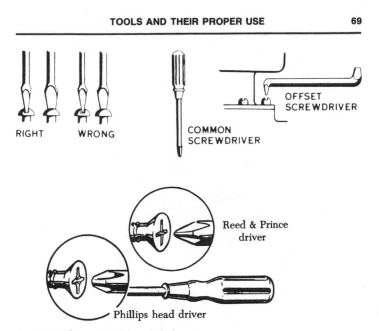

RIGHT   WRONG

COMMON
SCREWDRIVER

OFFSET
SCREWDRIVER

Reed & Prince
driver

Phillips head driver

Fig. 3-20. Screwdrivers and their uses.

The two types of recessed head screws in common use are the Phillips and the Reed and Prince. As shown in Fig. 3-20, the Reed and Prince recessed head forms a perfect cross. The screwdriver used with this screw is pointed on the end. Since the Phillips screw has a slightly larger center in the cross, the Phillips screwdriver is blunt on the end. The Phillips screwdriver is not interchangeable with the Reed and Prince. The use of the wrong type screwdriver results in mutilation of the screwdriver and the screwhead.

A screwdriver should not be used for chiseling or prying.

Pliers

There are several types of pliers, but those used most frequently in aircraft repair work include the slip-joint, longnose, diagonal-cutting, water-pump, and vise-grip types as shown in Fig. 3-21. The size of pliers indicates their overall length, usually ranging from 5 to 12 inches.

The 6-inch slip-joint plier is the preferred size for use in repair work.

Slip-joint pliers are used to grip flat or round stock and to bend small pieces of metal to desired shapes. Longnose pliers are used to reach where the fingers alone cannot and to bend small pieces of metal. Diagonal-cutting pliers or "diagonals" or "dikes" are used to perform work such as cutting safety wire and

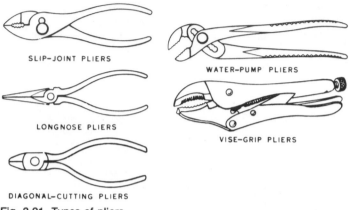

SLIP–JOINT PLIERS

WATER–PUMP PLIERS

LONGNOSE PLIERS

VISE–GRIP PLIERS

DIAGONAL–CUTTING PLIERS

Fig. 3-21. Types of pliers.

removing cotter pins. Water-pump pliers, which have extra long handles, are used to obtain a very powerful grip. Vise-grip pliers (sometimes referred to as vise-grip wrench) have many uses. Examples are to hold small work as a portable vise, to remove broken studs, and to pull cotter pins.

Pliers are not an all purpose tool. They are not to be used as a wrench for tightening a nut, for example. Tightening a nut with pliers causes damage to both the nut and the plier jaw serrations. Also, pliers should not be used as a prybar or as a hammer.

Punches

Punches are used to start holes for drilling, to punch holes in sheet metal, to remove damaged rivets, pins or bolts, and for aligning two or more parts for bolting together. A punch that has a mushroomed head should never be used. Flying pieces may cause an injury. Typical punches used by the aircraft mechanic are shown in Fig. 3-22.

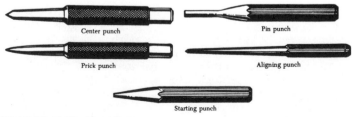

Center punch

Pin punch

Prick punch

Aligning punch

Starting punch

Fig. 3-22. Typical punches.

Wrenches

Wrenches are tools for tightening or removing nuts and bolts. The wrenches that are most often used are shown in Fig. 3-23. They include open-end, box-end, adjustable, socket, and Allen wrenches. All have special advantages. The good mechanic will choose the one best suited for the job at hand. Sockets are used with the various type handles (ratchet, hinge, and speed) and extension bar shown in Fig. 3-23. Extension bars come in various lengths. The ratchet handle and speed wrench can be used in conjunction with suitable adapters and various type screwdriver bits to quickly install or remove special-type screws. However, if screws must be torqued to a specific torque value, a torque wrench must be used. Adjustable type wrenches should be used only when other wrenches do not fit. To prevent rounding off the corners of a nut, properly adjust the wrench. The wrench should always be pulled so that the handle moves toward the adjustable jaw. A wrench should always be pulled. It is dangerous to push on it. A pipe should not be used to increase wrench leverage. Doing so may break the wrench. A wrench should never be used as a hammer.

Proper torquing of nuts and bolts is important. Overtorquing or under-torquing may set up a hazardous condition. Specified torque values and procedures should always be observed.

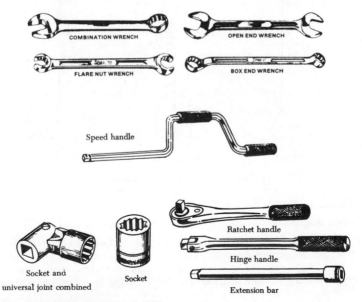

COMBINATION WRENCH

OPEN END WRENCH

FLARE NUT WRENCH

BOX END WRENCH

Speed handle

Socket and
universal joint combined

Socket

Ratchet handle

Hinge handle

Extension bar

Fig. 3-23. Wrenches and sockets.

Torque Wrenches

The three most commonly used torque wrenches are the flexible beam, rigid frame, and the ratchet types (Fig. 3-24). When using the flexible beam and the rigid frame torque wrenches, the torque value is read visually on a dial or scale mounted on the handle of the wrench.

To assure getting the correct amount of torque on the fasteners, all torque wrenches must be tested at least once a month or more often if necessary.

The standard torque table presented in Chapter 2 should be used as a guide in tightening nuts, studs, bolts, and screws whenever specific torque values are not called out in maintenance procedures.

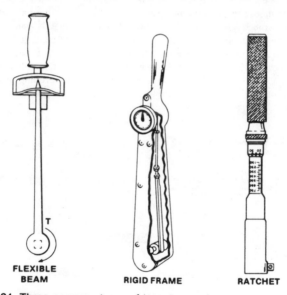

FLEXIBLE
BEAM   RIGID FRAME   RATCHET

Fig. 3-24. Three common types of torque wrenches.

METAL CUTTING TOOLS

Hand Snips

There are several kinds of hand snips, each of which serves a different purpose. Straight, curved, hawksbill, and aviation snips are in common use (Fig. 3-25). Straight snips are used for cutting straight lines when the distance is not great enough to use a squaring shear, and for cutting the outside of a curve. The other types are used for cutting the inside of curves or radii. Snips should never be used to cut heavy sheet metal.

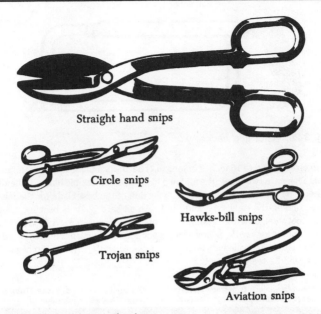

Straight hand snips

Circle snips

Hawks-bill snips

Trojan snips

Aviation snips

Fig. 3-25. Various types of snips.

Aviation snips are designed especially for cutting heat-treated aluminum alloy and stainless steel. They are also adaptable for enlarging small holes. The blades have small teeth on the cutting edges and are shaped for cutting very small circles and irregular outlines. The handles are the compound leverage type, making it possible to cut material as thick as 0.051 inch. Aviation snips are available in two types, those which cut from right to left and those which cut from left to right.

Unlike the hacksaw, snips do not remove any material when the cut is made, but minute fractures often occur along the cut. Therefore, cuts should be made about 1/32 inch from the layout line and finished by hand-filing down to the line.

Hacksaws

The common hacksaw has a blade, a frame, and a handle. The handle can be obtained in two styles, pistol grip and straight. A pistol grip hacksaw is shown in Fig. 3-26.

When installing a blade in a hacksaw frame, the blade should be mounted with the teeth pointing forward, away from the handle.

Blades are made of high-grade tool steel or tungsten steel and are availa-

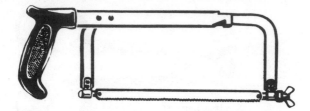

Fig. 3-26. Pistol grip hacksaw.

ble in sizes from 6 to 16 inches in length. The 10-inch blade is most commonly used. There are two types, the all-hard blade and the flexible blade. In flexible blades, only the teeth are hardened. Selection of the best blade for the job involves finding the right type and pitch. An all-hard blade is best for sawing brass, tool steel, cast iron, and heavy cross-section materials. A flexible blade is usually best for sawing hollow shapes and metals having a thin cross section.

The pitch of a blade indicates the number of teeth per inch. Pitches of 14, 18, 24, and 32 teeth per inch are available. See Fig. 3-27.

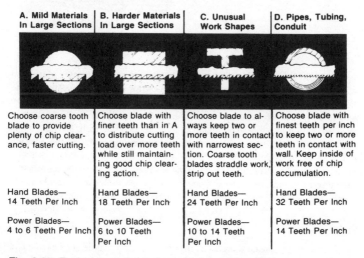

A. Mild Materials In Large Sections	B. Harder Materials In Large Sections	C. Unusual Work Shapes	D. Pipes, Tubing, Conduit
Choose coarse tooth blade to provide plenty of chip clearance, faster cutting.	Choose blade with finer teeth than in A to distribute cutting load over more teeth while still maintaining good chip clearing action.	Choose blade to always keep two or more teeth in contact with narrowest section. Coarse tooth blades straddle work, strip out teeth.	Choose blade with finest teeth per inch to keep two or more teeth in contact with wall. Keep inside of work free of chip accumulation.
Hand Blades— 14 Teeth Per Inch	Hand Blades— 18 Teeth Per Inch	Hand Blades— 24 Teeth Per Inch	Hand Blades— 32 Teeth Per Inch
Power Blades— 4 to 6 Teeth Per Inch	Power Blades— 6 to 10 Teeth Per Inch	Power Blades— 10 to 14 Teeth Per Inch	Power Blades— 14 Teeth Per Inch

Fig. 3-27. Typical uses for various pitch hacksaw blades.

Chisels

A chisel is a hard steel cutting tool which can be used for cutting and chipping any metal softer than the chisel itself. It can be used in restricted areas and for such work as shearing rivets, or splitting seized or damaged nuts from bolts (Fig. 3-28).

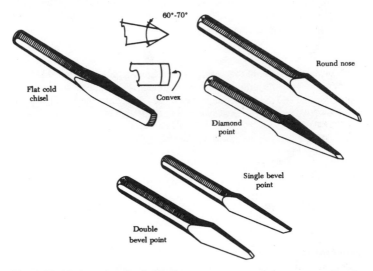

Fig. 3-28. Various types of chisels.

The size of a flat cold chisel is determined by the width of the cutting edge. Lengths will vary, but chisels are seldom under 5 inches or over 8 inches long.

A chisel should be held firmly in one hand. With the other hand, the chisel head is struck squarely with a ball-peen hammer.

When cutting square corners or slots, a special cold chisel called a cape chisel should be used. It is like a flat chisel except the cutting edge is very narrow. It has the same cutting angle and is held and used in the same manner as any other chisel.

Rounded or semicircular grooves and corners that have fillets should be cut with a roundnose chisel. This chisel is also used to recenter a drill which has moved away from its intended center.

The diamond point chisel is tapered square at the cutting end, then ground at an angle to provide the sharp diamond point. It is used for cutting grooves and inside sharp angles.

SHOP EQUIPMENT

Only the simpler metalworking machines, such as used in the service field, are presented in this manual. These include the powered and nonpowered metal-cutting machines, such as the various types of saws, powered and nonpowered shears, and nibblers. Also included is forming equipment (both power-driven and non-powered), such as brakes and forming rolls, the bar folder, and shrinking and stretching machines. Factory type equipment such as hydropresses, drop forge machines, and sparmills, for example, are not described.

Holding Devices

Vises and clamps are tools used for holding materials of various kinds on which some type of operation is being performed. The type of operation being performed and the type of metal being used determine the holding device to be used. A typical vise is shown in Fig. 3-29.

Fig. 3-29. A machinist's vise.

Squaring Shears

Squaring shears provide a convenient means of cutting and squaring metal. Three distinctly different operations can be performed on the squaring shears: (1) cutting to a line, (2) squaring, and (3) multiple cutting to a specific size. A squaring shear is shown in Chapter 6.

Throatless Shears

Throatless shears, Fig. 3-30, are best used to cut 10-gauge mild carbon

Fig. 3-30. Throatless shears.

sheet metal and 12-gauge stainless steel. The shear gets its name from its construction; it actually has no throat. There are no obstructions during cutting since the frame is throatless. A sheet of any length can be cut, and the metal can be turned in any direction to allow for cutting irregular shapes. The cutting blade (top blade) is operated by a hand lever.

Bar Folder

The bar folder, Fig. 3-31, is designed for use in making bends or folds along edges of sheets. This machine is best suited for folding small hems, flanges, seams, and edges to be wired. Most bar folders have a capacity for metal up to 22 gauge in thickness and 42 inches in length.

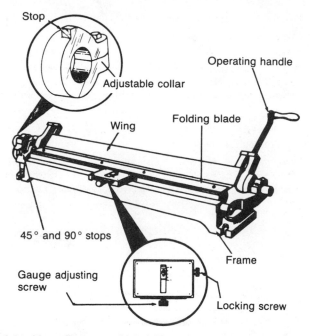

Fig. 3-31. Manually operated bar folder.

Sheet Metal Brake

The sheet metal brake, Fig. 3-32, has a much greater range of usefulness than the bar folder. Any bend formed on a bar folder can be made on the sheet

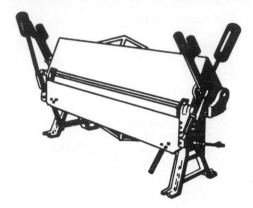

Fig. 3-32. Sheet metal brake.

metal brake. The bar folder can form a bend or edge only as wide as the depth of the jaws. In comparison, the sheet metal brake allows the sheet that is to be folded or formed to pass through the jaws from front to rear without obstruction.

Slip Roll Former

The slip roll former, Fig. 3-33, is manually operated and consists of three rolls, two housings, a base, and a handle. The handle turns the two front rolls through a system of gears enclosed in the housing. By properly adjusting the roller spacing, metal can be formed into a curve.

Fig. 3-33. Slip roll former.

Grinders

A grinding wheel is a cutting tool with a large number of cutting edges arranged so that when they become dull they break off and new cutting edges take their place.

Silicon carbide and aluminum oxide are the kinds of abrasives used in most grinding wheels. Silicon carbide is the cutting agent for grinding hard, brittle material, such as cast iron. It is also used in grinding aluminum, brass, bronze, and copper. Aluminum oxide is the cutting agent for grinding steel and other metals of high tensile strength.

The size of the abrasive particles used in grinding wheels is indicated by a number which corresponds to the number of meshes per linear inch in the screen through which the particles will pass. As an example, a number 30 abrasive will pass through a screen having 30 holes per linear inch, but will be retained by a smaller screen having more than 30 holes per linear inch.

A common type bench grinder found in most metalworking shops is shown in Fig. 3-34. This grinder can be used to dress mushroomed heads on chisels, and points on chisels, screwdrivers, and drills. It can be used for removing excess metal from work and smoothing metal surfaces.

As a rule, it is not good practice to grind work on the side of an abrasive wheel. When an abrasive wheel becomes worn, its cutting efficiency is reduced because of a decrease in surface speed. When a wheel becomes worn in this manner, it should be discarded and a new one installed.

Before using a bench grinder, the abrasive wheels should be checked to make sure that they are firmly held on the spindles by the flange nuts. If an abrasive wheel should come off or become loose, it could seriously injure the operator in addition to ruining the grinder.

Another hazard is loose tool rests. A loose tool rest could cause the tool or piece of work to be "grabbed" by the abrasive wheel and cause the operator's hand to come in contact with the wheel.

Goggles should always be worn when using a grinder, even if eye-shields

Fig. 3-34. A bench grinder.

are attached to the grinder. Goggles should fit firmly against the face and nose. This is the only way to protect eyes from the fine pieces of steel.

The abrasive wheel should be checked for cracks before using the grinder. A cracked abrasive wheel is likely to fly apart when turning at high speeds. A grinder should never be used unless it is equipped with wheel guards.

Chapter 4

Assembly and
Installation Methods

AIRCRAFT PLUMBING

Aircraft plumbing is, as the name implies, the system of tubing used for fuel, oil, coolant, hydraulic, instrument, and vent lines and carries the "life blood" of the aircraft. These lines are coded with colored bands to facilitate tracing and to avoid confusion on assembly or installation.

Seamless tubing is used exclusively for aircraft plumbing and all lines, excepting vent lines, are given a pressure test to eliminate any chance of leakage.

Materials used in the tubing for aircraft plumbing are aluminum alloy, stainless steel (18-8), and Inconel. Tubing sizes are designated by the outside diameter.

Fittings are made of aluminum alloy, brass and steel. The illustration shows two types of fittings joined to the tube end. The nut and sleeve are placed on the tube prior to the flaring of the tube. With the tube then flared, tightening the nut clamps the tube flare between the sleeve and the fitting.

The two fittings shown in Fig. 4-1 are similar but are different in design.

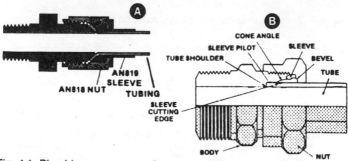

Fig. 4-1. Plumbing connectors; flared tube fitting using AN parts (A) and a flareless tube fitting (B).

The first (an AN fitting) is made specifically to AN sizes and specifications. The complete group of AN fittings are identified individually by AN numbers and are illustrated in the "Standard Parts" section—AN774 through AN928.

The flaring tool used for aircraft tubing has male and female dies ground to produce a flare of 35 degrees to 37 degrees. Under no circumstances is it permissible to use an automotive type flare tool which produces a flare of 45 degrees.

The MS (Military Standard) flareless-tube fittings are finding wide application in aircraft plumbing systems. Using this type fitting eliminates all tube flaring, yet provides a safe, strong, dependable tube connection. The fitting consists of three parts: a body, a sleeve, and a nut. The body has a counterbored shoulder, against which the end of the tube rests. (See Fig. 4-1). The angle of the counterbore causes the cutting edge of the sleeve to cut into the outside of the tube when the two are joined.

Installation. When tubing assemblies are being installed, the fittings should be properly aligned. With the nuts slipped back, the flares should sit easily in place and require no springing of the tubes to make them seat. The central axis of the tube and fitting should align properly to avoid cross threading (Fig. 4-2). Lines should be laid out with offsets as shown in Fig. 4-3A, avoiding point-to-point lines as shown in Fig. 4-3B.

Some compound, such as Parker Threadlube, is used on all threads *except on oxygen plumbing. Never use grease on oxygen lines. For oxygen fittings with straight threads, use Aguadag and for oxygen fittings with pipe threads, use litharge*

WRONG   RIGHT

Fig. 4-2. Tube assemblies and fittings must be properly aligned.

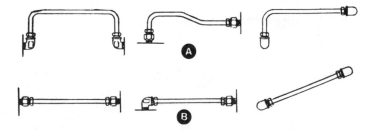

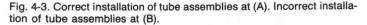

Fig. 4-3. Correct installation of tube assemblies at (A). Incorrect installation of tube assemblies at (B).

SIZE	– 4	– 6	– 8	– 10	– 12	– 16	– 24
TUBE O.D.	1/4	3/8	1/2	5/8	3/4	1	1 1/2
Torque inch-lbs Alum Alloy Tubing, Fitting or Nut	40-65	75-125	150-250	200-350	300-500	500-700	600-900
Steel Tubing, Fitting or Nut	135-150	270-300	450-500	650-700	900-1000	1200-1400	1500-1800
Hose End Fittings, MS28740 End Fittings	100-250	200-480	500-850	700-1150			

Fig. 4-4. Torque values for tightening flared tube fittings.

and glycerin. Threadlube is used sparingly, as the surplus entering the lines will cause trouble. Nuts are run down by hand, then tightened with smooth jaw wrenches, one on the nut and one on the fitting, according to the torque table in Fig. 4-4.

Identification of Fluid Lines

Fluid lines in aircraft are often identified by markers made up of color codes, words, and geometric symbols. These markers identify each line's function, content, and primary hazard, as well as the direction of fluid flow. The various color codes and symbols used to designate the type of system and its contents are shown in the Appendix.

In most instances, fluid lines are marked with 1-inch tape or decals, as shown in Fig. 4-5. On lines 4 inches in diameter (or larger), lines in oily environment, hot lines, and on some cold lines, steel tags may be used in place of tape or decals. Paint is used on lines in engine compartments, where there is the possibility of tapes, decals, or tags being drawn into the engine induction system.

Flexible Hose

Flexible hose is used in aircraft plumbing to connect moving parts with

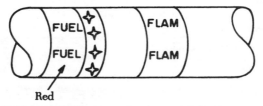

Red

Fig. 4-5. Fluid line identification using tape and decals.

stationary parts in locations subject to vibration or where a great amount of flexibility is needed. It can also serve as a connector in metal tubing systems.

Synthetic materials most commonly used in the manufacture of flexible hose are: Buna-N, Neoprene, Butyl and Teflon (trademark of DuPont Corp.). **Buna-N** is a synthetic rubber compound which has excellent resistance to petroleum products. Do not use for phosphate ester base hydraulic fluid (Skydrol®). **Neoprene** is a synthetic rubber compound which has an acetylene base. Its resistance to petroleum products is not as good as Buna-N but has better abrasive resistance. Do not use for phosphate ester base hydraulic fluid (Skydrol®). **Butyl** is a synthetic rubber compound made from petroleum raw materials. It is an excellent material to use with phosphate ester based hydraulic fluid (Skydrol®). Do not use with petroleum products. **Teflon** is the

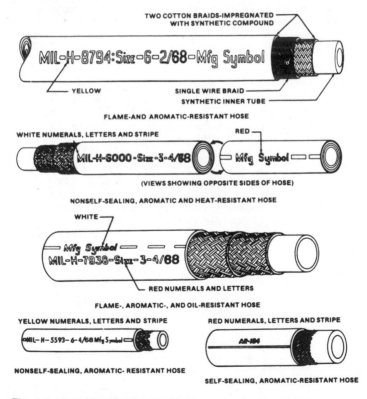

TWO COTTON BRAIDS-IMPREGNATED WITH SYNTHETIC COMPOUND

MIL-H-8794:Size-6-2/68-Mfg Symbol

YELLOW   SINGLE WIRE BRAID
SYNTHETIC INNER TUBE

FLAME-AND AROMATIC-RESISTANT HOSE

WHITE NUMERALS, LETTERS AND STRIPE   RED

MIL-H-6000-Size-3-4/68   Mfg Symbol

(VIEWS SHOWING OPPOSITE SIDES OF HOSE)

NONSELF-SEALING, AROMATIC AND HEAT-RESISTANT HOSE

WHITE

Mfg Symbol
MIL-H-7938-Size-3-4/68

RED NUMERALS AND LETTERS

FLAME-, AROMATIC-, AND OIL-RESISTANT HOSE

YELLOW NUMERALS, LETTERS AND STRIPE   RED NUMERALS, LETTERS AND STRIPE

MIL-H-5593-6-4/68 Mfg Symbol   AS-104

NONSELF-SEALING, AROMATIC- RESISTANT HOSE

SELF-SEALING, AROMATIC-RESISTANT HOSE

Fig. 4-6. Hose identification markings.

DuPont trade name for tetrafluoroethylene resin. It has a broad operating temperature range (– 65 degrees F. to + 450 degrees F.). It is compatible with nearly every substance or agent used.

Flexible rubber hose consists of a seamless synthetic rubber inner tube covered with layers of cotton braid and wire braid, and an outer layer of rubber-impregnated cotton braid. This type of hose is suitable for use in fuel, oil, coolant, and hydraulic systems. The types of hose are normally classified by the amount of pressure they are designed to withstand under normal operating conditions.

1. Low pressure, any pressure below 250 p.s.i. Fabric braid reinforcement.
2. Medium pressure, pressures up to 3,000 p.s.i.
   One wire braid reinforcement.
   Smaller sizes carry pressure up to 3,000 p.s.i.
   Larger sizes carry pressure up to 1,500 p.s.i.
3. High pressure (all sizes up to 3,000 p.s.i. operating pressures).

Identification markings consisting of lines, letters, and numbers are printed on the hose. These code markings show such information as hose size, manufacturer, date of manufacture, and pressure and temperature limits. Code markings assist in replacing a hose with one of the same specification or a recommended substitute. Hose suitable for use with phosphate ester base hydraulic fluid will be marked "Skydrol® use." In some instances several types of hose may be suitable for the same use. Therefore, in order to make the correct hose selection, always refer to the maintenance or parts manual for the particular airplane.

Installation of Flexible Hose Assemblies

Flexible hose must not be twisted on installation, since this reduces the life of the hose considerably and may loosen the fittings. Twisting of the hose can be determined from the identification stripe running along its length. This stripe should not spiral around the hose.

Flexible hose should be protected from chafing by wrapping it with tape, but only where necessary.

The minimum bend radius for flexible hose varies according to size and construction of the hose and the pressure under which the hose is to operate. Bends that are too sharp will reduce the bursting pressure of flexible hose considerably below its rated value (Fig. 4-7).

The size of flexible hose is determined by its inside diameter. Sizes are in one-sixteenth-inch increments and are identical to corresponding sizes of rigid tubing, with which it can be used.

Support clamps are used to secure the various lines to the airframe or powerplant assemblies. The rubber-cushioned clamp is used to secure lines subject to vibration; the cushioning prevents chafing of the tubing. The plain clamp is used to secure lines in areas not subject to vibration.

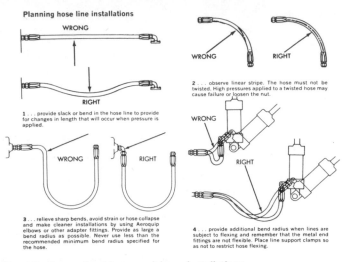

Planning hose line installations

WRONG

RIGHT

1 . . . provide slack or bend in the hose line to provide for changes in length that will occur when pressure is applied.

WRONG   RIGHT

WRONG   RIGHT

3 . . . relieve sharp bends, avoid strain or hose collapse and make cleaner installations by using Aeroquip elbows or other adapter fittings. Provide as large a bend radius as possible. Never use less than the recommended minimum bend radius specified for the hose.

WRONG   RIGHT

2 . . . observe linear stripe. The hose must not be twisted. High pressures applied to a twisted hose may cause failure or loosen the nut.

WRONG

RIGHT

4 . . . provide additional bend radius when lines are subject to flexing and remember that the metal end fittings are not flexible. Place line support clamps so as not to restrict hose flexing.

Fig. 4-7. Proper (and improper) hose installations.

A Teflon-cushioned clamp is used in areas where the deteriorating effect of Skydrol® 500, hydraulic fluid (MIL-0-5606), or fuel is expected. However, because it is less resilient, it does not provide as good a vibration-damping effect as other cushion materials. Use bonded clamps to secure metal hydraulic, fuel, and oil lines in place. Unbonded clamps should be used only for securing wiring.

AIRPLANE CONTROL SYSTEMS

Airplane control mechanisms transmit motion from the pilot's controls in the cockpit to the proper control surface or accessory using torque tubes, push-pull tubes, and cable-pulley arrangements (Fig. 4-8).

Torque tubes, as the name implies, transmit the load by a turning motion with push-pull tubes or cable-operated bell cranks on either end. Torque tubes are mounted on roller or ball bearings (Fig. 4-9). When torque tubes are being installed, the mounting brackets should be properly aligned so that they will not bind the bearings when bolts are tightened. Levers or bell cranks are riveted or "taper-pinned" to the tube. For example, a torque tube is generally used to couple and actuate the elevators, while a push-pull tube is used to couple and actuate double rudders.

Push-pull tubes used to operate wing flaps or other control surfaces are generally spliced or attached to the actuating fittings by taper pins to facilitate

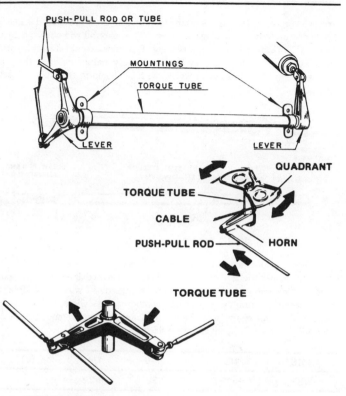

BELLCRANK

Fig. 4-8. Flight control system mechanical linkage.

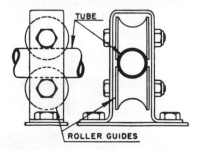
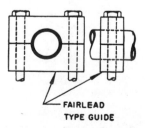

Fig. 4-9. Typical push-pull tube guides.

service and repair (Fig. 4-10). A push-pull tube carrying a heavy load is generally guided by Micarta bushings or rollers. This material will absorb a small amount of lubricant and serve as a bearing. The guides should always be carefully checked to be sure that they line up properly and do not draw the tube out of a straight line. For good results, the tube should fit the guides closely but freely.

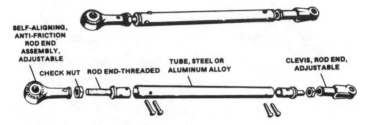

Fig. 4-10. Push-pull tube assembly.

Control cables are either flexible (7 × 7) or extraflexible (7 × 19). The latter is far more popular, except in sizes below 1/8 in. in diameter. 7 × 7 designates a cable composed of 7 strands, each composed of 7 wires; 7 × 19, a cable composed of 7 strands, each in turn composed of 19 wires. Control cables are generally made of stainless or galvanized steel, although some tinned steel cable still is used. The popular cable sizes are as follows:

1/16*	1/8	3/16	1/4	5/16
3/32*	5/32	7/32	9/32 †	

* 7 × 7 only.
† 7 × 19 only.

Figure 4-11 illustrates the construction of flexible (7 × 7) and extra-flexible (7 × 19) cables. Note the method of measuring cable diameter.

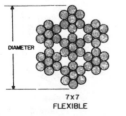
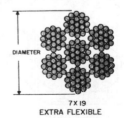

Fig. 4-11. Cable cross section.

Control cables are strung over AN210 pulleys and guided between pulleys by fair-leads when the span is long. Pulley brackets are equipped with cable guards to prevent the cable from dropping off the pulley when slackened (Fig. 4-12).

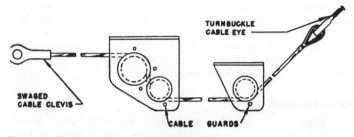

Fig. 4-12. Typical control cable installation.

Cable ends are either spliced around cable thimbles (AN100) or cable bushings (AN111), or the ends are swaged to cable terminals such as clevises, eyes, or threaded ends (AN666, 667, 668, and 669). The threaded ends are to fit in one end of a turnbuckle, the other ends to suit the installation.

When cables are being strung, it is usually necessary to remove the cable guards. After stringing, the cable should be checked to be sure that all guards are in place and properly safetied.

A group of control cables are often strung very close together. It is therefore of utmost importance that each cable is strung through its proper pulley, that no cables are twisted, and that ends are in the right direction.

"Pull-off" is serious and must be avoided at all times. This term denotes

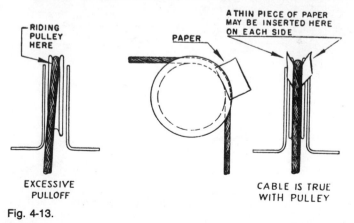

Fig. 4-13.

that the cable does not pull true with the pulley. Unless corrected, the cable will chafe the pulley sides and cause serious trouble. When a gauge to detect pull-off is not available, a thin piece of paper may be inserted between the cable and pulley side if there is no pull-off (Fig. 4-13).

To avoid pull-off, brackets should be set carefully by sighting through the pulley to the next pulley through which the cable runs, before the bolts holding the brackets are tightened. The system should be checked to see that cable terminals are properly secured and safetied, that cables have proper tension, and that turnbuckles are properly safetied. The safety wire should tend to tighten the turnbuckle as described later in this chapter.

Cable Terminals

Although hand-fabricated terminal ends are acceptable, modern methods of applying cable terminal ends consist of swaging and the Nicopress sleeve.

Swage-Type Terminals. Swage-type terminals, manufactured in accordance with Air Force-Navy Aeronautical Standard Specifications, are suitable for use in civil aircraft up to and including maximum cable loads. When swaging tools are used, it is important that all the manufacturers' instructions, including "go and no-go" dimensions (Fig. 4-14) be followed in detail to avoid defective and inferior swaging. Observance of all instructions should result in a terminal developing the full rated strength of the cable.

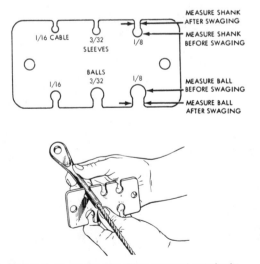

Fig. 4-14. A typical gauge for checking swaged terminals.

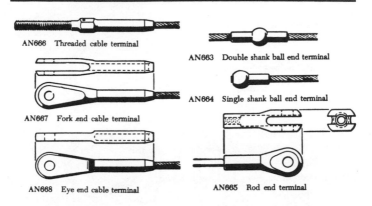

Fig. 4-15. Various types of terminal fittings.

Various types of swage terminal fittings are shown in Fig. 4-15.

Nicopress Process. A patented process using copper sleeves may be used up to the full rated strength of the cable when the cable is looped around a thimble. This process may also be used in place of the five-tuck splice on cables up to and including 3/8-inch diameter.

Before undertaking a Nicopress splice, the proper tool and sleeve for the cable must be determined based on the manufacturers instructions. A typical hand swager is shown in Fig. 4-16.

Fig. 4-16. A hand-operated nicopress swage for cables up to 3/16-inch diameter.

A typical Nicopress thimble eye splice is shown in Fig. 4-17.

To make a satisfactory copper sleeve installation, it is important that the amount of sleeve pressure be kept uniform. The completed sleeves should be checked periodically with the proper gauge. The gauge should be held so that it contacts the major axis of the sleeve. The compressed portion at the center of the sleeve should enter the gauge opening with very little clearance, as shown in Fig. 4-18. If it does not, the tool must be adjusted accordingly.

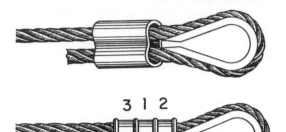

Fig. 4-17. Typical thimble-eye splice. The sleeve should be compressed in the 1-2-3 sequence shown.

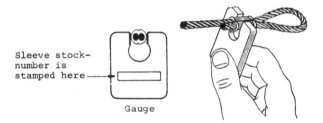

Fig. 4-18. Typical go/no-go gauge for nicopress terminals.

Turnbuckles

A turnbuckle assembly is a mechanical screw device consisting of two threaded terminals and a threaded barrel. Figure 4-19 illustrates a typical turnbuckle assembly.

Turnbuckles are fitted in the cable assembly for the purpose of making minor adjustments in cable length and for adjusting cable tension. One of the

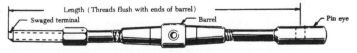

Fig. 4-19. A typical turnbuckle assembly.

terminals has right-hand threads and the other has left-hand threads. The barrel has matching right- and left-hand internal threads. The end of the barrel with the left-hand threads can usually be identified by a groove or knurl around that end of the barrel.

When installing a turnbuckle in a control system, it is necessary to screw both of the terminals an equal number of turns into the barrel. It is also essential that all turnbuckle terminals be screwed into the barrel until not more than three threads are exposed on either side of the turnbuckle barrel.

Safety Methods for Turnbuckles. After a turnbuckle has been properly adjusted, it must be safetied. There are several methods of safetying turnbuckles; however, only two methods will be discussed in this section. These methods are illustrated in Figs. 4-20 and 4-21. The clip-locking method, Fig. 4-20, is used only on modern aircraft. The older type aircraft still use the type turnbuckles that require the wire-wrapping method.

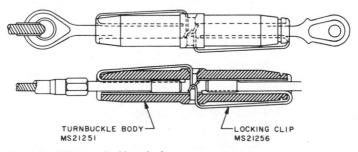

Fig. 4-20. Clip-type locking device.

Fig. 4-21. Double wrapped method for safetying turnbuckles.

Double-Wrap Method. Of the methods using safety wire for safetying turnbuckles, the double-wrap method is preferred, although the single-wrap method is satisfactory. The method of double-wrap safetying is shown in Fig. 4-21. Two separate lengths of the proper wire as shown in Fig. 4-22 are used. One end of the wire is run through the hole in the barrel of the turnbuckle. The ends of the wire are bent toward opposite ends of the turnbuckle. Then the second length of the wire is passed into the hole in the barrel and the ends bent along the barrel on the side opposite the first. Then the wires at the end of the turnbuckle are passed in opposite directions through the holes in the

Cable Size (in.)	Type of Wrap	Diameter of Safety Wire	Material (Annealed Condition)
1/16	Single	0.020	Copper, brass.[1]
3/32	Single	0.040	Copper, brass.[1]
1/8	Single	0.040	Stainless steel, Monel and "K" Monel.
1/8	Double	0.040	Copper, brass.[1]
1/8	Single	0.057 min	Copper, brass.[1]
5/32 and greater.	Double	0.040	Stainless steel, Monel and "K" Monel.[1]
5/32 and greater.	Single	0.057 min	Stainless steel, Monel or "K" Monel.[1]
5/32 and greater.	Double	0.051[2]	Copper, brass.

[1] Galvanized or tinned steel, or soft iron wires are also acceptable.
[2] The safty wire holes in 5/32-inch diameter and larger turnbuckle terminals for swaging may be drilled sufficiently to accommodate the double 0.051-inch diameter copper or brass wires when used.

Fig. 4-22. Guide for selecting turnbuckle safety wire.

turnbuckle eyes or between the jaws of the turnbuckle fork, as applicable. The laid wires are bent in place before cutting off the wrapped wire. The remaining length of safety wire is wrapped at least four turns around the shank and cut off. The procedure is repeated at the opposite end of the turnbuckle.

When a swaged terminal is being safetied, the ends of both wires are passed, if possible, through the hole provided in the terminal for this purpose and both ends are wrapped around the shank as described above.

If the hole is not large enough to allow passage of both wires, the wire should be passed through the hole and looped over the free end of the other wire, and then both ends wrapped around the shank as described.

Cable Tension Adjustment

Control cable tension should be carefully adjusted in accordance with the airframe manufacturer's recommendations. On large aircraft, the temperature of the immediate area should be taken into consideration when using a tensiometer, Fig. 4-23. For long cable sections, the average of two or three temperature readings should be used to obtain accurate tension values. If necessary,

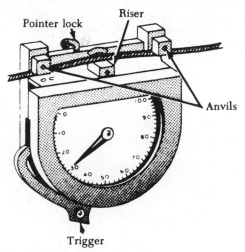

Fig. 4-23. A typical cable tensiometer.

compensation should be made for extreme surface temperature variations that may be encountered if the aircraft is operated primarily in unusual geographic or climatic conditions such as arctic, arid, or tropic locations. Figure 4-24 shows a typical cable rigging chart.

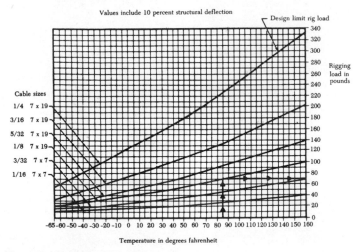

Fig. 4-24. Typical cable rigging chart.

Rigging pins and gust locks should be used as necessary to assure satisfactory results. At the completion of rigging operations, turnbuckle adjustment and safetying should be checked in accordance with previous instructions.

Chapter 5
Electrical Wiring
and Installation

MATERIAL SELECTION

Aircraft service imposes severe environmental conditions on electric wire. To assure satisfactory service, the wire should be inspected at regular intervals for abrasions, defective insulation, condition of terminal posts, and buildup of corrosion under or around swaged terminals.

For the purpose of this discussion, a **wire** is described as a single, solid conductor, or as a stranded conductor covered with an insulating material. Figure 5-1 illustrates these two definitions of a wire.

Wire single solid conductor

Conductors

Solid conductor.

Stranded   conductor

Fig. 5-1. Single solid conductor and a conductor consisting of many strands.

The term **cable**, as used in aircraft electrical installations, includes:

1. Two or more separately insulated conductors in the same jacket (multi-conductor cable).

2. Two or more separately insulated conductors twisted together (twisted pair).

3. One or more insulated conductors, covered with a metallic braided shield (shielded cable).

4. A single insulated center conductor with a metallic braided outer conductor (radio frequency cable). The concentricity of the center conductor and the outer conductor is carefully controlled during manufacture to ensure that they are coaxial.

Wire Size

Wire is manufactured in sizes according to a standard known as the AWG (American wire gauge). As shown in Fig. 5-2, the wire diameters become smaller as the gauge numbers become larger. See Appendix for a table of wire gauges.

To use the wire gauge, the wire to be measured is inserted in the smallest slot that will just accommodate the bare wire. The gauge number corresponding to that slot indicates the wire size. The slot has parallel sides and should not be confused with the semicircular opening at the end of the slot. The opening simply permits the free movement of the wire all the way through the slot.

Gauge numbers are useful in comparing the diameter of wires, but not all types of wire or cable can be accurately measured with a gauge. Large wires are usually stranded to increase their flexibility. In such cases, the total area can be determined by multiplying the area of one strand (usually computed in circular mils when diameter or gauge number is known) by the number of strands in the wire or cable.

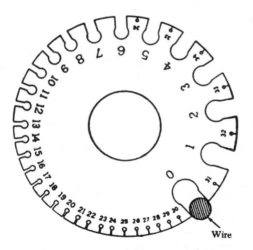

Fig. 5-2. An AWG wire gauge.

Factors Affecting the Selection of Wire Size

Tables and procedures are available for selecting correct wire sizes. For purposes of this manual, it is assumed that wire sizes were specified by the manufacturer of the aircraft or equipment.

Factors Affecting Selection of Conductor Material

Although silver is the best conductor, its cost limits its use to special circuits where a substance with high conductivity is needed.

The two most generally used conductors are copper and aluminum. Each has characteristics that make its use advantageous under certain circumstances. Also, each has certain disadvantages.

Copper has a higher conductivity; it is more ductile (can be drawn), has relatively high tensile strength, and can be easily soldered. It is more expensive and heavier than aluminum.

Although aluminum has only about 60 percent of the conductivity of copper, it is used extensively. Its lightness makes possible long spans, and its relatively large diameter for a given conductivity reduces corona (the discharge of electricity from the wire when it has a high potential). The discharge is greater when small diameter wire is used than when large diameter wire is used. Some bus bars are made of aluminum instead of copper where there is a greater radiating surface for the same conductance.

The type of conductor insulation material varies with the type of installation. Such types of insulation as rubber, silk, and paper are no longer used extensively in aircraft systems. More common today are such materials as vinyl, cotton, nylon, Teflon, and Rockbestos.

Stripping Insulation

Attachment of wire to connectors or terminals requires the removal of insulation to expose the conductors. This practice is commonly known as stripping. When performing the stripping operation, remove no more insulation than is necessary. Stripping may be accomplished in many ways; however, the following basic principles should be practiced:

Make sure all cutting tools used for stripping are sharp.

When using special wire stripping tools, adjust the tool to avoid nicking, cutting, or otherwise damaging the strands.

Automatic stripping tools should be carefully adjusted; the manufacturer's instructions should be followed to avoid nicking, cutting, or otherwise damag-

Fig. 5-3. A light-duty hand operated wire stripper.

ing strands. This is especially important for aluminum wires and for copper wires smaller than No. 10.

A light duty hand-operated wire stripper is shown in Fig. 5-3.

TERMINALS

Terminals are attached to the ends of electric wires to facilitate connection of the wires to terminal strips or items of equipment. Terminals specifically designed for use with the standard sizes of aircraft wire are available through normal supply channels. Haphazard choice of commercial terminals may lead to overheated joints, vibration failures, and corrosion difficulties.

For most applications, soldered terminals have been replaced by solderless terminals. The solder process has disadvantages that have been overcome by use of the solderless terminals.

The terminal manufacturer will normally provide a special crimping or swaging tool for joining the solderless terminal to the electric wire. Aluminum wire presents special difficulty in that each individual strand is insulated by an oxide coating. This oxide coating must be broken down in the crimping process and some method employed to prevent its reforming. In all cases, terminal manufacturer's instructions should be followed when installing solderless terminals.

Copper wires are terminated with solderless, preinsulated straight copper terminal lugs. The insulation is part of the terminal lug and extends beyond its barrel so that it will cover a portion of the wire insulation, making the use of an insulation sleeve unnecessary (Fig. 5-4).

In addition, preinsulated terminal lugs contain an insulation grip (a metal reinforcing sleeve) beneath the insulation for extra gripping strength on the

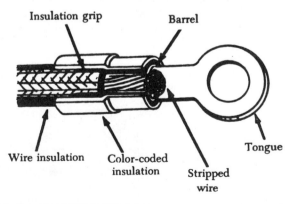

Fig. 5-4. A preinsulated terminal lug.

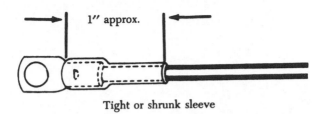

1″ approx.

Tight or shrunk sleeve

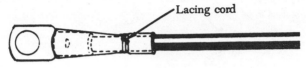

Lacing cord

Loose sleeve

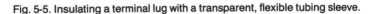

Fig. 5-5. Insulating a terminal lug with a transparent, flexible tubing sleeve.

wire insulation. Preinsulated terminals accommodate more than one size of wire; the insulation is usually color-coded to identify the wire sizes that can be terminated with each of the terminal lug sizes.

Some types of uninsulated terminal lugs are insulated after assembly to a wire by means of pieces of transparent flexible tubing called "**sleeves.**" The sleeve provides electrical and mechanical protection at the connection. When the size of the sleeving used is such that it will fit tightly over the terminal lug, the sleeving need not be tied; otherwise, it should be tied with lacing cord as illustrated in Fig. 5-5.

Aluminum Wire Terminals

The use of aluminum wire in aircraft systems is increasing because of its weight advantage over copper. However, bending aluminum will cause "work hardening" of the metal, making it brittle. This results in failure or breakage of strands much sooner than in a similar case with copper wire. Aluminum also forms a high-resistant oxide film immediately upon exposure to air. To compensate for these disadvantages, it is important to use the most reliable installation procedures.

Only aluminum terminal lugs are used to terminate aluminum wires. All aluminum terminals incorporate an inspection hole (Fig. 5-6), which permits checking the depth of wire insertion. The barrel of aluminum terminal lugs is filled with a petrolatum-zinc dust compound. This compound removes the oxide film from the aluminum by a grinding process during the crimping oper-

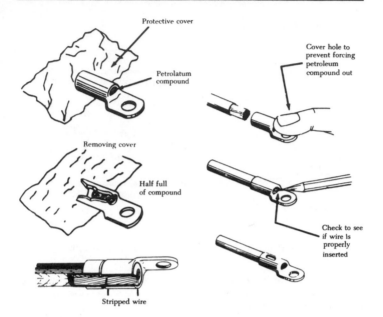

Fig. 5-6. Inserting aluminum wire into aluminum terminal lugs.

ation. The compound will also minimize later oxidation of the completed connection by excluding moisture and air. The compound is retained inside the terminal lug barrel by a plastic or foil seal at the end of the barrel.

Connecting Terminal Lugs to Terminal Blocks

Terminal lugs should be installed on terminal blocks so that they are locked against movement in the direction of loosening (Fig. 5-7).

Terminal blocks are normally supplied with studs secured in place by a plain washer, an external tooth lockwasher, and a nut. In connecting terminals, a recommended practice is to place copper terminal lugs directly on top of the nut, followed with a plain washer and elastic stop nut, or with a plain washer, split steel lockwasher, and plain nut.

Aluminum terminal lugs should be placed over a plated brass plain washer, followed with another plated brass plain washer, split steel lockwasher, and plain nut or elastic stop nut. The plated brass washer should have a diameter equal to the tongue width of the aluminum terminal lug. The manufacturer's instructions should be consulted for recommended dimensions of these plated

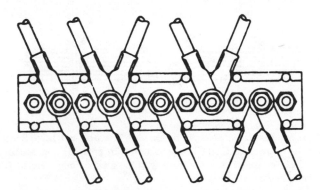

Fig. 5-7. Connecting terminals to a terminal block.

brass washers. No washer should be placed in the current path between two aluminum terminal lugs or between two copper terminal lugs. Also, no lockwasher should be placed directly against the tongue or pad of the aluminum terminal.

To join a copper terminal lug to an aluminum terminal lug, a plated brass plain washer should be placed over the nut that holds the stud in place, followed with the aluminum terminal lug, a plated brass plain washer, the copper terminal lug, plain washer, split steel lockwasher, and plain nut or self-locking, all-metal nut. As a general rule, a torque wrench should be used to tighten nuts to ensure sufficient contact pressure. Manufacturer's instructions provide installation torques for all types of terminals.

Identifying Wire and Cable

Aircraft electrical system wiring and cable may be marked with a combination of letters and numbers to identify the wire, the circuit it belongs to, the gauge number, and other information necessary to relate the wire or cable to a wiring diagram. Such markings are called the **identification code**. There is no standard procedure for marking and identifying wiring; each manufacturer normally develops his own identification code. Wires are usually marked at intervals of not more than 15 inches lengthwise and within 3 inches of each junction or terminating point.

WIRE GROUPS AND BUNDLES

Grouping or bundling certain wires, such as electrically unprotected power wiring and wiring going to duplicate vital equipment, should be avoided.

Fig. 5-8. Groups and bundle ties.

Wire bundles should generally be less than 75 wires, or 1 1/2 to 2 inches in diameter where practicable. When several wires are grouped at junction boxes, terminal blocks, panels, etc., the identity of the group within a bundle (Fig. 5-8) can be retained.

Single wires or wire bundles should not be installed with excessive slack. Slack between supports should normally not exceed a maximum of 1/2 inch deflection with normal hand force (Fig. 5-9).

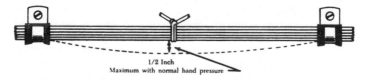

Fig. 5-9. Maximum recommended slack in wire bundles between supports.

Bend Radii

Bends in wire groups or bundles should be not less than 10 times the outside diameter of the wire group or bundle. However, at terminal strips, where wire is suitably supported at each end of the bend, a minimum radius of three times the outside diameter of the wire, or wire bundle, is normally acceptable. There are, of course, exceptions to these guidelines in the case of certain types of cable; for example, coaxial cable should never be bent to a smaller radius than six times the outside diameter.

Routing and Installations

All wiring should be installed so that it is mechanically and electrically sound and neat in appearance. Whenever practicable, wires and bundles should be routed parallel with, or at right angles to, the stringers or ribs of the area involved. An exception to this general rule is coaxial cable, which is routed as directly as possible.

The wiring must be adequately supported throughout its length. A sufficient number of supports must be provided to prevent undue vibration of the unsupported lengths.

When wiring must be routed parallel to combustible fluid or oxygen lines for short distances, as much fixed separation as possible should be maintained. The wires should be on a level with, or above, the plumbing lines. Clamps should be spaced so that if a wire is broken at a clamp it will not contact the line. Where a 6-inch separation is not possible, both the wire bundle and the plumbing line can be clamped to the same structure to prevent any relative motion. If the separation is less than 2 inches but more than 1/2 inch, a polyethylene sleeve may be used over the wire bundle to give further protection. Also two cable clamps back-to-back, as shown in Fig. 5-10, can used be used to maintain a rigid separation only, and not for support of the bundle. No wire should be routed so that it is located nearer than 1/2 inch to a plumbing line. Neither should a wire or wire bundle be supported from a plumbing line that carries flammable fluids or oxygen.

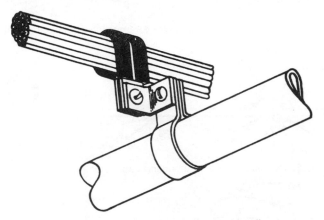

Fig. 5-10. Method of separating wires from plumbing lines.

Wiring should be routed to maintain a minimum clearance of at least 3 inches from control cables. If this cannot be accomplished, mechanical guards should be installed to prevent contact between wiring and control cables.

Cable clamps should be installed with regard to the proper angle, as shown in Fig. 5-11. The mounting screw should be above the wire bundle. It is also desirable that the back of the cable clamp rest against a structural member where practicable.

Care should be taken that wires are not pinched in cable clamps. Where possible, the cables should be mounted directly to structural members, as shown in Figs. 5-12 and 5-13. Clamps can be used with rubber cushions to secure wire

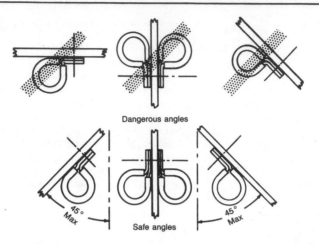

Dangerous angles

Safe angles

Fig. 5-11. Proper and improper angles for installation of cable clamps.

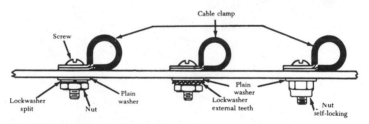

Cable clamp

Screw

Lockwasher split

Plain washer

Nut

Plain washer

Lockwasher external teeth

Nut self-locking

Fig. 5-12. Various methods of mounting cable clamps.

MS 21919 Cable clamps

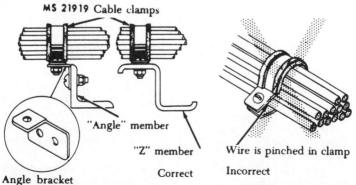

"Angle" member

"Z" member

Correct

Angle bracket

Wire is pinched in clamp

Incorrect

Fig. 5-13. Mounting cable clamp to structure.

bundles to tubular structures. Such clamps must fit tightly, but should not be deformed when locked in place.

Protection Against Chafing

Wires and wire groups should be protected against chafing or abrasion in those locations where contact with sharp surfaces or other wires would damage the insulation. Damage to the insulation can cause short circuits, malfunction, or inadvertent operation of equipment. Cable clamps should be used to support wire bundles at each hole through a bulkhead (Fig. 5-14). If wires come

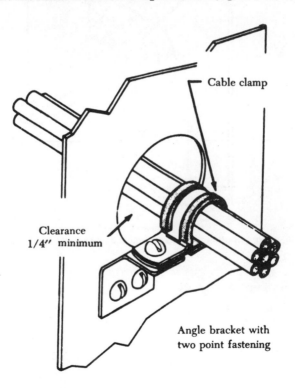

Fig. 5-14. Cable clamp at large bulkhead hole.

closer than 1/4 inch to the edge of the hole, a suitable grommet is used in the hole as shown in Fig. 5-15.

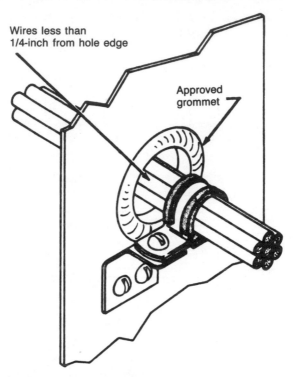

Wires less than
1/4-inch from hole edge

Approved
grommet

Fig. 5-15. A grommet is used to protect a cable routed through a small bulkhead hole.

BONDING AND GROUNDING

Bonding is the electrical connecting of two or more conducting objects not otherwise adequately connected. **Grounding** is the electrical connecting of a conducting object to the primary structure for a return path for current. Primary structure is the main frame, fuselage, or wing structure of the aircraft, commonly referred to as **ground**. Bonding and grounding connections are made in aircraft electrical systems to:

☐ Protect aircraft and personnel against hazards from lightning discharge.
☐ Provide current return paths.
☐ Prevent development of radio frequency potentials.
☐ Protect personnel from shock hazards.

☐ Provide stability of radio transmission and reception.
☐ Prevent accumulation of static charge.

Bonding jumpers should be made as short as practicable, and installed in such manner that the resistance of each connection does not exceed .003 ohm. The jumper must not interfere with the operation of movable aircraft elements, such as surface controls, nor should normal movement of these elements result in damage to the bonding jumper.

To ensure a low-resistance connection, nonconducting finishes such as paint and anodizing films should be removed from the attachment surface to be contacted by the bonding terminal. Electric wiring should not be grounded directly to magnesium parts.

Electrolytic action may rapidly corrode a bonding connection if suitable precautions are not taken. Aluminum alloy jumpers are recommended for most cases; however, copper jumpers should be used to bond together parts made of stainless steel, cadmium plated steel, copper, brass, or bronze. Where contact between dissimilar metals cannot be avoided, the choice of jumper and hardware should be such that corrosion is minimized, and the part likely to corrode would be the jumper or associated hardware. Figure 5-16 shows the proper hardware combination for making a bond connection. At locations where finishes are removed, protective finish should be applied to the completed connection to prevent subsequent corrosion.

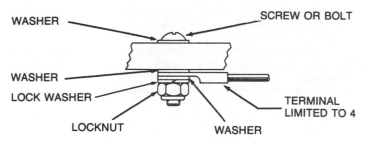

Fig. 5-16. Bolt and nut bonding or grounding to flat surface.

The use of solder to attach bonding jumpers should be avoided. Tubular members should be bonded by means of clamps to which the jumper is attached. Proper choice of clamp material will minimize the probability of corrosion.

Chapter 6

Materials and Fabricating

ALUMINUM AND ALUMINUM ALLOYS

Aluminum is one of the most widely used metals in modern aircraft construction. It is vital to the aviation industry because of its high strength-to-weight ratio and its comparative ease of fabrication. The outstanding characteristic of aluminum is its light weight. Aluminum melts at the comparatively low temperature of 1,250° F. It is nonmagnetic and is an excellent conductor.

Commercially pure aluminum is a white lustrous metal. Aluminum combined with various percentages of other metals forms alloys which are used in aircraft construction.

Aluminum alloys in which the principal alloying ingredients are either manganese, chromium, or magnesium and silicone show little attack in corrosive environments. Alloys in which substantial percentages of copper are used are more susceptible to corrosive action. The total percentage of alloying elements is seldom more than 6 or 7 percent in the wrought alloys.

Commercially pure aluminum has a tensile strength of about 13,000 p.s.i., but by rolling or other cold-working processes its strength may be approximately doubled. By alloying with other metals, or by using heat-treating processes, the tensile strength may be raised to as high as 65,000 p.s.i. or to within the strength range of structural steel.

Aluminum alloys, although strong, are easily worked because they are malleable and ductile. Most aluminum alloy sheet stock used in aircraft construction ranges from .016 to .096 inch in thickness; however, some of the larger aircraft use sheet stock which may be as thick as .356 inch.

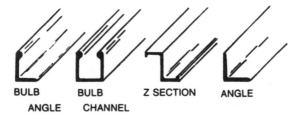

BULB   BULB   Z SECTION   ANGLE
ANGLE   CHANNEL

Fig. 6-1. Extrusions.

The various types of aluminum may be divided into two general classes: (1) The casting alloys (those suitable for casting in sand, permanent mold, die castings), and (2) the wrought alloys (those which may be shaped by rolling, drawing, or forging). Of these two, the wrought alloys are the most widely used in aircraft construction, being used for stringers, bulkheads, skin, rivets, and extruded sections (Fig. 6-1).

Aluminum Casting Alloys

Aluminum casting alloys are divided into two basic groups. In one, the physical properties of the alloys are determined by the alloying elements and cannot be changed after the metal is cast. In the other, the alloying elements make it possible to heat treat the casting to produce the desired physical properties.

The casting alloys are identified by a letter preceeding the alloy number. When a letter precedes a number, it indicates a slight variation in the composition of the original alloy. This variation in composition is simply to impart some desirable quality. In casting alloy 214, for example, the addition of zinc to improve its pouring qualities is indicated by the letter A in front of the number, thus creating the designation A214.

When castings have been heat treated, the heat treatment and the composition of the casting is indicated by the letter T, followed by an alloying number. An example of this is the sand casting alloy 355, which has several different compositions and tempers and is designated by 355-T6, 355-T51, or C355-T51.

Aluminum alloy castings are produced by one of three basic methods: (1) Sand mold, (2) permanent mold, or (3) die cast. In casting aluminum, different types of alloys are used for different types of castings. Sand castings and die castings require different types of alloys than those used in permanent molds.

Wrought Aluminum Alloys

Wrought aluminum and wrought aluminum alloys are divided into two general classes, nonheat-treatable alloys and heat-treatable alloys.

Nonheat-treatable alloys are those in which the mechanical properties are determined by the amount of cold-work introduced after the final annealing operation. The mechanical properties obtained by cold working are destroyed by any subsequent heating and cannot be restored except by additional cold working, which is not always possible. The "full hard" temper is produced by the maximum amount of cold-work that is commercially practicable. Metal in the "as fabricated" condition is produced from the ingot without any subsequent controlled amount of cold working or thermal treatment. There is, consequently, a variable amount of strain hardening, depending upon the thickness of the section.

For heat-treatable aluminum alloys the mechanical properties are obtained by heat treating to suitable temperature, holding at that temperature long enough to allow the alloying constituent to enter into solid solution, and then quenching to hold the constituent in solution. The metal is left in a supersaturated, unstable state and is then age hardened either by natural aging at room temperature or by artificial aging at some elevated temperature.

Typical mechanical properties of wrought aluminum alloys are shown in chart form in the Appendix.

Aluminum Designations

Wrought aluminum and wrought aluminum alloys are designated by a four-digit index system. The system is broken into three distinct groups: 1xxx group, 2xxx through 8xxx group, and 9xxx group (which is at present unused).

The first digit of a designation identifies the alloy type. The second digit indicates specific alloy modifications. Should the second number be zero, it would indicate no special control over individual impurities. Digit 1 through 9, however, when assigned consecutively as needed for the second number in this group, indicate the number of controls over individual impurities in the metal.

The last two digits of the 1xxx group are used to indicate the hundredths of 1 percent above the original 99 percent designated by the first digit. Thus, if the last two digits were 30, the alloy would contain 99 percent plus 0.30 percent of pure aluminum, or a total of 99.30 percent pure aluminum. Examples of alloys in this group are:

1100—99.00 percent pure aluminum with one control over individual impurities.
1130—99.30 percent pure aluminum with one control over individual impurities.
1275—99.75 percent pure aluminum with two controls over individual impurities.

In the 2xxx through 8xxx groups, the first digit indicates the major alloying element used in the formation of the alloy as follows:

2xxx—copper.
3xxx—manganese.
4xxx—silicon.
5xxx—magnesium.
6xxx—magnesium and silicon.
7xxx—zinc.
8xxx—other elements.

In the 2xxx through 8xxx alloy groups, the second digit in the alloy designation indicates alloy modifications. If the second digit is zero; it indicates the original alloy, while digits 1 through 9 indicate alloy modifications.

The last two of the four digits in the designation identify the different alloys in the group.

Where used, the temper designation follows the alloy designation and is separated from it by a dash; i.e., 7075-T6, 2024-T4, etc. The temper designation consists of a letter indicating the basic temper which may be more specifically defined by the addition of one or more digits. These designations are as shown in Fig. 6-2.

Nonheat-Treatable Alloys		Heat-Treatable Alloys	
Temper designation	**Definition**	**Temper designation**	**Definition**
– O	Annealed recrystallized (wrought products only) applies to softest temper of wrought products.	– O	Annealed recrystallized (wrought products only) applies to softest temper of wrought products.
– H12	Strain-hardened one-quarter-hard temper.	– T2	Annealed (castings only.)
		– T3	Solution heat-treated and cold-worked by the flattening or straightening operation.
– H14	Strain-hardened half-hard temper.		
– H16	Strain-hardened three-quarters-hard temper.		
		– T36	Solution heat-treated and cold-worked by reduction of 6 percent.
– H18	Strain-hardened full-hard temper.		
– H22	Strain-hardened and partially annealed to one-quarter-hard temper.	– T4	Solution heat-treated.
		– T42	Solution heat-treated by the user regardless of prior temper (applicable only to 2014 and 2024 alloys).
– H24	Strain-hardened and partially annealed to half-hard temper.		
– H26	Strain-hardened and partially annealed to three-quarters-hard temper.	– T5	Artificially aged only (castings only).
		– T6	Solution heat-treated and artificially aged.
– H28	Strain-hardened and partially annealed to full-hard temper.		
– H32	Strain-hardened and then stabilized. Final temper is one-quarter hard.	– T62	Solution heat-treated and aged by user regardless of prior temper (applicable only to 2014 and 2024 alloys).
– H34	Strain-hardened and then stabilized. Final temper is one-half hard.	– T351, – T451 – T3510, – T3511, – T4510, – T4511.	Solution heat-treated and stress relieved by stretching to produce a permanent set of 1 to 3 percent, depending on the product.
– H36	Strain-hardened and then stabilized. Final temper is three-quarters hard.	– T651, – T851, – T6510, – T8510, – T6511, – T8511.	Solution heat-treated, stress relieved by stretching to produce a permanent set of 1 to 3 percent, and artifically aged.
– H38	Strain-hardened and then stabilized. Final temper is full-hard.		
– H112	As fabricated; with specified mechanical property limits.	– T652	Solution heat-treated, compressed to produce a permanent set and then artificially aged.
– F	For wrought alloys; as fabricated. No mechanical properties limits. For cast alloys; as cast.	– T81	Solution heat-treated, cold-worked by the flattening or straightening operation, and then artificially aged.
		– T86	Solution heat-treated, cold-worked by reduction of 6 percent, and then artificially aged.
		– F	For wrought alloys; as fabricated. No mechanical properties limits. For cast alloys; as cast.

Fig. 6-2. Aluminum alloy temper designation chart.

In the wrought form, commercially pure aluminum is known as 1100. It has a high degree of resistance to corrosion and is easily formed into intricate shapes. It is relatively low in strength, however, and does not have the strength required for structural aircraft parts. Higher strengths are generally obtained by the process of alloying. The resulting alloys are less easily formed and, with some exceptions, have lower resistance to corrosion than 1100 aluminum.

Alloying is not the only method of increasing the strength of aluminum. Like other materials, aluminum becomes stronger and harder as it is rolled, formed, or otherwise cold-worked. Since the hardness depends on the amount of cold working done, 1100 and some wrought aluminum alloys are available in several strain-hardened tempers. The soft or annealed condition is designated O. If the material is strain hardened, it is said to be in the H condition.

The most widely used alloys in aircraft construction are hardened by heat treatment rather than by cold-work. These alloys are designated by a somewhat different set of symbols:—T4 and W indicate solution heat treated and quenched but not aged, and T6 indicates an alloy in the heat treated hardened condition.

Aluminum alloy sheets are marked with the specification number on approximately every square foot of material. If for any reason this identification is not on the material, it is possible to separate the heat-treatable alloys from the nonheat-treatable alloys by immersing a sample of the material in a 10-percent solution of caustic soda (sodium hydroxide). The heat-treatable alloys will turn black due to the copper content, whereas the others will remain bright. In the case of clad material, the surface will remain bright, but there will be a dark area in the middle when viewed from the edge.

Clad Aluminum

The terms "Alclad" and "Pureclad" (tradenames) are used to designate sheets that consist of an aluminum alloy core coated with a layer of pure aluminum to a depth of approximately 5 1/2 percent on each side. The pure aluminum coating affords a dual protection for the core, preventing contact with any corrosive agents, and protecting the core electrolytically by preventing any attack caused by scratching or from other abrasions.

Heat Treatment of Aluminum Alloys

Heat treatment is a series of operations involving the heating and cooling of metals in the solid state. Its purpose is to change a mechanical property or combination of mechanical properties so that the metal will be more useful, serviceable, and safe for a definite purpose. By heat treating, a metal can be made harder, stronger, and more resistant to impact. Heat treating can also make a metal softer and more ductile. No one heat-treating operation can produce all of these characteristics. In fact, some properties are often improved at the expense of others. In being hardened, for example, a metal may become brittle.

The various heat-treating processes are similar in that they all involve the heating and cooling of metals. They differ, however, in the temperatures to which the metal is heated, the rate at which it is cooled, and, of course, in the final result.

Successful heat treating requires close control over all factors affecting the heating and cooling of metals. Such control is possible only when the proper equipment is available and the equipment is selected to fit the particular job. Thus, the furnace must be of the proper size and type and must be so controlled that temperatures are kept within the limits prescribed for each operation. Even the atmosphere within the furnace affects the condition of the part being heat treated. Further, the quenching equipment and the quenching medium must be selected to fit the metal and the heat-treating operation. Finally, there must be equipment for handling parts and materials, for cleaning metals, and for straightening parts.

Heat treating requires special techniques and equipment which are usually associated with manufacturers or large repair stations. Since these processes are usually beyond the scope of the field mechanic, the heat treatment of aluminum alloys will only be discussed briefly.

There are two types of heat treatments applicable to aluminum alloys. One is called solution heat treatment, and the other is known as precipitation heat treatment. Some alloys, such as 2017 and 2024, develop their full properties as a result of solution heat treatment followed by about 4 days of aging at room temperature. Other alloys, such as 2014 and 7075, require both heat treatments.

The alloys that require precipitation heat treatment (artificial aging) to develop their full strength also age to a limited extent at room temperature; the rate and amount of strengthening depends upon the alloy. Some reach their maximum natural or room-temperature aging strength in a few days, and are designated as—T4 or —T3 temper. Others continue to age appreciably over a long period of time. Because of this natural aging, the —W designation is specified only when the period of aging is indicated, for example 7075-W (1/2 hour). Thus, there is considerable difference in the mechanical and physical properties of freshly quenched (—W) material and material that is in the —T3 or —T4 temper.

The hardening of an aluminum alloy by heat treatment consists of four distinct steps:

1. Heating to a predetermined temperature.
2. Soaking at temperature for a specified length of time.
3. Rapidly quenching to a relatively low temperature.
4. Aging or precipitation hardening either spontaneously at room temperature, or as a result of a low-temperature thermal treatment.

The first three steps above are known as solution heat treatment, although it has become common practice to use the shorter term, "heat treatment." Room-temperature hardening is known as natural aging, while hardening done at moderate temperature is called artificial aging, or precipitation heat treatment.

Solution Heat Treatment

Temperature

The temperatures used for solution heat treating vary with different alloys and range from 825 degrees F. to 980 degrees F. As a rule, they must be controlled within a very narrow range (plus or minus 10 degrees) to obtain specified properties. Heating is accomplished in either a fused salt bath or an air furnace. The soaking time varies, depending upon the alloy and thickness from 10 minutes for thin sheets to approximately 12 hours for heavy forgings. For the heavy sections, the nominal soaking time is approximately 1 hour for each inch of cross-sectional thickness. The soaking time is chosen so that it will be the minimum necessary to develop the required physical properties.

Quenching

After the soluble constituents are in solid solution, the material is quenched to prevent or retard immediate re-precipitation. Three distinct quenching methods are employed. The one to be used in any particular instance depends upon the part, the alloy, and the properties desired.

Cold Water Quenching

Parts produced from sheet, extrusions, tubing, small forgings, and similar type material are generally quenched in a cold water bath. The temperature of the water before quenching should not exceed 85 degrees F. Such a drastic quench ensures maximum resistance to corrosion. This is particularly important when working with such alloys as 2017, 2024, and 7075. This is the reason a drastic quench is preferred, even though a slower quench may produce the required mechanical properties.

Hot Water Quenching

Large forgings and heavy sections can be quenched in hot or boiling water. This type of quench minimizes distortion and alleviates cracking which may be produced by the unequal temperatures obtained during the quench. The use of a hot water quench is permitted with these parts because the temperature of the quench water does not critically affect the resistance to corrosion of the forging alloys. In addition, the resistance to corrosion of heavy sections is not as critical a factor as for thin sections.

Spray Quenching

High-velocity water sprays are useful for parts formed from clad sheet and for large sections of almost all alloys. This type of quench also minimizes distortion and alleviates quench cracking. However, many specifications forbid the use of spray quenching for bare 2017 and 2024 sheet materials because of the effect on their resistance to corrosion.

Lag Between Soaking and Quenching

The time interval between the removal of the material from the furnace and quenching is critical for some alloys and should be held to a minimum.

Re-Heat Treatment

The treatment of material which has been previously heat treated is considered a re-heat treatment. The unclad heat-treatable alloys can be solution heat treated repeatedly without harmful effects.

The number of solution heat treatments allowed for clad sheet is limited due to increased diffusion of core and cladding with each reheating. Existing specification allow one to three re-heat treatments of clad sheet depending upon cladding thickness.

Straightening after Solution Heat Treatment

Some warping occurs during solution heat treatment, producing kinks, buckles, waves, and twists. These imperfections are generally removed by straightening and flattening operations.

Where the straightening operations produce an appreciable increase in the tensile and yield strengths and a slight decrease in the percent of elongation, the material is designated—T3 temper. When the above values are not materially affected, the material is designated—T4 temper.

Precipitation Heat Treating

As previously stated, the aluminum alloys are in a comparatively soft state immediately after quenching from a solution heat-treating temperature. To obtain their maximum strengths, they must be either naturally aged or precipitation hardened.

Precipitation hardening produces a great increase in the strength and hardness of the material with corresponding decreases in the ductile properties. The process used to obtain the desired increase in strength is therefore known as aging, or precipitation hardening.

The aging practices used depend upon many properties other than strength. As a rule, the artificially aged alloys are slightly overaged to increase their resistance to corrosion. This is especially true with the artificially aged high-copper content alloys that are susceptible to intergranular corrosion when inadequately aged.

The heat-treatable aluminum alloys are subdivided into two classes, those that obtain their full strength at room temperature and those that require artificial aging.

The alloys that obtain their full strength after 4 or 5 days at room temperature are known as natural aging alloys. Precipitation from the supersaturated solid solution starts soon after quenching, with 90 percent of the maximum strength generally being obtained in 24 hours. Alloys 2017 and 2024 are natural aging alloys.

The alloys that require precipitation thermal treatment to develop their full strength are artificially aged alloys. However, these alloys also age a limited amount at room temperature, the rate and extent of the strengthening depending upon the alloys.

Many of the artificially aged alloys reach their maximum natural or room temperature aging strengths after a few days. These can be stocked for fabrication in the —T4 or —T3 temper. High-zinc content alloys such as 7075 continue to age appreciably over a long period of time, their mechanical property changes being sufficient to reduce their formability.

The advantage of —W temper formability can be utilized, however, in the same manner as with natural aging alloys; that is, by fabricating shortly after solution heat treatment, or retaining formability by the use of refrigeration.

Refrigeration retards the rate of natural aging. At 32 degrees F., the beginning of the aging process is delayed for several hours, while dry ice (– 50 degrees F. to – 100 degrees F.) retards aging for an extended period of time.

Precipitation Practices

The temperatures used for precipitation hardening depend upon the alloy and the properties desired, ranging from 250 degrees F. to 375 degrees F. They should be controlled within a very narrow range (plus or minus 5 degrees) to obtain best results.

The time at temperature is dependent upon the temperature used, the properties desired, and the alloy. It ranges from 8 to 96 hours. Increasing the aging temperature decreases the soaking period necessary for proper aging. However, a closer control of both time and temperature is necessary when using the higher temperatures.

After receiving the thermal precipitation treatment, the material should be air cooled to room temperature. Water quenching, while not necessary, produces no ill effects. Furnace cooling has a tendency to produce overaging.

Annealing of Aluminum Alloys

The annealing procedure for aluminum alloys consists of heating the alloys to an elevated temperature, holding or soaking them at this temperature for a length of time depending upon the mass of the metal, and then cooling in still air. Annealing leaves the metal in the best condition for cold-working. However, when prolonged forming operations are involved, the metal will take on a condition known as "mechanical hardness" and will resist further working. It may be necessary to anneal a part several times during the forming process to avoid cracking. Aluminum alloys should not be used in the annealed state for parts or fittings.

Clad parts should be heated as quickly and carefully as possible, since long exposure to heat tends to cause some of the constitutents of the core to diffuse into the cladding. This reduces the corrosion resistance of the cladding.

Heat-treatment of Rivets. Rivets are made from various alloys and, of course, should be heat-treated before being used. In this condition, some alloyed rivets are too hard and will crack upon upsetting. This tendency may be controlled by retarding the age hardening of the rivets until the time of use. If they are placed in freezing boxes immediately after heating and quenching, their age hardening will be arrested and will continue when the rivets are removed and used in a structure. After their removal from the low temperature, they should be used within approximately 20 min. before age hardening prevents riveting.

Typical Uses of Aluminum and Its Alloys

A summary of the various aluminum alloys as related to aircraft fabrication is indicated below:

1000 series—Aluminum of 99 percent or higher purity has little application in the aerospace industry. These alloys are characterized by excellent corrosion resistance, high thermal and electrical conductivity, low mechanical properties, and excellent workability. Moderate increases in strength may be obtained by strain-hardening. Soft, 1100 rivets are used in non-structural applications.

2000 series—Copper is the principal alloying element in this group. These alloys require solution heat-treatment to obtain optimum properties; in the heat-treated condition mechanical properties are similar to, and sometimes exceed, those of mild steel. In some instances artificial aging is employed to further increase the mechanical properties. This treatment materially increases yield strength. These alloys in the form of sheet are usually clad with a high-purity alloy. Alloy 2024 is perhaps the best known and most widely used aircraft alloy. Most aircraft rivets are of alloy 2117.

3000 series—Maganese is the major alloying element of alloys in this group, which are generally non-heat-treatable. One of these is 3003, which has limited use as a general-purpose alloy for moderate-strength applications requiring good workability such as cowlings and non-structural parts. Alloy 3003 is easy to weld.

4000 series—This alloy is seldom used in the aerospace industry.

5000 series—Magnesium is one of the most effective and widely used alloying elements for aluminum. When it is used as the major alloying element or with manganese, the result is a moderate to high strength non-heat-treatable alloy. Alloys in this series possess good welding characteristics and good resistance to corrosion in various atmospheres. It is widely used for the fabrication of tanks and fluid lines.

6000 series—Alloys in this group contain silicon and magnesium in approximate proportions to form magnesium silicide, thus making them heat-treatable. Major alloy in this series is 6061, one of the most versatile of the heat-treatable alloys. Though less strong than most of the 2000 or 7000 alloys, the magnesium-silicon (or magnesium-silicide) alloys possess good formability and corrosion resistance, with medium strength.

7000 series—Zinc is the major alloying element in this group, and when coupled with a smaller percentage of magnesium results in heat-treatable alloys of very high strength. Usually other elements such as copper and chromium are also added in small quantities. Outstanding member of this group is 7075, which is among the highest strength alloys available and is used in airframe structures and for highly stressed parts.

Fabricating

Forming. The forming of aluminum is generally confined to sheet stock and employs such standard practice machines as drop hammers, presses, power brakes, and punch presses.

Figure 6-3 shows a hand operated brake used for bending sheet metal. Larger brakes are power operated.

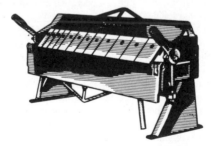

Fig. 6-3. Hand operated brake.

Of most importance is the manner in which the dies or tools used on these machines are made and cared for during their operation, for the action of forming the metal must be done over exceedingly smooth and polished dies, using lubricants where necessary, such that the movement of the material over the tool surfaces will not scratch or smear the Alclad finish.

The simplest type of forming is the bending of a straight flange. Even this operation requires great care. First, in designing the part, consideration should be given to the sharpness of the bend, or bend radius, which depends on the temper of the material. For aluminum in the T condition this radius must not be less than 2 1/2 times the thickness of the material; for O material the radius may be as little as the thickness of the material. It is practical to increase calculated minimum radii to conform to standard dies generally available in sizes varying by 1/32 in. Disregard for these minimum radii or the use of roughly finished tools may result in small flaws or cracks that will necessitate the rejection of the part.

An exercise to illustrate the understanding of sheet metal fabrication is the use of "bend allowance" in the forming of a simple part such as shown in Fig. 6-4.

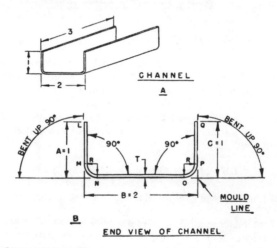

Fig. 6-4. Channel dimensions.

Flat pattern layout by bend allowance (BA) is most universally accepted. By the use of the bend allowance chart and the following equations, any straight bend may be accurately developed.

The length of the channel will, of course, remain unchanged from flat pattern to finished part. On the other hand, the material necessary to make the channel web and the two flanges will not be the sum of their dimensions in the finished part, as it might at first seem, but rather, this "developed length" will be less than that sum, owing to the short cuts taken around the curved corners.

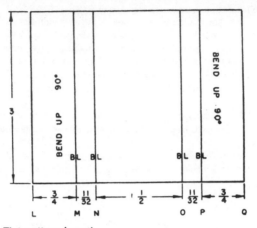

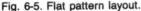

Fig. 6-5. Flat pattern layout.

One might figure that each corner is a quarter of a circle and calculate its length in that manner, but practice has developed the *empirical formula* for bend allowance, which is much easier. The procedure for its use is

1. Imagine that the length around the cross section of the channel is divided into sections according to the letters L, M, N, O, P, and Q (Fig. 6-4B). Length $LM = 1$ in. $- R$ (radius of bend) $- T$ (thickness of metal). If $R = 3/16$ and $T = 1/16$ (.064), then

$$LM = 1 \text{ in.} - (3/16 \text{ in.} + 1/16 \text{ in.}) = 3/4 \text{ in.}$$

Lay this length out along the metal as shown in Fig. 6-5 and draw the bend line (BL).

2. Next, for the length MN, called the "bend allowance," refer to the bend allowance chart (Fig. 6-9), for 1-deg. bend allowance and multiply it by the number of degrees of bend (90 deg.). The chart gives .00377 for 3/16 R and .064 T; when multiplied by 90, we get .3393 or 11/32 (closest fraction) to the next bend line.

3. The web of the channel has two bends to be subtracted. Therefore it is 2 in. $- 2(T + R)$ or 2 in. $- 1/2$ in. $= 1\ 1/2$ in. from N to O. Repeat the first two operations in reverse order to complete the pattern.

A computation of this kind for aircraft is generally done in decimals for greater accuracy. Therefore, using decimals, the lengths would be

$A = 1.0000$	$B = 2.0000$	$C = 1.0000$
$T + R = \underline{.2515}$	$2TR = \underline{.5030}$	$T + R = \underline{.2515}$
$LM = .7485$	$NO = 1.4970$	$PQ = .7485$

$MN = CP =$ bend allowance $= 90° \times .00377 = .3393$

Therefore, the developed length (sum $LM + MN + NO + OP + PQ$) equals 3.6726. Referring back, this is less than the sum of the dimensioned sides in Fig. 6-5B.

Formed angles of open or closed bevels may be developed in the same manner except that the distance from the corner mold line to the bend line is found by the formula:

$(T + R) \times$ (the tangent of half the "bent-up" angle) (Fig. 6-6).

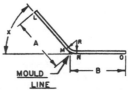

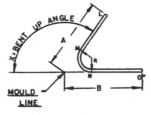

CLOSED BEVEL   **OPEN BEVEL**

Fig. 6-6. Typical bends.

Bend Allowance Derivation

The coefficients for bend allowance are computed from the bend allowance empirical formula. This formula, as the name implies, was developed by experimentation after a mathematical formula had been found, as shown in Fig. 6-7.

The neutral axis was found, by experimentation, to lie slightly inside the $1/2T$, therefore the formula $(.01743R + .0078T)$ gives the bend allowance for 1-deg. bend. The table (Fig. 6-9) gives the 1-deg. bend allowances for certain given radii and thicknesses. These are multiplied by the number of degrees bend to arrive at the total bend allowance.

Values are for 1-deg. bend. Values derived from:

$$\text{B.A.} = (.0078T + .01743R)N$$

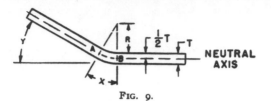

Fig. 9.

Bend allowance = BA along neutral axis

$$BA = 2\pi \cdot \left(R + \frac{T}{2}\right) \cdot \frac{X}{360}$$

$$BA = (2\pi R + \pi T) \cdot \frac{X}{360}$$

$$BA = \frac{(2\pi R + \pi T) \cdot X}{360}$$

$$BA = \frac{(6.2832R)}{(360)} + \frac{(3.1416T)}{(360)} \cdot X$$

$$BA = (.01743R + .00872T) \cdot X$$

Fig. 6-7. Example of bend allowance derivation.

Example: T = .032, R = 1/8, angle = 90°.
B.A. = .00243 × 90 = .2187.

Bends of a more complicated design, as a sheet-metal rib having flanges around its contour, should be made over a form block shaped to fit the inside contour of the finished part. Bending the flanges over this die may be accomplished by "hand forming," a slow but practical method for experimental work (Fig. 6-8).

A speedier and better production method is the use of the hydropress (Fig. 6-10). The form block is laid on the base of the press with the material held in place by pin guides in the form block at locations where the pin holes will not affect the designed strength of the part. The upper platen of the press is covered with rubber from 4 to 6 in. thick. When it is lowered, a pressure of several tons is applied. The rubber forces the material edges down over the sides of the form block, either shrinking or stretching the material to fit its contour. This method, though used extensively, also has limitations such as the depth to which it may form a part, and the amount of shrinking it will successfully perform before the material will wrinkle or fold over.

For such irregular shapes as cowlings and fairings where extreme forming is necessary, the drop hammer is applicable (Fig. 6-11). Drop hammers use heavy dies and punches. The die, of Kirksite (a lead and zinc alloy) or steel, is generally cast to the shape of the part from a plaster pattern. After being finished by scraping or grinding, it may then by used to pour a lead punch. The drop

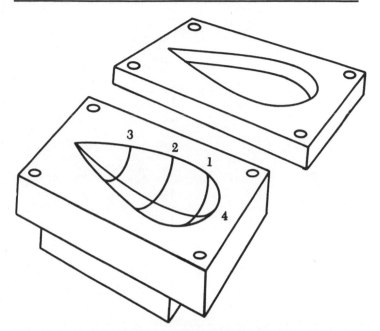

Fig. 6-8. A simple form block and holddown plate for hand forming. A speedier and better production is the use of the hydropress.

hammer does not press the part into shape. The punch is raised by the upper platen and dropped into the die, forcing or ramming the metal to fit the shape of the die.

Parts that require deep forming, when fabricated on the drop hammer, often must be made progressively by the use of graduated dies forming the part in several stages. Another method uses the finish die in a progressive manner by the stacking of several layers of plywood rings between the punch and the die. This prevents the punch from bottoming until all the wood rings have been removed, one after each stroke. The falling of the punch on the rings serves two purposes; it stops the punch at a desired height and it holds the overlapping sheet metal in a flat plane, preventing wrinkling and thus producing a drawing action as each layer of plywood is removed.

Forming of irregular shapes may be speedily accomplished if the part is small and used in such quantity as to warrant making punch and dies for the punch press. The punch press is activated by a crankshaft, operated rapidly by engaging a clutch to a power-driven flywheel. Dies for punch press forming are more complicated and intricate than for other types of presses and gener-

R \ T	.020 .022	.023 .025	.028 .029	.031 .032	.038 .040	.050 .051	.063 .064	.081	.091 .094	.125 .129
1/32	00072	00073	00076	00079	00086	00094	00104	00117	00125	00154
1/16	00126	00128	00131	00135	00140	00149	00159	00172	00180	00209
3/32	00180	00183	00185	00188	00195	00203	00213	00226	00234	00263
1/8	00235	00237	00240	00243	00249	00258	00268	00281	00289	00317
5/32	00290	00292	00294	00297	00304	00312	00322	00335	00343	00372
3/16	00344	00346	00349	00352	00358	00367	00377	00390	00398	00426
7/32	00398	00401	00403	00406	00412	00421	00431	00444	00452	00481
1/4	00454	00455	00458	00461	00467	00476	00486	00500	00507	00535
9.32	00507	00510	00512	00515	00521	00530	00540	00553	00561	00590
5/16	00562	00564	00567	00570	00576	00584	00595	00608	00616	00644
11/32	00616	00619	00620	00624	00630	00639	00649	00662	00670	00699
3/8	00671	00673	00675	00679	00685	00693	00704	00717	00725	00753
13/32	00725	00728	00730	00733	00739	00748	00758	00771	00779	00808
7/16	00780	00782	00784	00767	00794	00802	00812	00826	00834	00862
15/32	00834	00836	00839	00842	00848	00857	00867	00853	00888	00917
1/2	00889	00891	00893	00896	00903	00911	00921	00935	00943	00971
17/32	00943	00945	00948	00951	00957	00966	00976	00989	00997	01025
9/16	00998	01000	01002	01005	01012	01020	01030	01044	01051	01080
19/32	01051	01054	01055	01058	01065	01073	01083	01098	01105	01133
5/8	01107	01109	01111	01114	01121	01129	01139	01152	01160	01189
21/32	01161	01163	01166	01170	01175	01183	01193	01207	01214	01245
11/16	01216	01218	01220	01223	01230	01238	01248	01261	01269	01298
23/32	01269	01272	01273	01276	01283	01291	01301	01316	01322	01351
3/4	01324	01327	01329	01332	01338	01347	01357	01370	01378	01407
25/32	01378	01381	01383	01386	01392	01401	01411	01425	01432	01461
13/16	01433	01436	01438	01441	01447	01456	01466	01479	01487	01516
27/32	01487	01490	01491	01494	01501	01509	01519	01534	01540	01569
7/8	01542	01545	01548	01550	01556	01565	01575	01588	01596	01625
29/32	01596	01600	01601	01604	01610	01619	01629	01643	01650	01679
15/16	01651	01654	01655	01657	01665	01674	01684	01697	01705	01734
31/32	01705	01708	01709	01712	01718	01727	01737	01752	01758	01787
1	01760	01763	01765	01768	01774	01783	01793	01806	01814	01834

Minimum allowance below line _____ for hard alloy
Minimum allowance below line - - - - - - - - - - for soft alloy and steel.

Fig. 6-9. Sheet metal bend allowance chart for 1-degree angle.

ally perform a "drawing" operation. Such dies should be equipped with pressure pads that hold the material tightly against the face of the die while the punch draws the material in and down over the edges of the die.

Parts of a symmetrical concentric shape may often be best formed by spinning. Lathe chucks are formed to the inside contour of the part. Over these the metal is forced by pressure of a hard wood or polished steel spin tool. Spinning also is done on tubing that may need a flange turned outward on the end or an alteration in its diameter for special designs.

Fig. 6-10. Double action hydraulic press, and deep drawn section of wingtip tank.

Fig. 6-11. Drop hammer showing sheet-metal part being formed to die contour by successive strokes or hits.

There are many special tools and applications of the foregoing machines to handle special forming jobs that arise from intricate designs. For instance, the power brake, though primarily used for bending straight flanges, has been adapted to use in forming dies for small parts and such special work as setting joggles in preformed parts and extrusions.

In the fabrication of aluminum where shrinking or stretching is severe, the metal is used in the O condition. After forming, the part is heat-treated to the T condition. Though the material used is in the O condition, the forming, if very severe, work-hardens the material. Often this work hardening is so pronounced as to hinder completion of the part; then it is necessary to anneal the material before forming is continued.

Machining involves all forms of cutting, whether preformed on sheet stock, castings, or extrusions, and involves such operations as shearing (Fig. 6-12), sawing, routing, lathe and millwork, and such hand operations as drilling, tapping, and reaming.

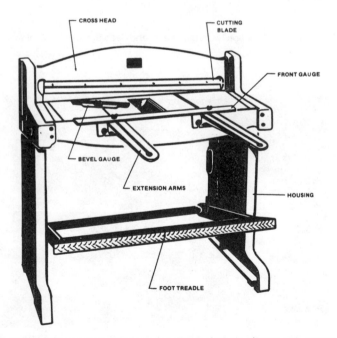

Fig. 6-12. A foot-operated squaring shear. Larger shears are power-operated.

Lathe and millwork and all turning operations performed on aluminum are governed by general machine-shop practices and differ from similar operations upon steels in that the turning is done at higher speeds taking lighter cuts. The cutting tools should be kept very sharp with more top and side rake than for steels. Cuts requiring a smooth finish generally are made under a flow of kerosene and lard oil lubricants. These oils are excellent for such hand cutting as drilling and tapping, but the more common soluble lubricants may be used equally as well for lighter work.

Cutting operations on sheet material are principally the blanking out of parts prior to forming or assembly. Small parts are blanked most quickly on a punch press while the larger patterns must be sheared, sawed, or routed.

Routing of irregularly shaped parts is one of the most extensively used practices, since it permits the cutting of several parts at one time by stacking several sheets. Using templates clamped to the material, a milling cutter of small diameter turning at high speed is guided around the template, routing a path equal to the diameter of the cutter. A small amount of lubricant supplied to the surface of the material makes a smoother cut and prolongs the life of the cutter (Fig. 6-13).

Fig. 6-13. Master router cutting several sheets of metal as it follows the large template clamped on the material.

The router is adaptable to several types of machines. For the above-mentioned cutting, the router head is mounted on movable arms to follow the profile of the part. This machine is called the "master router." Another type is the "pin router" where the router head is stationary and the material is run against the cutter and guided by the template touching a pin directly below the cutter. Other stationary routers use jigs that nest small parts such as extruded sections, and on passing the cutter are trimmed, beveled, or tapered, and perform highspeed milling operations.

Chemical Milling

Chemical milling is a dimensional etching process for metal removal. In working aluminum, it is the preferred method for removing less than 0.125 inch from large, intricate surfaces. Sodium-hydroxide-base or other suitable alkaline solutions are generally used for milling aluminum. The process is carried out at elevated temperatures. The metal removal (dissolution) is controlled by masking, rate of immersion, duration of immersion, and composition and temperature of the bath.

Dissolution of 0.001 inch thickness of aluminum per minute is a typical removal rate. Economics dictates removal of thickness above 0.250 inch by mechanical means. Choice of method between the aforementioned 0.125 and 0.250 inch metal removal thickness depends on fillet ratio and weight penalty.

Welding

Flame welding of aluminum is generally confined to the non-heat-treatable alloys. Obviously, an alloy selected for high strength and used in the heat-treated condition should not have local portions partly annealed as a result of welding. Alloys 1100 and 3003, being nearly pure aluminum and practical for use in nonstructural components such as fairings, air scoops, and cowlings, may be welded with practically no loss of their original strength. Of the heat-treatable alloys. 6053 may be welded quite satisfactorily. The welding action simulates that of heat-treatment, in that as the torch moves along there is a heating followed by an air quench which hardens this material approximately to its temper in the W condition.

The selection of the proper welding rod or wire is most important for good results. The non-heat-treatable alloy 3003 should ordinarily be welded with 3003 wire, while the heat-treatable alloy should ordinarily be welded with a silicon wire.

The production of a sound weld in aluminum necessitates the use of a flux to clean the material in the area of the weld and to remove the aluminum oxide present on the surface of the aluminum. The flux is generally a powder mixed with water and may be brushed on the surface to be welded, or the welding rod may be dipped in the solution prior to welding with satisfactory results. On completion of welds, this flux should be removed by washing, as the residual flux is corrosive to the material and its presence under a painted finish will lift the paint in a short while. If the welded area is readily accessible, hot water and brushing are sufficient. For inaccessible welds, the parts may be immersed in a solution of 10 percent sulphuric acid for 30 min. or 3 percent sulphuric acid, heated to 150 °F, for 10 min.

Resistance Welding. Spot welding is practiced extensively on sheet aluminum of nearly all alloys. The principal requirements are good equipment with accurate current adjustment, timing devices to produce accurate and uniform spots, and material free of grease or dirt.

Cleaning is done with a fine abrasive cloth or light etching solution in the immediate area of the weld. Unless cleaned, the aluminum oxide on the surface of the material will offer high resistance and cause surface heating at the point of contact between the electrode and the aluminum, resulting in the electrodes either picking up a part of the aluminum surface or depositing some copper on the aluminum.

The spot-welding machine, equipped with copper electrodes for spot welding or rolls for seam welding, should be kept clean and smooth by frequent polishing. In polishing, extreme care should be used to keep a slight crown on the contact points. Rolls used in seam welding are electrically driven; timing devices form overlapping spots or seams. The timing may be adjusted to allow greater space between spots and thus will spot intermittently to any desired spacing.

Surface Protection

Pure aluminum is inherently resistant to corrosion. It is this quality that prompted the use of Alclad finishes to the alloyed materials. However, aircraft are often subject to adverse weather conditions and, especially on sea-going craft, it is important that as much protection as possible be afforded.

Anodic Treatment is a means of oxydizing the surface of aluminum, providing a very thin and hard surface of aluminum oxide. This aluminum oxide provides a greater resistance to corrosion and an excellent base for paint primers to be applied later, if still greater protection is necessary.

Anodizing is electroplating in reverse. The aluminum part is made the anode in a chromic acid or sulphuric acid solution. By electrolysis, oxygen is deposited on the surface, forming aluminum oxide.

Various processes of anodizing are applicable depending on the finish desired. Alumiliting is an anodic process, practical for producing a finish that may include dye or pigment to provide color effects. It is often the final finish applied.

Chromodizing, a slightly less effective treatment that eliminates the expense of electrolysis, is accomplished by a simple chemical dip. Applied on such parts where requirements permit, it involves a 5-min. immersion in a heated chromic acid bath.

MAGNESIUM AND MAGNESIUM ALLOYS

Magnesium, the world's lightest structural metal, is a silvery-white material weighing only two-thirds as much as aluminum. Magnesium does not possess sufficient strength in its pure state for structural uses, but when alloyed with zinc, aluminum, and manganese it produces an alloy having the highest strength-to-weigh ratio of any of the commonly used metals.

Some of today's aircraft require in excess of one-half ton of this metal for use in hundreds of vital spots. Some wing panels are fabricated entirely from magnesium alloys, weigh 18 percent less than standard aluminum panels, and have flown hundreds of satisfactory hours. Among the aircraft parts that have been made from magnesium with a substantial savings in weight are nosewheel, doors, flap cover skin, aileron cover skin, oil tanks, floorings, fuselage parts, wingtips, engine nacelles, instrument panels, radio masts, hydraulic fluid tanks, oxygen bottle cases, ducts, and seats.

Magnesium alloys possess good casting characteristics. Their properties compare favorably with those of cast aluminum. In forging, hydraulic presses are ordinarily used, although, under certain conditions, forging can be accomplished in mechanical presses or with drop hammers.

Magnesium alloys are subject to such treatments as annealing, quenching, solution heat treatment, aging, and stabilizing. Sheet and plate magnesium are annealed at the rolling mill. The solution heat treatment is used to put as much of the alloying ingredients as possible into solid solution, which results in high tensile strength and maximum ductility. Aging is applied to castings following heat treatment where maximum hardness and yield strength are desired.

Magnesium embodies fire hazards of an unpredictable nature. When in large sections, its high thermal conductivity makes it difficult to ignite and prevents it from burning. It will not burn until the melting point is reached, which is 1,204 degrees F. However, magnesium dust and fine chips are ignited easily. Precautions must be taken to avoid this if possible. Should a fire occur, it can be extinguished with an extinguishing powder, such as powdered soapstone, or graphite powder. Water or any standard liquid or foam fire extinguishers cause magnesium to burn more rapidly and can cause explosions.

Magnesium alloys produced in the United States consist of magneisum alloyed with varying proportions of aluminum, manganese, and zinc. These alloys are designated by a letter of the alphabet, with the number 1 indicating high purity and maximum corrosion resistance.

Heat Treatment of Magnesium Alloys

Magnesium alloy castings respond readily to heat treatment, and about 95 percent of the magnesium used in aircraft construction is in the cast form.

The heat treatment of magnesium alloy castings is similar to the heat treatment of aluminum alloys in that there are two types of heat treatment: (1) Solution heat treatment and (2) precipitation (aging) heat treatment. Magnesium, however, develops a negligible change in its properties when allowed to age naturally at room temperatures.

Solution Heat Treatment

Magnesium alloy castings are solution heat treated to improve tensile strength, ductility, and shock resistance. This heat-treatment condition is indicated by using the symbol —T4 following the alloy designation. Solution heat treatment plus artificial aging is designated —T6. Artificial aging is necessary to develop the full properties of the metal.

Solution heat-treatment temperatures for magnesium alloy castings range from 730 degrees F. to 780 degrees F., the exact range depending upon the type of alloy. The temperature range for each type of alloy is listed in Specification MIL-H-6857. The upper limit of each range listed in the specification is the maximum temperature to which the alloy may be heated without danger of melting the metal.

The soaking time ranges from 10 to 18 hours, the exact time depending upon the type of alloy as well as the thickness of the part. Soaking periods longer than 18 hours may be necessary for castings over 2 inches in thickness. Magnesium alloys must never be heated in a salt bath as this may result in an explosion.

A serious potential fire hazard exists in the heat treatment of magnesium alloys. If through oversight or malfunctioning of equipment, the maximum temperatures are exceeded, the casting may ignite and burn freely. For this reason, the furnace used should be equipped with a safety cutoff that will turn off the power to the heating elements and blowers if the regular control equipment malfunctions or fails.

Some magnesium alloys require a protective atmosphere of sulphur dioxide gas during solution heat treatment. This aids in preventing the start of a fire even if the temperature limits are slightly exceeded.

Air-quenching is used after solution heat treatment of magnesium alloys since there appears to be no advantage in liquid cooling.

Precipitation Heat Treatment

After solution treatment, magnesium alloys may be given an aging treatment to increase hardness and yield strength. Generally, the aging treatments are used merely to relieve stress and stabilize the alloys in order to prevent dimensional changes later, especially during or after machining. Both yield strength and hardness are improved somewhat by this treatment at the expense of a slight amount of ductility. The corrosion resistance is also improved, making it closer to the "as cast" alloy.

Precipitation heat-treatment temperatures are considerably lower than solution heat-treatment temperatures and range from 325 degrees F. to 500 degrees

F. Soaking time ranges from 4 to 18 hours.

TITANIUM AND TITANIUM ALLOYS

In aircraft construction and repair, titanium is used for fuselage skins, engine shrouds, firewalls, longerons, frames, fittings, air ducts, and fasteners. Titanium is used for making compressor disks, spacer rings, compressor blades and vanes, through bolts, turbine housings and liners, and miscellaneous hardware for turbine engines.

Titanium falls between aluminum and stainless steel in terms of elasticity, density, and elevated temperature strength. It has a melting point of from 2,730 degrees F. to 3,155 degrees, low thermal conductivity, and a low coefficient of expansion. It is light, strong, and resistant to stress-corrosion cracking. Titanium is approximately 60 percent heavier than aluminum and about 50 percent lighter than stainless steel.

Because of the high melting point of titanium, high-temperature properties are disappointing. The ultimate yield strength of titanium drops rapidly above 800 degrees F. The absorption of oxygen and nitrogen from the air at temperatures above 1,000 degrees F. makes the metal so brittle on long exposure that it soon becomes worthless. However, titanium does have some merit for short-time exposure up to 3,000 degrees F. where strength is not important. Aircraft firewalls demand this requirement.

Titanium is nonmagnetic and has an electrical resistance comparable to that of stainless steel. Some of the base alloys of titanium are quite hard. Heat treating and alloying do not develop the hardness of titanium to the high levels of some of the heat-treated alloys of steel. It was only recently that a heat-treatable titanium alloy was developed. Prior to the development of this alloy, heating and rolling was the only method of forming that could be accomplished. However, it is possible to form the new alloy in the soft condition and heat treat it for hardness.

Iron, molybdenum, and chromium are used to stabilize titanium and produce alloys that will quench harden and age harden. The addition of these metals also adds ductility. The fatigue resistance of titanium is greater than that of aluminum or steel.

Titanium Designations

The A-B-C classification of titanium alloys was established to provide a convenient and simple means of describing all titanium alloys. Titanium and titanium alloys possess three basic types of crystals: A (alpha), B (beta), and C (combined alpha and beta). Their characteristics are:

A (alpha)—All-around performance; good weldability; tough and strong both cold and hot, and resistant to oxidation.

B (beta)—Bendability; excellent bend ductility; strong both cold and hot, but vulnerable to contamination.

C (combined alpha and beta for compromise performances)—Strong when cold and warm, but weak when hot; good bendability; moderate contamination resistance; excellent forgeability.

Titanium is manufactured for commercial use in two basic compositions; commercially pure titanium and alloyed titanium. A-55 is an example of a commercially pure titanium. It has a yield strength of 55,000 to 80,000 p.s.i. and is a general-purpose grade for moderate to severe forming. It is sometimes used for nonstructural aircraft parts and for all types of corrosion resistant applications, such as tubing.

Type A-70 titanium is closely related to type A-55 but has a yield strength of 70,000 to 95,000 p.s.i. It is used where higher strength is required, and it is specified for many moderately stressed aircraft parts. For many corrosion applications, it is used interchangeably with type A-55. Both type A-55 and type A-70 are weldable.

One of the widely used titanium-base alloys is designated as C-110M. It is used for primary structural members and aircraft skin, has 110,000 p.s.i. minimum yield strength, and contains 8 percent manganese.

Type A-110AT is a titanium alloy which contains 5 percent aluminum and 2.5 percent tin. It also has a high minimum yield strength at elevated temperatures with the excellent welding characteristics inherent in alpha-type titanium alloys.

Corrosion Characteristics

The corrosion resistance of titanium deserves special mention. The resistance of the metal to corrosion is caused by the formation of a protective surface film of stable oxide or chemi-absorbed oxygen. Film is often produced by the presence of oxygen and oxidizing agents.

Corrosion of titanium is uniform. There is little evidence of pitting or other serious forms of localized attack. Normally, it is not subject to stress corrosion, corrosion fatigue, intergranular corrosion, or galvanic corrosion. Its corrosion resistance is equal or superior to 18-8 stainless steel.

Heat Treatment of Titanium

Titanium is heat treated for the following purposes:

1. Relief of stresses set up during cold forming or machining.

2. Annealing after hot working or cold working, or to provide maximum ductility for subsequent cold working.

3. Thermal hardening to improve strength.

Stress Relieving

Stress relieving is generally used to remove stress concentrations resulting from forming of titanium sheet. It is performed at temperatures ranging from 650 degrees F. to 1,000 degrees F. The time at temperature varies from a few minutes for a very thin sheet to an hour or more for heavier sections. A typical stress-relieving treatment is 900 degrees F. for 30 minutes, followed by an air cool.

The discoloration or scale which forms on the surface of the metal during stress relieving is easily removed by pickling in acid solutions. The recommended solution contains 10 to 20 percent nitric acid and 1 to 3 percent hydrofluoric acid. The solution should be at room temperature or slightly above.

Full Annealing

The annealing of titanium alloys provides toughness, ductility at room temperature, dimensional and structural stability at elevated temperatures, and improved machinability.

The full anneal is usually called for as preparation for further working. It is performed at 1,200 degrees F. to 1,650 degrees F. The time at temperature varies from 16 minutes to several hours, depending on the thickness of the material and the amount of cold work to be performed. The usual treatment for the commonly used alloys is 1,300 degrees F. for 1 hour, followed by an air cool. A full anneal generally results in sufficient scale formation to require the use of caustic descaling, such as sodium hydride salt bath.

Thermal Hardening

Unalloyed titanium cannot be heat treated , but the alloys commonly used in aircraft construction can be strengthened by thermal treatment, usually at some sacrifice in ductility. For best results, a water quench from 1,450 degrees F., followed by re-heating to 900 degrees F. for 8 hours is recommended.

Casehardening

The chemical activity of titanium and its rapid absorption of oxygen, nitrogen, and carbon at relatively low temperatures make casehardening advantageous for special applications. Nitriding, carburizing, or carbonitriding can be used to produce a water-resistant case of 0.0001 to 0.0002 inch in depth.

STEEL
Source

Steel is a metal resulting from the purification of iron and the reduction of its carbon content. Iron is obtained from ore extracted from the earth in various degrees of impurity and purified and refined by smelting to oxidize the carbon and other impurities. Steel is iron containing less than 2 percent of carbon. Other elements present in steel are manganese, important to the increase of toughness, and silicon, acting as a gas eliminator to prevent blowholes. Also present are sulphur and phosphorus in very small amounts.

Classification

The alloying of steels by adding other metals, singly or in combination, results in alloys of varied uses and properties. These many alloys are classified by an S.A.E. numbering system to identify them in drawings, specifications, etc.

The principal alloy combinations are classified by basic numerals as follows:

Alloy	Number	Alloy	Number
Carbon steels.......	1	Chromium steels....	5
Nickel steels........	2	Chromium-vanadium steels.............	6
Nickel-chromium steels.............	3	Tungsten steels.....	7
Molybdenum steels..	4	Silicomanganese steels.............	9

The use of these assigned numerals in coding steel specifications is as follows. The class of the alloy is indicated first in the code; for example in the code 4130, the class is a molybdenum steel indicated by the number 4. The second numeral, 1, indicates the percentage of this predominating alloying element, 1 percent chromium. The last two numerals, 30, indicate the average carbon content in hundredths of 1 percent, or .30 percent.

Plain carbon steels, not being an alloy steel, may be indicated as follows:

Steel 1020: The first numeral, 1, indicates carbon steel. The second numeral, 0, indicates no alloy. The last two numerals, 20, indicate .20 percent carbon range.

NOTE: Carbon range is considered to vary 5 points above or below its coded number. Thus, in the example, the carbon range is .15 to .25 percent carbon.

The first two numerals, indicating the type and percentage of the predominating element, may necessarily require three numerals instead of two. For example, after a first numeral of 7 (tungsten steel), it may contain 13 percent tungsten, indicated 713; if the carbon range is .50 percent, it becomes 71350.

Identification

Supplementing the S.A.E. classification of steels, the Air Force has adapted a standard method of readily identifying material in stock by painting color combinations on the surface. Parallel stripes are painted at the ends and in the middle of bar and sheet stock. These bands are combinations of broad and narrow stripes of different colors. The broad stripes (4 to 5 inches wide) indicate the first two or first three digits of the code. The narrow stripes (2 inches wide) indicate that last two digits of the code.

By referring to the following table: to identify 1020 steel, select the color red, from the broad stripe column, indicating 10, and from the narrow stripe column, the color yellow indicating 20. These colors are painted across the material separated by a 1-inch space. In other cases, it may require two colors to identify one pair of numerals. In this case, each color will take one-half of the 5-inch stripe if indicating the first two numerals, or one-half of the 2-inch stripe if indicating the second pair of numerals.

Figure 6-14 shows such a sample in the coding of 4130 steel.

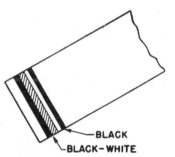

Fig. 6-14. Example of color coding to identify steel alloy.

BLACK
BLACK-WHITE

Broad stripes, 4 to 5 in. wide		Narrow stripes, 2 in. wide	
Red	10	Red and black	00
Red and white	12	Red	10
Red and yellow	13	Red and green	12
Yellow	23	Red and white	15
Yellow and green	25	Yellow	20
Green	31	Yellow and white	25
Blue	32	Black	30
Brown	33	Black and white	35
Black	34	Green	40
Black and white	41	Green and white	45
Red and black	46	Black and green	46
Khaki	51	Blue	50
Red and blue	53	Brown	60
White	61	Brown and white	65
Red and brown	72	Khaki	95
Blue and yellow	76		

Broad stripes, 4 to 5 in. wide
Blue and brown........ 92
Brown and white....... 512
Brown and yellow...... 521
Purple................ 713
Purple and yellow...... 716

The addition of an orange stripe indicates annealed stock. The addition of a gray stripe indicates heat-treated stock. This color scheme does not apply to corrosion-resistant steels, since they are not classified by S.A.E. numbers.

Properties

The properties and uses of commonly used steels in aircraft are as follows:

1010-1025, low-carbon steels are soft and ductile steels used for low stressed parts where cold working is required. Fittings made of these steels may be readily machined and welded but are not adaptable to heat-treatment, except casehardening.

1050-1095, high-carbon steels are heat-treatable after forming or machining and are used for parts requiring high shear strength and wearing surfaces such as drills, taps, and similar hand tools or springs, provided heat-treatment is done after forming.

2330-2350, nickel steels are heat-treatable after fabrication and are excellent for parts requiring high stress and wear, such as bolts, clevises, turn-buckles, and small fittings.

4130-4150, molybdenum steels, high-strength steels used in sheet form and tubing, are employed extensively for fuselage and landing gear structures where heat-treatment is impractical owing to structural size or shape. It has the excellent quality of retaining most of its strength after being welded. Fittings requiring higher strength may be fabricated and heat-treated to high strengths.

Corrosion-and Heat-Resistant Steels

General. Stainless steels are used where corrosion resistance and heat resistance are important factors in the design of the part. There are many varieties of stainless steels and variations in the basic analysis and, as yet, S.A.E. classifications have not been assigned to all types. The A.I.S.I. (American Iron and Steel Institute) has however, assigned numbers to several of the commonly used alloys.

Basically, stainless steels contain 18 percent of chromium and 8 percent of nickel and are commonly referred to as 18-8 steels. These steels can be either flame- or spot-welded, are drawn and formed easily, are non-heat-treatable, but are available in various degrees of hardness from annealed to full hard condition, the result of strain hardening by cold rolling or cold drawing in their manufacture.

The commonly used alloys have A.I.S.I. numbers as follows, and also a common name designation.

A.I.S.I. Number	Common Designation
302	18-8
303	18-8 free machining
321	Stabilized titanium
347	Stabilized columbium
None	Inconel

Identification. Since these steels do not have S.A.E. classifications for all alloys, the steel color scheme for identifying is not applicable, but they are rubber-stamped with A.I.S.I. numbers. Example: 302 1/2 H is 18-8 corrosion-resistant steel, 1/2 hard. Inconel must be stamped Inconel followed by 1A or 1H. The properties of commonly used corrosion-resistant steels are as follows:

302 alloy is most commonly used in the machining of sheet-metal parts. It is available in the annealed condition, designated 1A, or various degrees of hardness, 1/4 H, 1/2 H, 3/4 H or 1 H (fully hardened).

303 alloy contains selenium or zirconium to reduce the work-hardening characteristics of 18-8 steels and to provide easier machining.

321 alloy contains titanium to increase its corrosion resistance when subjected to welding or other extreme temperatures.

347 alloy contains columbium, resulting in characteristics similar to 321 steels.

Inconel is another corrosion-resistant steel, of high nickel content, having the advantage of easier formability with slight work-hardening characteristics. It does not tend to corrode at welded joints, nor is it susceptible to inner granular corrosion when subjected to high temperatures; therefore it is best adaptable to exhaust collectors, etc.

Fabrication

Forming of steel is accomplished by any of the methods and machines described under Aluminum, the essential difference being the workability of the material used. Steel is a stronger material and requires harder dies and more powerful machines, according to the type of steel being formed.

The stronger steels, such as 4130, are more difficult to work and, where possible, are limited to simple forming; assembly is completed by welding or bolting. Forming is easier in the case of low-carbon steels, stainless steels, or Inconel; these being more ductile steels and well suited to drawing operations.

The bend radii of steels are subject to minima, particularly the high-strength alloys. The grain in high-strength steels is almost always apparent to the eye; whenever possible they should be bent across the grain.

Cutting of sheet steel is done principally by shearing and sawing or by punch press dies. Routing is not applicable except at slow speeds. For the trimming of irregular parts, there are several types of small machines and power-driven hand tools performing shearing or nibbling operations. The nibbler is used extensively for trimming the ends of tubing where intersecting tubes necessitate a developed curve. The nibbler uses a small (1/8 to 1/4 inch in diameter) punch and die, which punch circular blanks from the parts as it is fed into the machine, cutting a path equal to the diameter of the punch. The rough scalloped edge left on the part requires only a small amount of handwork to finish smooth.

Machining of steel parts and fittings for aircraft must follow the best machine-shop practices and requires a knowledge of proper setups, cutting requirements of various metals, cutting speeds, and sharpening of tools. Machining operations are varied, owing to the wide range of hardness of different steels. In Chapter 3 are tables of cutting speeds for different materials, which will aid in setting the turning speeds according to the diameter of the part.

The automatic lathe is the most highly productive type in aircraft shops but requires tedious setup. The turret lathe is most common; while not so fast as the automatic lathe, it requires considerably less setup time. The engine lathe requires least setup but is so slow that it is used principally for tool work and small lots.

For parts requiring exceedingly close tolerances and smooth finish, grinding is the common practice; for close fits, as required by portions of the hydraulic systems, honing and lapping produce the desired finish.

Heat-Treatment

Heat-treatment of steels involves the heating and cooling of the metal; the rate of this heating and cooling determines the crystalline structure of the material. Almost all metals have a critical temperature at which the grain structure changes. Steel at its critical temperature changes structure when carbon and iron are said to form a solid solution. Common forms of heat-treatment are hardening, tempering, annealing, normalizing, and casehardening.

Hardening. To obtain maximum hardness, the steel should be heated to a temperature in excess of its critical temperature to ensure a complete change of state (upper critical temperature). Exceeding this temperature by 25 to 50 °F is necessary to ensure thorough heating of the inside of the piece. Rapid quenching from this temperature will result in maximum hardness.

The required temperature of heating varies for different alloys, from 1500 to 1650 °F; for best results, parts should be put in the oven when its heat is approximately 1000 °F and gradually increased to its hardening temperature.

Quenching is accomplished in water, air, oil, or salt brine. Oil results in the slowest cooling rate but is sometimes necessary for alloys that require higher heating temperatures to prevent cracking and excess warping from the strain of uneven cooling.

Accurate methods of measuring and controlling temperatures of the oven should be available for best results; however, where necessary, the change in color can be used to determine temperatures.

Tempering (Drawing). Metal that has been hardened by rapid cooling from a point above its critical temperature is often harder than necessary, too brittle for most purposes, and under internal strains. In order to relieve the strains and reduce brittleness, the metal is usually tempered after being hardened. This is accomplished by heating the hardened steel to a temperature below the critical range (400 to 1200 °F). The degree of strength and the hardness remaining depend on the temperature of heating, the less this temperature the more hardness remaining. Tempering, like hardening, requires accurate methods of heating and measuring temperatures for good results, but the temperatures may also be approximated by noting the change of color as the temperature rises. These colors appear in the well-cleaned or polished surface accomplished by buffing or grinding to remove the oxide film formed during hardening.

Annealing of steels, the reverse of hardening, is performed when necessary to reduce or remove hardness and to increase their ductility. Heating to the critical temperature removes any hardness caused by previous heat-treatments or working strains. From this critical temperature, slow cooling will restore them to a state of minimum hardness. This is accomplished simply by allowing them to cool with the furnace. Annealing is often done to allow severe forming of the material; on completion of the part, it may be hardened and tempered again to a desired strength.

Normalizing is a special case of annealing for the purpose of removing strains in fabricated parts induced by machining, bending, or welding. It is accomplished by heating to a point above its critical temperature and allowing to cool in still air, avoiding drafts that would cause uneven cooling and set up strains again in the part.

Casehardening, a special treatment for iron base alloys, produces a hard surface but leaves the core tough and resilient. This may be accomplished by carburizing, nitriding, or cyaniding.

Carburizing is done by heating the metal while it is in contact with a solid, liquid, or gas, rich in carbon. Several hours of this treatment is required for the surface of the material to absorb carbon and thus become a high-carbon steel.

Nitriding is a similar process applied to special steels. The heated material is held in contact with anhydrous ammonia. Iron nitrides, formed in the surface of the metal, produce a greater hardness that carburizing but to a lesser depth and only in certain special steels.

Cyaniding is a rapid method of casehardening by immersing the heated steel in a molten bath of cyanide or applying powdered cyanide to the surface of the material.

Surface Protection

Surface protection of steels is generally accomplished by painting, by plating with a corrosion-resistant metal, or by plating followed by painting. In any case, an essential prerequisite is the proper cleaning of the material.

Cleaning of steel parts prior to painting necessitates the removal of all grease or oil formerly applied for corrosion resistance during shipment or for a manufacturing lubricant. Degreasing may be done most simply by washing in a solvent such as carbon tetrachloride followed by thorough drying; if facilities are available, the parts may be vapor cleaned. In this process the parts are passed through tanks containing vaporized solvent, which condenses on the parts, dissolves, and carries away the grease or oil.

Pickling is a chemical cleaning process, involving an acid or electrolytic dip, applied to nearly all metals for cleaning. It varies in its formula and method for various metals and cannot be considered a standard process. This treatment, if not followed immediately by washing and painting, must be washed in an alkaline solution to neutralize the acid.

For stainless steels, the pickling solution is a strong acid, which will loosen particles of steel, scale of welding, or materials imbedded from forming dies. Stainless steel fabricated parts generally require pickling, particularly after welding, when scale must be loosened and removed by brushing.

Passivate. Stainless steel used in manifolds or in areas subject to heat may be further protected from corrosion by an oxidizing finish resulting from passivating, which is a chemical dip producing a very thin and invisible oxide surface.

Sandblasting is a fast method of removing scale and dirt by an air blast carrying sand or finely divided steel particles, frequently applied on steel parts previously welded. This method when employed on stainless steels should not contain steel particles as some may be imbedded in the material and later corrode.

Plating. Probably the most extensively used method of preventing corrosion on small fittings is cadmium plating, an electrolytic process depositing a layer of cadmium on the surface of the part. This, of course, is impractical if the parts are too large or if the part is of a laminated nature where the acid solution may enter crevices from which it cannot be washed out. Chromium plating is also used for corrosion protection but is generally applied where use can be made of its hard surface for wearing qualities or, if desired, for its appearance.

Painting may be applied directly to the cleaned steel and be the only corrosion protection or it may be applied after any of the other protecting processes. A paint primer is first applied, generally zinc chromate P-27, or the newer epoxy chromate, followed by colored lacquers or polyuethane enamel.

Greasing. Wearing surfaces of machined parts, such as bearings and bushings, should be protected from painting and any of the acid treatments by masking or plugging. Later they will require an application of grease or oil to protect the surface during stocking.

HARDNESS TESTING

Hardness testing of both raw materials and finished parts is necessary to determine whether the materials and the heat-treatment have met the strength values used in design. By one of three common methods, Rockwell, Brinell, or Shore scleroscope, a close approximation can be made of a material's tensile strength, which is closely related to its hardness. The hardness of steels is indicated by a number derived from tests on materials of a known tensile strength.

Rockwell testing for hardness is accomplished by a device that applies a known load to a penetrator on the surface of the material being tested (Fig. 6-15). A minor load is first applied seating the penetrator in the material; penetration is then effected by the application of a major load. A dial mounted on the instrument will measure this penetration, and, as the pointer comes to a rest, the major load is released; the pointer will then return to a position indicating the depth still penetrated by the minor load. The greater the difference between these two readings, the less the hardness number and the softer the material.

Fig. 6-15. Rockwell hardness tester.

The penetrator may be a 1/16-diameter steel ball with a 100-kg weight for the major load, or a diamond-cone penetrator with a 150-kg weight. The former is used for the softer materials and indicated on a red *B* scale about the circumference of the dial; readings for the diamond penetrator are taken from a black *C* scale. The minor load is 10-kg with either penetrator.

Brinell testing for hardness is done with a small hydraulic press applying a known load (3,000 kg for steels) to a steel ball that makes a spherical impression in the surface of the material being tested. The area of the impression is measured by a microscope with micrometer eyepiece. The load in kilograms divided by the area of the impression in square millimeters gives the Brinell number.

Shore scleroscope testing for hardness consists of dropping a diamond-tipped hammer on the material from a definite height and measuring the rebound. Several tests are generally made and an average of all readings is taken as the Shore number.

X-RAY

In this inspection an actual x-ray photograph of the part is studied for flaws. This examination is generally applied to castings where gas pockets, slag inclusions, cracks, or other faults of casting might be present. X-ray inspection is generally required only on designated parts, either highly stressed or vital to the airplane's operation. Whether a 10 percent inspection is needed to determine the "run" of the castings in a special lot, or 25, or 100 percent, is specified by the structures and process engineers.

MAGNAFLUX

Magnaflux inspection is applicable to ferromagnetic materials, such as iron and steel, and is a dependable method of detecting cracks and flaws in or near the surface of fabricated parts. Highly stressed steel parts are generally magnafluxed to detect cracks, resulting from heat-treatment or machining strains, or welding, which may leave cracks resulting from the heating and cooling of the metal or from improper welding procedure.

The parts to be magnafluxed are first magnetized, setting up flux lines around the part. If the part is cracked, opposite poles are formed at the break in the material. Finely divided ferromagnetic particles sprayed over the part will tend to gather at this break and form a pattern outlining its boundaries. An operator inspecting parts by this method should be skilled and experienced in judging which defects are cause for rejection. Irregularly shaped parts having sharp corners or machined recesses tend to cause confusing indications and should be carefully analyzed before judgment is passed.

Magnafluxing equipment consists of electrical apparatus for magnetizing parts, a tank holding a supply of kerosene or special oil in which the ferromagnetic particles are suspended, and a spray system to apply this solution to the parts being tested. After inspection, the parts are demagnetized by passing them through an alternating field (demagnetizing coils) and then rinsed clean.

Chapter 7
Aircraft Drawings

A **drawing** is a method of conveying ideas concerning the construction or assembly of objects. This is done with the help of lines, notes, abbreviations and symbols. It is very important that the aviation mechanic who is to make or assemble the object understand the meaning of the different lines, notes, abbreviations and symbols that are used in a drawing.

Although blueprints as such are no longer used, the term **blueprint** or **print** is generally used in place of drawing.

Interpreting a drawing and visualizing the appearance of a part or assembly necessitate an understanding of drafting practices and of the principles of orthographic projection, which establish the methods of illustrating and dimensioning a part.

The following notes are intended to aid the production mechanic only in determining from the print how the part is made, not how the print was drawn.

Although the various manufacturers' drafting systems will differ in detail, there is central agreement in the broad arrangement of drawings. This arrangement serves as an index for the quick location of the specific information required from the print being studied.

A line drawing of the part itself makes up the greater portion of the print; supplemented by dimensions and notes, it completely describes the part. In the lower right-hand corner is a block, referred to as the "legend" or "title block," containing reference material pertaining to the part. The information given here should be the first portion of the print to be analyzed.

The legend or title block will contain such information as:

Name of the print—indentifies the part.

Number of the print—indexes this part for filing reference.

Model—of the airplane, or of the airplane unit if an aircraft accessory.

Signatures of draftsmen, engineer, checker, and project engineer.

Material—notes its form, dimensions, and pertinent specifications.

Finish—notes any painting, anodizing, plating required, and determines the final condition and appearance of the part. (This information may be indicated by code, which varies with each manufacturer.)

Scale—indicated as full, half, etc., giving the proportion of the drawing to the actual part.

Tolerance—designates the degree of precision necessary in fabricating the part and guides the inspector in determining the conformance to the print.

Immediately outside the legend are found such notes as are necessary to label the views or to elaborate any information not sufficiently detailed in the legend.

Change block is the space allotted to recording design changes. Located directly over the legend or at the top right of the print, it records the date of each change in the drawing and is important when supplying replacement parts for existing aircraft.

The foregoing facts may be applied to interpret the illustrations of the drafting practices that follow.

Orthographic projection is almost universally accepted as the most accurate method to describe fully a part or assembly. Figure 7-1 illustrates the arrangement of views. The front, side, and top views are arranged with the top (or plan) view directly over the front, and the side views directly to the side and in line with the front view.

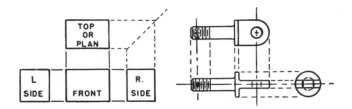

Fig. 7-1. Orthographic projection.

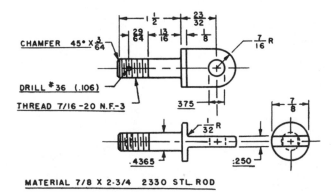

Fig. 7-2. A dimensional drawing.

It will be noted, in the part drawn at the right, that only those views needed to describe the part are shown. The left view is omitted since it adds no information not given in the right side view. Generally, three views, or even two or one, may be sufficient. The illustration alone does not, however, fully describe the part if dimensional and material information is lacking. Drawings should be complete and give every requirement for making the part.

The completed drawing (Fig. 7-2) follows such standard drafting room practices as follows:

Index of Lines. Lines are drawn of different boldness and composition to identify the assortment of boundary lines, center lines, hidden lines, etc., needed to represent the part (Fig. 7-3).

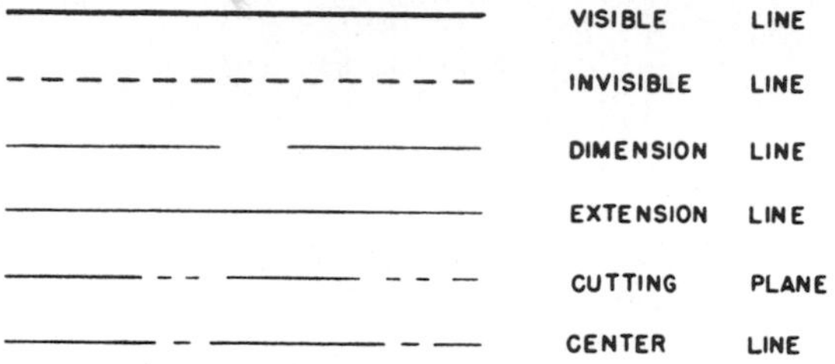

	VISIBLE	LINE
	INVISIBLE	LINE
	DIMENSION	LINE
	EXTENSION	LINE
	CUTTING	PLANE
	CENTER	LINE

Fig. 7-3. Index of lines.

Dimensioning. It will first be noted that dimensions show size or length of the part, not the size of the drawing. This rule should always be adhered to. Although the drawing, if to full scale, would coincide with the part, it is poor practice to scale a drawing to take a dimension.

The dimension line will always be drawn parallel to the dimension indicated and be bounded by extension lines at right angles. The dimension is printed in the break of the dimension line and always reads horizontally regardless of the direction of the dimension line. Dimensions on aircraft drawings are always given in inches, even when the full airplane length is given.

Stations are established at definite points along the fuselage and outward along the wing to aid in locating parts and to make it unnecessary to draw long and overlapping dimension lines. These stations are not placed at random but at such important structural members as ribs and bulkheads. Although in a few drafting systems station designations have no dimensional significance, fuselage stations usually are measurements in inches from the nose of the aircraft aft (from the fire wall, if a single-engine aircraft); wing stations are from the center line of the airplane measuring outboard (Fig. 7-4).

Station lines will be found on other drawings than that of the completed

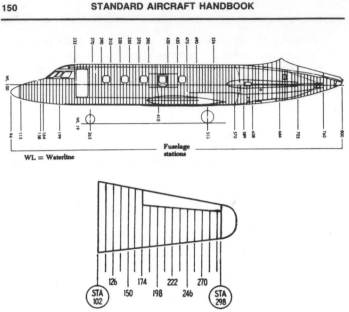

WL = Waterline

Fuselage stations

Fig. 7-4. Examples of station designation.

airplane; for example, the drawing of an aileron will show station lines at rib locations. The station line dimensions will however be dimensioned from the center line of the airplane, as on the wing, and will coincide with the same stations along the wing.

Sectional views (Fig. 7-5) are drawn to show the cross-sectional profile

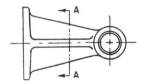

Fig. 7-5. A sectional view.

SECTION A-A

of a part. The location from which this view is taken is indicated by a cutting plane line which suggests that the part is cut in two at this line. The view of the exposed surface is rotated to an end view. The arrows at the ends of the cutting plane point toward the surface to be shown.

The sectional view is crosshatched according to the drafting room practices of the manufacturer to indicate the material. However, to eliminate confusing lines, sheet metal and such thin sections are not crosshatched.

The illustration of view B-B (Fig. 7-6) is another application of the cutting plane line. Not actually a cross section of a part, it is used to eliminate the necessity of drawing a rotated view of the complete part. Here only the approximate portion represented by the length of the cutting plane is given in a rotated view to show the detail of the splice in this particular part. The letters used in the illustration do not identify the type of view but alphabetically identify and locate the sectional view on the principal view.

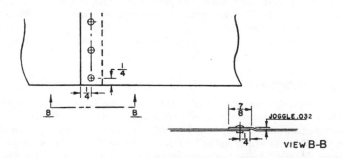

Fig. 7-6. Example of sectional view of thin sheet structure.

WORKING DRAWINGS

Working drawings must give such information as size of the object and all of its parts, its shape and that of all of its parts, specifications as to the material to be used, how the material is to be finished, how the parts are to be assembled, and any other information essential to making and assembling the particular object.

Working drawings may be divided into three classes: (1) Detail drawings, (2) assembly drawings, and (3) installation drawings.

Detail Drawing. A detail drawing is a description of a single part, given in such a manner as to describe by lines, notes, and symbols the specifications as to size, shape, material, and methods of manufacture that are to be used in making the part. Detail drawings are usually rather simple: and, when single parts are small, several detail drawings may be shown on the same sheet or print.

Assembly Drawing. An assembly drawing is a description of an object made up of two or more parts. It describes the object by giving, in a general way, the size and shape. Its primary purpose is to show the relationship of the various parts. An assembly drawing is usually more complex than a detail drawing, and is often accompanied by detail drawings of various parts.

Installation Drawing. An installation drawing is one which includes all necessary information for a part or an assembly of parts in the final position in the aircraft. It shows the dimensions necessary for the location of specific parts with relation to the other parts and reference dimensions that are helpful in later work in the shop.

PICTORIAL DRAWINGS

A pictorial drawing is similar to a photograph. It shows an object as it appears to the eye, but it is not satisfactory for showing complex forms and shapes. Pictorial drawings are useful in showing the general appearance of an object and are used extensively with orthographic projection drawings. Pictorial drawings are used in maintenance and overhaul manuals.

REFERENCE LINES

There are various numbering systems in use to facilitate location of specific wing ribs, fuselage bulkheads, or other structural members on an aircraft. Most manufacturers use some system of station marking; for example, the nose of the aircraft may be designated zero station, and all other stations are measured distances in inches behind the zero station. Thus, when a drawing (blueprint) reads "fuselage frame station 90," that particular frame station can be located 90 inches behind the nose of the aircraft. Figure 7-7 shows a typical station diagram.

To locate structures to the left or right of the centerline of the aircraft, many manufacturers consider the center line as a zero station for structural member location to its left or right. With such a system the stabilizer ribs can be designated as being so many inches left or right of the aircraft centerline.

The applicable manufacturer's numbering system and abbreviated designations or symbols should always be reviewed before attempting to locate a structural member.

The following list includes location designations typical of those used by many manufacturers.

Fuselage Stations (F.S.)

Fuselage Stations are numbered in inches from a reference or zero point

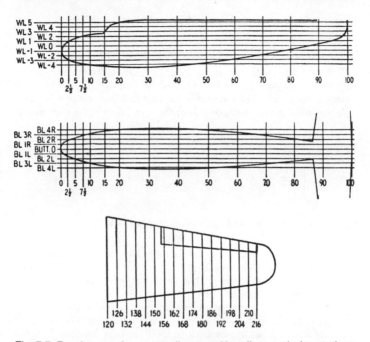

Fig. 7-7. Fuselage stations, waterlines, and butt lines and wing stations .

known as the **reference datum**. The reference datum is an imaginary vertical plane at or near the nose of the aircraft from which all horizontal distances are measured.

Buttock or Butt Lines (B.L.)

Butt lines are width measurements left or right of the vertical centerline.

Water Lines (W.L.)

Water lines are height measurements perpendicular from a horizontal plane located at a fixed location (within the fuselage as in Fig. 7-7, or a fixed distance below the bottom of the fuselage).

Wing Station, Horizontal Stabilizer Stations (W.S.), (H.S.S.)

These stations are measured left or right of the aircraft centerline or sometimes referenced to the root of the wing or horizontal stabilizer.

RIVET SYMBOLS USED ON DRAWINGS (BLUEPRINTS)

Rivet locations are shown on drawings by symbols. These symbols provide the necessary information by the use of code numbers or code letters or a combination of both. The meaning of the code numbers and code letters is explained in the general notes section of the drawing on which they appear.

Fig. 7-8. Basic rivet symbol quandrant configuration.

The rivet code system has been standardized by the National Aerospace Standards Committee (NAS Standard) and has been adopted by most major companies in the aircraft industry. This system has been assigned the number NAS523 in the NAS Standard book.

The NAS523 basic rivet symbol consists of two lines crossing at 90 degrees which form four quadrants. Code letters and code numbers are placed in these quadrants to give the desired information about the rivet. Each quadrant has been assigned a name: Northwest (NW), Northeast (NE), Southwest (SW), and Southeast (SE), as shown in Fig. 7-8.

The rivet type, head type, size, material, and location are shown on the field of the drawing by means of the rivet code, with one exception. Rivets to be installed flush on both sides are not coded, but are called out and detailed

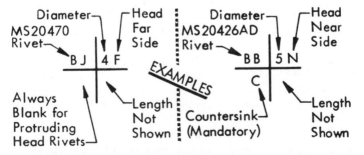

Fig. 7-9. Examples of rivet coding on a drawing.

CODE	BASIC PART NO.	MATERIAL	DESCRIPTION OF RIVET
BA	MS20426A	1100F	Solid, 100° Flush
BB	MS20426AD	2117-T3	Solid, 100° Flush
CY	MS20426DD	2024-T31	Solid, 100° Flush
BH	MS20470A	1100F	Solid, Universal Head
BJ	MS20470AD	2117-T3	Solid, Universal Head
CX	MS20470DD	2024-T31	Solid, Universal Head
AAR	NAS1738E	5056	Blind, Protruding Head
AAP	NAS1738M	MONEL	Blind, Protruding Head
AAV	NAS1739E	5056	Blind, 100° Flush
AAW	NAS1739M	MONEL	Blind, 100° Flush

Fig. 7-10. Typical examples of rivet coding. This list will vary according to requirements of each manufacturer.

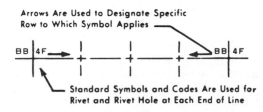

Fig. 7-11. Method of illustrating rivet code and location where there are a number of identical rivets in a row.

on the drawing. An explanation of the rivet codes for each type of rivet used is shown on the field of the drawing. Figure 7-9 shows examples of rivet coding on the drawing and Fig. 7-10 is a sample of rivet coding.

Hole and countersink dimensions for solid shank and blind rivets are omitted on all drawings since it is understood that the countersink angle is 100 degrees, and the countersink should be of such depth that the fastener fits flush with the surface after driving. When there are a number of rivets in a row which are identical, the rivet code is shown for the first and last rivet in the row only, and an arrow will show the direction in which the rivet row runs. The location of the rivets between the rivet codes are marked only with crossing centerlines as shown in Fig. 7-11.

Chapter 8
Standard Parts

STANDARD PARTS IDENTIFICATION

Since the manufacture of aircraft requires a large number of miscellaneous small fasteners and other items usually called "hardware," some degree of standardization is required. These standards have been derived by the various military organizations and described in detail in a set of specifications with applicable identification codes. These military standards have been universally adopted by the civil aircraft industry.

The derivation of a uniform "standard" is of necessity an evolutionary process. Originally, each of the military services derived their own standards. The old Army Air Corps set up AC (Air Corps) standards whereas the Navy used NAF (Naval Aircraft Factory) standards. In time, these were consolidated into AN (Air Force-Navy) standards and NAS (National Aerospace Standards). Still later these were consolidated into MS (Military Standard) designations.

At present, the three most common standards are:

- ☐ AN, Air Force Navy
- ☐ MS, Military Standard
- ☐ NAS (National Aerospace Standards)

The aircraft mechanic however, will also occasionally be confronted with the following standard parts on older aircraft:

- ☐ AC (Air Corps)
- ☐ NAF (Naval Aircraft Factory)

Each of these standard parts is identified by its specification number and various dash numbers and letters to fully describe its name, size and material.

Additional information on AN, MS, NAS as well as AMS and AND specifications and schedule of prices for specification sheets can be obtained from: National Standards Association, 1321 Fourteenth St. N.W., Washington, D.C. 20005.

Most airframe manufacturers have need for special small parts and use their own series of numbers and specifications. However, they use the universal "Standard Parts" wherever practicable.

Since the purpose of this *Standard Aircraft Handbook* is to provide the mechanic with a handy reference, only the most common "Standard Parts" are mentioned here with sufficient information to identify them.

STANDARD PARTS ILLUSTRATIONS

AN Standard Parts are shown on the following pages and are listed numerically according to their AN number. The equivalent and/or superceding MS numbers are shown where applicable.

—— AN3 to AN20 ——
BOLT, HEX HEAD

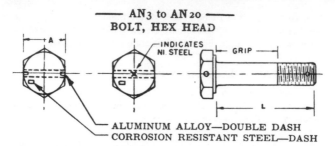

ALUMINUM ALLOY—DOUBLE DASH
CORROSION RESISTANT STEEL—DASH

Material: Nickel steel (S.A.E. 2330). Process: heat-treat harden and cadmium plate.

2024-T4 Alum. Process: heat-treat harden and anodic treatment. Corrosion resistant steel.

Thread: Class 3NF (unless otherwise noted).

DIAMETER—BY PART NUMBER

Part No.	Dia.	A, in.	Part No.	Dia.	A, in.	Part No.	Dia.	A, in.
AN3*	3/16	.375	AN7	7/16	.625	AN12	3/4	1.0625
AN4	1/4	.4375	AN8	1/2	.750	AN14	7/8	1.250
AN5	5/16	.500	AN9	9/16	.875	AN16	1	1.4375
AN6	3/8	.5825	AN10	5/8	.9375			

* SPECIAL NOTE: An AN3 bolt is made to a No. 10-32 screw size (see p. 223) to avoid confusion, since the two measurements are so nearly the same. (No. 10 screw is .190 dia., 3/16 is .187.)

LENGTH—BY DASH NUMBER

Dash No.	L, in.	Dash No.	L, in.	Dash No.	L, in.	Dash No.	L, in.
-3	3/8	-7	7/8	-13	1 3/8	-17	1 7/8
-4	1/2	-10	1	-14	1 1/2	-20	2
-5	5/8	-11	1 1/8	-15	1 5/8	-21	2 1/8
-6	3/4	-12	1 1/4	-16	1 3/4	-22	2 1/4

Additional lengths correspondingly coded in 8ths of an inch.

AN CODE: The material is indicated in the code by a letter preceding the dash number as follows:

Nickel steel ....No letter
Corrosion resistant steel.....................................Letter C
Aluminum alloy...Letters DD

The bolt may be supplied with or without the hole in either the shank or the head. This is indicated in code as follows:

UNDRILLED BOLT............................Add A after dash number
DRILLED SHANK ONLY...............No letter required
DRILLED HEAD ONLY...................Add H before dash number and A after dash number
DRILLED HEAD AND DRILLED SHANK..........Add H before dash number

—— AN21 to AN36 ——

BOLT, CLEVIS

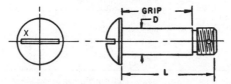

Material: Nickel steel (S.A.E. 2330). Process: heat-treat harden and cadmium plate.

Thread: Class 3NF.

DIAMETER—BY PART NUMBER

Part No.	Size	Part No.	Dia., in.	Part No.	Dia., in.	Part No.	Dia., in.
AN21	6–40	AN24	$\frac{1}{4}$	AN27	$\frac{7}{16}$	AN30	$\frac{5}{8}$
AN22	8–36	AN25	$\frac{5}{16}$	AN28	$\frac{1}{2}$	AN32	$\frac{3}{4}$
AN23	10–32	AN26	$\frac{3}{8}$	AN29	$\frac{9}{16}$	AN34	$\frac{7}{8}$
						AN36	1

LENGTH—BY DASH NUMBER

Dash No.	L, in.	Dash No.	L, in.	Dash No.	L, in.	Dash No.	L, in.	Dash No.	L, in.
–5	$\frac{5}{16}$	–9	$\frac{9}{16}$	–13	$1\frac{3}{16}$	–17	$1\frac{1}{16}$	–21	$1\frac{5}{16}$
–6	$\frac{3}{8}$	–10	$\frac{5}{8}$	–14	$\frac{7}{8}$	–18	$1\frac{1}{8}$	–22	$1\frac{3}{8}$
–7	$\frac{7}{16}$	–11	$1\frac{1}{16}$	–15	$1\frac{5}{16}$	–19	$1\frac{3}{16}$	–23	$1\frac{7}{16}$
–8	$\frac{1}{2}$	–12	$\frac{3}{4}$	–16	1	–20	$1\frac{1}{4}$	–24	$1\frac{1}{2}$

Additional lengths, on large sizes, to 7 in. are given similarly in 16ths by the dash number.

Example: AN23–12 is clevis bolt size 10–32 and $\frac{3}{4}$ in. long.

Description: AN clevis bolts are made from .001 to .002 small to allow a fit in fractional size drill holes. The short thread requires AN320 nut or AN364 self-locking nut. The hole in the threaded end is for a safety cotter; its absence is indicated by the letter A immediately following the dash number in the code.

Example: AN24–15A.

—— AN42 to AN49 ——

BOLT, EYE

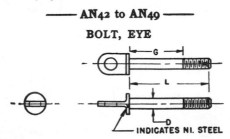

Material: Nickel steel (S.A.E. 2330)   Process: heat-treat harden and cadmium plate.

Size: Eye size and shank diameter combination by part number according to chart. Length by dash number in 8ths, same as hex-head bolts.

Part No.	Dia., in.		Clevis strength, lb.	Part No.	Dia., in.		Clevis strength, lb.
	Eye	Shank			Eye	Shank	
AN42	3/16	No. 10–32	1,000	AN47	3/8	7/16–20	8,000
AN43	3/16	1/4–28	2,100	AN48	7/16	1/2–20	11,500
AN45	5/16	5/16–24	4,600	AN49	1/2	9/16–18	15,500
AN46	3/8	3/8–24	6,100				

Shank made 2½ to 4 thousandths undersize and eye is to 10 thousandths oversize.

Example: AN 43—12 is an eyebolt, ¼ in. dia., 3/16 eye, and 1¼ in. long. (Add A for absence of hole.)

—— AN73 to AN81 ——

Superseded by MS20073/74

BOLT, AIRCRAFT-DRILLED HEAD

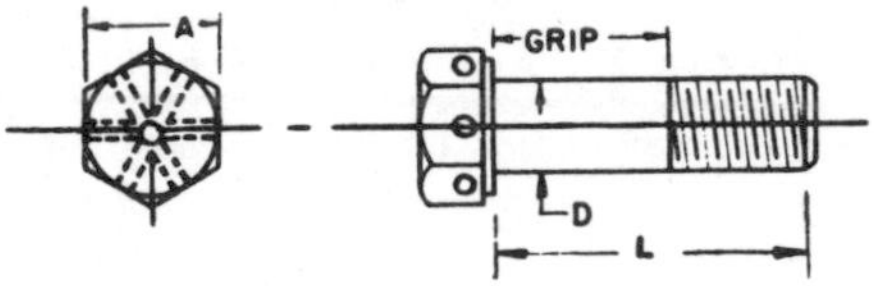

Material: Nickel steel (S.A.E. 2330). Process: heat-treat harden and cadmium plate.

Thread: Class 3NF or class 3NC. (NC indicated by A inserted in code in place of the usual dash.)

Size: A is the same as A for the corresponding sizes AN3 to AN16.

Diameter—by Part Number

Part No.	Dia., in.	Part No.	Dia., in.	Part No.	Dia., in.
AN73*	3/16	AN76	3/8	AN79	9/16
AN74	1/4	AN77	7/16	AN80	5/8
AN75	5/16	AN78	1/2	AN81	3/4

* See special note AN3.

Length—by Dash Number

Dash No.	*L*, in.	Dash No.	*L*, in.	Dash No.	*L*, in.	Dash No.	*L*, in.
–3	3/8	–7	7/8	–13	1 3/8	–17	1 7/8
–4	1/2	–10	1	–14	1 1/2	–20	2
–5	5/8	–11	1 1/8	–15	1 5/8	–21	2 1/8
–6	3/4	–12	1 1/4	–16	1 3/4	–22	2 1/4

Additional lengths correspondingly coded in 8ths of an inch.

Example: AN74–10 is drilled-head bolt, ¼ dia. and 1 in. long.

Description: The hole in the bolthead is for a safety wire. There is no hole in the threaded end for a cotter.

AN turnbuckle assemblies will be found on older aircraft. However, they have been superseded by MS (Military Standard) turnbuckle assemblies. See page 184 for a description of MS turnbuckle assemblies.

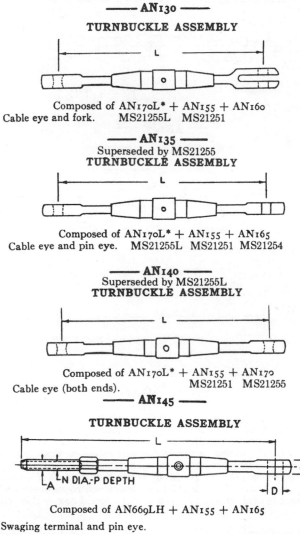

——— **AN130** ———

TURNBUCKLE ASSEMBLY

Composed of AN170L* + AN155 + AN160
Cable eye and fork. MS21255L MS21251

——— **AN135** ———
Superseded by MS21255
TURNBUCKLE ASSEMBLY

Composed of AN170L* + AN155 + AN165
Cable eye and pin eye. MS21255L MS21251 MS21254

——— **AN140** ———
Superseded by MS21255L
TURNBUCKLE ASSEMBLY

Composed of AN170L* + AN155 + AN170
Cable eye (both ends). MS21251 MS21255

——— **AN145** ———

TURNBUCKLE ASSEMBLY

Composed of AN669LH + AN155 + AN165

Swaging terminal and pin eye.
* Left-hand thread.

—— AN146 ——

TURNBUCKLE ASSEMBLY

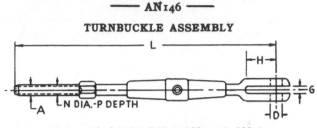

Composed of AN669LH + AN155 + AN161
Superseded by MS21252

Swaging terminal and fork.

—— AN147 ——

TURNBUCKLE ASSEMBLY

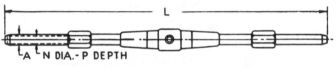

Composed of AN669LH + AN155 + AN669RH

Swaging terminal, both ends.

—— AN150 ——
Superseded by MS21252L
TURNBUCKLE ASSEMBLY

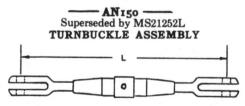

Composed of AN161L* + AN155 + AN161

Fork (both ends).   Use AN111 bushing.

Description: The turnbuckle length equals the length of the barrel plus the effective lengths of both ends with the ends screwed clear in. Notice that the dash numbers of the ends are the same as the dash numbers for the barrels or turnbuckle assemblies in which they fit. Notice also that the lockwire tends to tighten the turnbuckle (Fig.4-21, p. 93). These turnbuckles are, as already noted, combinations of the basic components described below. All turnbuckles and components are in two general classifications: long and short indicated by L or S in code.

* Left-hand thread.

The various sizes are indicated by dash numbers designating the rated pounds strength. The short types come in 8-, 16-, 21-, 32-, and 46-hundred pound strengths, while the long types come in 16-, 21-, 32-, 46-, 61-, 80-, 125-, and 175-hundred pound strengths. Class 3NF threads as follows are used on all turnbuckle parts:

Dash No.	Thread	Dash No.	Thread	Dash No.	Thread	Dash No.	Thread
−8	6–40	−21	12–28	−46	$\frac{5}{16}$–24	−125	$\frac{7}{16}$–20
−16	10–32	−32	$\frac{1}{4}$–28	−61 + −80	$\frac{3}{8}$–24	−175	$\frac{1}{2}$–20

Examples: AN130–8S is turnbuckle assembly, cable eye and fork, short, 8 hundred pounds strength. AN135–21L is turnbuckle assembly, cable eye and pin eye, long, 21 hundred pounds strength. AN140–32S is turnbuckle assembly, cable eyes, short, 32 hundred pounds strength. AN150–16S is turnbuckle assembly, fork ends, short, 16 hundred pounds strength.

—— AN155 ——

TURNBUCKLE BARREL

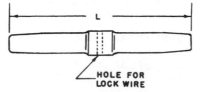

HOLE FOR
LOCK WIRE

Material: Brass.

Size: Lengths as follows: −8S to −46S incl., $2\frac{1}{4}$ in.; −16L to −80L incl., 4 in.; −125L and −175L, $4\frac{1}{4}$ in.

—— AN160 ——

TURNBUCKLE FORK

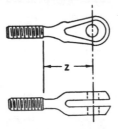

Material: Steel.   Process: heat-treat and cadmium plate.

Description: Right-hand thread. *Z*, or effective length, as follows: −8S to −46S incl., $1\frac{1}{8}$ in.; −16L to −80L incl., 2 in.; −125L, $2\frac{3}{8}$; −175L, $2\frac{5}{8}$ in.

—— **AN161** ——
MS21252
TURNBUCKLE FORK

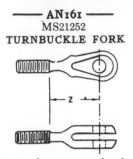

Material: Steel.   Process: heat-treat and cadmium plate.
Description: Right- or left-hand thread, indicated by R or L. Z, or effective lengths, as follows:

Dash No.	Z, in.	Dash No.	Z, in.	Dash No.	Z, in.	Dash No.	Z, in.
−16S	$1\frac{1}{8}$	−46S	$1\frac{9}{32}$	−32L	$2\frac{7}{64}$	−80L	$2\frac{5}{16}$
−21S	$1\frac{5}{32}$	−16L	2	−46L	$2\frac{5}{32}$	−125L	$2\frac{7}{16}$
−32S	$1\frac{7}{32}$	−21L	$2\frac{1}{32}$	−61L	$2\frac{9}{32}$	−175L	$2\frac{11}{16}$

—— **AN165** ——
MS21254
TURNBUCKLE EYE FOR PIN

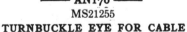

Material: Steel.   Process: heat-treat and cadmium plate.
Description: Right-hand thread. Z, or effective lengths, same as AN160.

—— **AN170** ——
MS21255
TURNBUCKLE EYE FOR CABLE

Material: Steel.   Process: heat-treat and cadmium plate.
Description: Right- or left-hand thread, indicated by R or L Z, or effective length, same as AN160.

—— **AN 173 to AN 186** ——

BOLT — CLOSE TOLERANCE

This marking on head of close tolerance bolts.

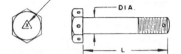

Description: These bolts are made of nickel steel (S.A.E. 2330). Head and threads are cadmium-plated. Shank is ground with a tolerance of .0005 of an inch. Diameter is ±.0005. The shank is greased after grinding. Thread is NF.

Size: Diameter given by part number. Length is given in 8ths by the second dash number according to Table 4, page 195. These bolts may be obtained with or without drilled shank and with or without drilled head. (Code like AN3 to AN20)

—— **AN310** ——

NUT, AIRCRAFT—CASTLE

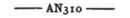
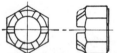

Material: Steel. Process: heat-treat harden and cadmium plate. 2024-T4 Alum. indicated by D preceding dash number.
Corrosion resistant steel indicated by C preceding dash number.

Thread: Class 3 NF.
Size: Made in sizes 3/16 to 1 in., indicated in 16ths of an inch by the dash number. Fits AN hex-head bolts of same designated size.

Example: AN310—5 is AN castle nut made of steel and fits a 5/16 AN bolt.

—— **AN315** ——

NUT, AIRCRAFT—PLAIN

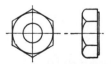

Material, Thread, and Sizes: Same as AN310, except that thread is also left-hand indicated by L or R following dash number and is made in size 640

Examples: AN315D5L is plain aircraft nut made of dural. Fits a $\frac{5}{16}$ bolt and has a left-hand thread. AN315D5R is same nut with a right-hand thread.

——— AN316 ———

NUT, AIRCRAFT—CHECK

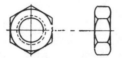

Material: Steel. Process: heat-treat harden and cadmium plate.
Thread: Class 3 NF, left or right indicated by L or R.
Sizes: Made in sizes $\frac{1}{4}$ to 1 in. incl. indicated in 16ths of an inch by this dash number.
Description: Much thinner than AN315.
Examples: AN316–6R is aircraft check nut to fit a $\frac{3}{8}$ bolt with right-hand thread. AN316–6L is same nut with left-hand thread.

——— AN320 ———

NUT, AIRCRAFT—SHEAR

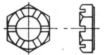

Material and Thread: Same as AN310.
Size: Same as AN310 except –1 is size 6–40, –2 is size 8–36, and –20 is 1$\frac{1}{4}$–12.
Description: Much thinner than AN310 as illustration indicates.
Examples: AN320–4 is aircraft shear nut made of steel and fits a $\frac{1}{4}$-in. AN bolt. AN320D4 is same nut made of aluminum alloy.

——— AN340 ———

NUT, MACHINE SCREW—HEX (COARSE THREAD)

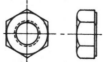

Material: Steel, cadmium-plated.
Corrosion resistant steel
Brass, commercial.
2024-T4 Alum., anodized.

Thread: Class 2 NC.

Size: Machine screw sizes; steel, 2 to 416; brass, 2 to 10; dural, 6 to 616. Refer to dash number table, page 195

Examples: AN340DD6 is machine screw hex nut made of 2024 aluminum to fit a size 6-32 machine screw. AN340B6 is same nut made of brass. AN340-6 is same nut made of steel. AN340C6 is same nut made of corrosion resistant steel.

—— AN345 ——

NUT, PLAIN HEX (FINE THREAD)

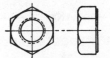

Material: Carbon steel, commercial, cadmium-plated.

Brass, commercial, indicated by B in code.

Corrosion-resistant steel, passivated. Indicated by C in code.

2024-T4 aluminum alloy, anodized. Indicated by DD in code.

Thread: Class 2 NF.

Sizes: Machine screw, dural No. 10 and 416; brass 0 to 10 incl.; carbon steel 0 to 416 incl.; and corrosion-resistant 0 to 416 incl.

Examples: AN345C4 is machine screw hex nut (fine thread) made of stainless (corrosion-resistant) steel, size 4. AN345B4 is the same screw made of brass. AN345DD4 is the same screw made of 2024-T4 Alum AN345-4 is the same screw made of carbon steel.

—— AN350 ——

NUT, WING

Material: Steel, cadmium-plated, or brass.

Thread: Class 2 NF.

Sizes: 6, 8, and 10 machine screw sizes coded according to dash number Table 1, page 195 and ¼, ⁵⁄₁₆, ⅜, ⁷⁄₁₆, and ½ indicated by dash number giving diameter of bolt that it fits in 16ths of an inch.

Examples: AN350-1032 is wing nut made of steel and fits a 10–32 machine screw. AN350B4 is wing nut made of brass and fits a ¼-in. bolt.

—— AN355 ——

NUT, ENGINE—SLOTTED

These nuts are designed specifically for engines and are *not* to be used on aircraft.

Material: Steel.   Process: heat-treat harden.   Spec. AN–QQ–S–689, AN–QQ–690, AN–QQ–687.   Spec. 29–26 except material.

Thread: Class 3 NF.

Size: Made in $\frac{3}{16}$ to $\frac{3}{4}$ sizes indicated by dash number in 16ths giving diameter of bolt that it fits (–3 is 10–32).

Example: AN355–5 is slotted engine nut made of steel and fits a $\frac{5}{16}$ bolt.

—— **AN356** ——

NUT, LOCK (PALNUT)

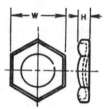

Material: Steel.   Process: cadmium plate (Spec. AN–QQ–P–421).

Description: *Not to be used in aircraft structures*.   Is made in National Coarse (No. 4–36 to $\frac{3}{4}$–10) and National Fine (No. 10–32 to $\frac{3}{4}$–16) threads.

Sizes: Sizes are indicated according to thread Table 1, page 195 .

Example: AN356-524 is AN palnut 5/6 in. diameter with 24 threads per inch.

—— **AN360** ——

NUT, ENGINE—PLAIN

These nuts are designed specifically for engines and are *not* to be used on aircraft.

Material, Thread, and Size: Same as AN355 except finish is black rustproof (Spec. 57–0–2).

Example: AN360–5 is plain engine nut made of steel and fits a $\frac{5}{16}$ bolt.

NUT, SELF-LOCKING PLATE (HIGH TEMPERATURE)

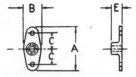

Material: Steel.
Corrosion resistant steel

Thread: NF and NC.

Sizes: No. 6 machine screw through ⅜ dia. Coded according to dash number, Table 1 on page 195.

Code: F — Steel
C — Corrosion resistant steel
WC — Weldable corrosion resistant steel

NUT, SELF-LOCKING (HIGH TEMPERATURE)

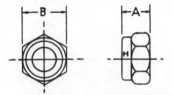

Material: Steel .Corrosion resistant steel or brass.

Thread: NF and NC.

Sizes: No. 10 machine screw through ¾ dia. Coded according to Table 1 on page 195 . Shall not be used where temperature exceeds 650°F.

Description: Similar in appearance to AN365.

Superseded by MS20364
NUT, SELF-LOCKING—THIN

Material: Steel. Process: cadmium plate.
Brass.
Dural 24S, heat-treat hardened and anodized.

Thread: Class 2 NF on 6–40 and 8.36.   Class 3 NF on 10–32 through 1 in.

Size: Steel 6–40 through 1 in., brass 8–36 through 1 in. and dural 10–32 through 1 in. All sizes designated according to dash number Table 1 on page 195.

Examples: AN364-1032 is thin self-locking nut made of steel to fit a 10-32 machine screw. AN364B1032 is same nut made of brass. AN364D1032 is same nut made of dural.

Description: Add A after dash number for non-metalic inserts. Add C after dash number for all metal.

——— **AN365** ———
Superseded by MS20365
NUT, SELF-LOCKING

Material: Same as AN364.

Thread: Class 2 NF or NC on machine screw sizes 4, 6, and 8. Class 3 NF or NC on machine screw size 10 through $\frac{1}{2}$ in. dia.

Size: Steel machine screw size 4 through $\frac{1}{2}$ dia.; brass fine thread size 8 through $\frac{1}{2}$ in. dia. and in coarse thread size 4 through $\frac{1}{2}$ in. dia.; dural fine thread size 10 through $\frac{1}{2}$ in. dia., and coarse thread size 4 through $\frac{3}{8}$ dia. All sizes designated according to dash number table 1, page 195.

Examples: AN365-1032 is self-locking nut made of steel and fits a 10-32 screw. AN365B524 is self-locking nut made of brass and fits a 5/16 fine thread bolt. AN365D832 is self-locking nut made of dural and fits an 8-32 machine screw.

Description: Add A after dash number for non-metalic inserts. Add C after dash number for all metal.

——— **AN366** ———
Superseded by MS21048
NUT, PLATE

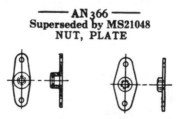

Material: Steel.   Process: cadmium plate.
2024-T4 Alum: Process: heat-treat harden and anodize.
Thread: Class 2 NF.
Size: No. 8, No. 10, and $\frac{1}{4}$ in. except self-locking steel, which also has No. 6. All sizes designated according to Table 1, page 195.

Description: Self-locking nuts shall not be used where the temperature exceeds 250°F. To be riveted in place where nut is inaccessible to a wrench. Self-locking type indicated in code by F preceding the dash number. Add A after dash number for non-metalic inserts. Add C after dash number for all metal.

Examples: AN366-836 is plain plate nut made of steel, size 8-36. AN366DF420 is self-locking plate nut made of dural and fits a ¼ in. dia. coarse thread bolt. AN366F428 is same plate nut made of steel to fit a fine thread bolt.

—— AN380 ——
Superseded by MS24665
PIN, COTTER

Material: Low carbon steel.   Process: cadmium plate.
Size: See following table:

First dash No.	Dia., in.	Second dash No.	Length, in.	Second dash No.	Length, in.
−2	¹⁄₁₆	−2	½	−8	2
−3	³⁄₃₂	−3	¾	−10	2½
−4	⅛	−4	1	−12	3
−5	⁵⁄₃₂	−5	1¼	−14	3½
−6	³⁄₁₆	−6	1½	−16	4
−8	¼	−7	1¾		

—— AN381 ——
Superseded by MS24665
PIN, COTTER

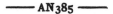

Description: Same as above except made of corrosion resistant steel.

—— AN385 ——

PIN, TAPER

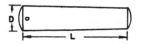

Material: Steel, plain carbon and alloy steel.

SIZES

First dash No.	Dia. large end, in.	First dash No.	Dia. large end, in.	First dash No.	Dia. large end, in.
–60	.078	–20	.141	–3	.219
–50	.094	–10	.156	–4	.250
–40	.109	–1	.172	–5	.289
–30	.125	–2	.193	–6	.341

Second dash No.	Length, in.	Second dash No.	Length, in.	Second dash No.	Length, in.
–3	3/8	–8	1	–18	2 1/4
–4	1/2	–10	1 1/4	–20	2 1/2
–5	5/8	–12	1 1/2	–22	2 3/4
–6	3/4	–14	1 3/4	–24	3
–7	7/8	–16	2		

Add H before dash Number for drilled head.
Add A before dash number for alloy steel.
Add P before second dash number for cadmium plate.

Examples: AN385–30–6 is taper pin, size 3/0, Morse taper (1/4 in. per foot), 3/4 in. long. AN385–3–12 is taper pin, size 3, Morse taper, 1 1/2 in. long. Use Morse standard taper pin reamer, same designated size as pin. Use drill as specified or, when not specified, .003 to .005 smaller than small end of pin.

—— **AN386** ——

PIN, TAPER—THREADED

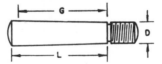

Material: Steel. Process: heat-treat harden and cadmium plate.
Thread: Class 3 NF.

SIZES

First dash No.	Dia., in.	Thread	First dash No.	Dia., in.	Thread	First dash No.	Dia., in.	Thread
–1	.2052	10–32	–5	.4552	3/8–24	–9	.9052	3/4–16
–2	.2052	10–32	–6	.5052	7/16–20	–10	1.0502	7/8–14
–3	.3172	1/4–28	–7	.6052	1/2–20	–10A	1.1527	7/8–14
–4	.3552	5/16–24	–8	.7552	9/16–18	–11	1.2552	7/8–14
$L = \text{grip} + 1/8$			$L = \text{grip} + 3/16$			$L = \text{grip} + 1/4$		

Second dash No.*	Grip, length,† in.	Second dash No.*	Grip, length,† in.	Second dash No.*	Grip, length,† in.
–6	3/4	–13	1 5/8	–19	2 3/8
–7	7/8	–14	1 3/4	–20	2 1/4
–8	1	–15	1 7/8	–21	2 5/8
–9	1 1/8	–16	2	–22	2 3/4
–10	1 1/4	–17	2 1/8	–23	2 7/8
–11	1 3/8	–18	2 1/4	–24	3
–12	1 1/2			–25	3 3/8

* A following second dash number indicates no cotter pin hole.
† Additional lengths to 6 in. are correspondingly indicated in 8ths.

Examples: AN386–6–12 is threaded taper pin, Brown & Sharpe taper (½ in. per foot except No. 10 and No. 10A, on which taper is .5161 in. per foot), size 6 with a 1½ in. grip length. AN386–612A is same pin without cotter pin hole. Use Brown & Sharpe taper reamer with same number size as pin. Use drill as specified or, when not specified, 3 to 5 thousandths smaller than small end of taper.

——— AN392 to AN406 ———
Superseded by MS20392
PIN, FLAT HEAD

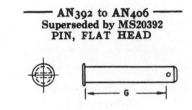

Material: Steel.　Process: heat-treat harden and cadmium plate.

SIZES

Part No.	Dia.,* in.	Part No.	Dia.,* in.	Part No.	Dia.,* in.
392	⅛	396	⅜	400	⅝
393	³⁄₁₆	397	⁷⁄₁₆	402	¾
394	¼	398	½	404	⅞
395	⁵⁄₁₆	399	⁹⁄₁₆	406	1

Dash No.	Grip length†	Dash No.	Grip length†	Dash No.	Grip length†
–7	⁷⁄₃₂	–17	1⁷⁄₃₂	–29	2⁹⁄₃₂
–9	⁹⁄₃₂	–19	1⁹⁄₃₂	–31	3¹⁄₃₂
–11	1¹⁄₃₂	–21	2¹⁄₃₂	–33	1¹⁄₃₂
–13	1³⁄₃₂	–23	2³⁄₃₂	–35	1³⁄₃₂
–15	1⁵⁄₃₂	–25	2⁵⁄₃₂	–37	1⁵⁄₃₂
		–27	2⁷⁄₃₂		

* 0 to .002 under indicated size.
† Additional grip lengths to 4⁹⁄₃₂ given similarly in odd 32nds.

Example: AN394–25 is flathead pin ¼ dia. and ²⁵⁄₃₂ grip length.

——— AN415 ———

PIN, LOCK

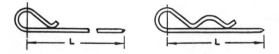

Material: Corrosion resistant steel
Size: Length of AN415 given in increments of 1 in. by dash number.
Example: AN415–3 is lock pin 3 in. long.

—— AN416 ——

PIN, RETAINING—SAFETY

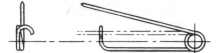

Material: Steel wire.   Process: cadmium-plate.

SIZES

Dash No.	A, in.	B, in.	D, in.
—1	$1\frac{1}{16}$	$1\frac{3}{8}$	.051
—2	$\frac{3}{4}$	$1\frac{5}{16}$	.041

—— AN426 ——
MS20426 (100°)
RIVET, 100° COUNTERSUNK HEAD—ALUMINUM ALLOY

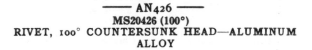

Material: Alloy 5056-H12 (B), ¼ hard.
Alloy 2117-T4 (AD), heat-treat hardened.
Alloy 2024-T4 (DD), heat-treat hardened.
Alloy 2017-T4 (D), heat-treat hardened.
Size: Indicated by dash numbers according to Table 4, page 195.
Example: AN426B3-5 is 100-deg. countersunk-head rivet, made of 5056-H12, 3/32 dia. and 5/16 long. AN426AD3-5 is same rivet made of 2117-T4, AN426DD3-5 is same rivet made of 2024-T4. AN426D3-5 is same rivet made of 2017-T4

—— AN427 ——
MS20427
RIVET, 100° COUNTERSUNK

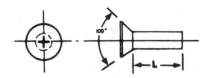

Material: Steel, monel, corrosion resistant steel and copper.

Size: Indicated by dash numbers according to table 4, page 195.
     Add before the dash number:—
             F—for corrosion resistant steel
             M—for monel
             C—for copper
     Add after the dash number:—
             C—for cadmium plated carbon steel
             Z—for zinc plated
             U—for unplated
The monel rivet is indicated by the triangle on the rivet head.

——— AN430 ———
MS20430
RIVET, ROUND HEAD—ALUMINUM ALLOY✳

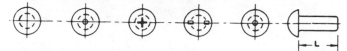

✳These rivets have been superseded by AN470 for most applications.
Material: Alloy 1100-H14 (A), not applicable for new design.
Alloy 2117-T4 (AD), heat-treat hardened.
Alloy 5056-H12 (B), ¼ hard.
Alloy 2024-T4 (DD), heat-treat hardened.
Alloy 2017-T4 (D), heat-reat hardened.
Size: Indicated by dash numbers according to Table 4, page 195.
Example: AN430A3-5 is roundhead rive made of 2S½H, 3/32 dia.,
5/16 long. AN430AD3-5 is same rivet made of 2117-T4. AN430B3-5
is same rivet made of 5056-H12. AN430DD3-5 is same rivet made of
2024-T4. AN430D3-5 is same rivet made of 2017-T4.

——— AN442 ———

RIVET, FLAT HEAD—ALUMINUM ✳

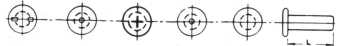

✳These rivets have been superseded by AN470 for most applications.
Material: Alloy 2017-T4 (D), heat-treat hardened;
Alloy 2024-T4 (DD), heat-treat hardened;
Alloy 5056-F
Alloy 1100-H14 (A), half hard.
Alloy 2117-T4 (AD), heat-treat hardened.
Size: Indicated by dash numbers according to Table 4, page 195.
Example: AN442A3-5 is flathead rivet made of 1100-H14, 3-32 dia.,
5/16 long. AN442AD3-5 is same rivet made of 2117-T4

—— AN456 ——

RIVET, BRAZIER HEAD—ALUMINUM ALLOY *

*These rivets have been superseded by AN470 for most applications.

Material: Alloy 2017-T4 (D), 2117-T4 (AD), 2024-T4 (DD), 5056-F (B).
Size: Inidcated by dash numbers according to Table 4, page 195.
Example: AN456AD3-5 is brazier head rivet, made of 2117-T4, 3/32 dia., 5/16 long. AN456D3-5 is same rivet made of 2017-T4.

—— AN470 ——
MS20470
RIVET — UNIVERSAL HEAD

Material and **Size** of this rivet are the same as AN430. This rivet is a replacement rivet to suit the requirements of AN430, AN442, and AN456.

—— AN481 ——

ROD END, CLEVIS

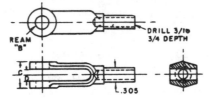

Material: Steel forging (Spec. 57–107–20). Finish: heat-treat normalize. Cadmium plate indicated by P following dash number. Unplated parts to be finished at assembly.

SIZE

Dash No.	B, in.	C, in.	D, in.	Dash No.	B, in.	C, in.	D, in.
—1	.250	½	$1\frac{7}{64}$	—3	.1875	½	$1\frac{7}{16}$
—2	.250	$\frac{5}{16}$	$\frac{9}{64}$	—4	.1875	$\frac{5}{16}$	$\frac{9}{64}$

AN486 same as AN481 except that the end opposite the clevis has Y4-28 NF3 internal thread.

—— AN665 ——

TERMINAL, TIE ROD

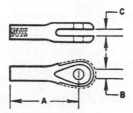

Types: Threader—clevis.

Material: Nickel steel.   Process: heat-treat.

Threads: NF–3.   Left and right hand, denoted by L or R following dash number.

SIZES

Dash No.	Tie rod strength, lb.	Tap T	A, in.	B, in.	C, in.
–10	1,200	6–40	$1\frac{5}{16}$	.188	.109
–21	2,400	10–32	$1\frac{17}{32}$	.188	.150
–34	4,200	$\frac{1}{4}$–28	$1\frac{13}{16}$	.250	.203
–46	4,600	$\frac{5}{16}$–24	$1\frac{7}{8}$	.313	.203
–61	6,900	$\frac{5}{16}$–24	2	.375	.203
–80	10,000	$\frac{3}{8}$–24	$2\frac{1}{4}$	.375	.266
–115	13,700	$\frac{7}{16}$–20	$2\frac{1}{2}$	.438	.344
–155	18,500	$\frac{1}{2}$–20	$2\frac{13}{16}$	.500	.406
–202	24,000	$\frac{9}{16}$–18	$3\frac{1}{8}$	.563	.453
–247	29,500	$\frac{5}{8}$–16	$3\frac{3}{8}$	.625	.516
–430	42,000	$\frac{3}{4}$–16	$4\frac{1}{8}$	.750	.656
–580	58,000	$\frac{7}{8}$–14	$4\frac{7}{8}$	.875	.781
–760	76,000	1–14	$5\frac{3}{4}$	1.	.906

Examples: AN665–61L.   AN665–80R.

——AN500——

SCREW, FILLISTER HEAD—DRILLED OR PLAIN HEAD (COARSE THREAD)

Material: Steel (S.A.E. 1120).   Process: cadmium plate.
Stainless steel (corrosion-resistant 18–8) passivated; C in code.
Brass (commercial); B in code.
Thread: Class 2 NC.
Size: Machine screw size or diameter of longer sizes is given by first dash number according to screw size Table 2, page 195 .   Sizes are No. 2 through ⅜ dia.   Length in 16ths of an inch is given by second dash number according to Table 3, page 195 .
Examples: AN500-10-14 is fillister-head screw, made of carbon steel, size No. 10-24, and ⅞ in. long. AN500C10-14 is the same screw made of stainless steel. AN500B10-14 is the same screw made of brass.

Description: Drilled head is indicated by A immediately following the part number.

––––– **AN501** –––––

SCREW, FILLISTER HEAD

Drilled or plain head (fine thread).   Identical with AN500 except that thread is class 2 NF.   Sizes are No. 0 through ⅜ dia.

––––– **AN502** –––––

SCREW, AIRCRAFT—FILLISTER HEAD, DRILLED (FINE THREAD)

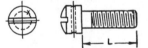

Material: Steel (S.A.E. 2330) (S.A.E. 3140 or 6150 optional).   Process: heat-treat harden and cadmium plate.
Thread: Class 3 NF.
Size: Machine-screw size or diameter of large sizes is given by first dash number according to Table 2, page 195 .   Sizes are 6, 8, 10, ¼, and ⁵⁄₁₆.   Length in 16ths of an inch is given by second dash number according to Table 3, page 195 .
Example: AN502–8–10 is fillister-head screw, size 8–36 and ⅝ in. long.

––––– **AN503** –––––

SCREW, AIRCRAFT—FILLISTER HEAD, DRILLED (COARSE THREAD)

Identical with AN502 except that thread is class 3 NC.

—— AN505 ——

SCREW, FLAT HEAD (COARSE THREAD)

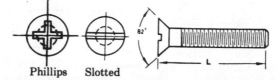

Phillips   Slotted

Material: Steel (S.A.E. 2330).   Process: cadmium plate.
Brass.
Aluminum alloy   Process: heat-treat harden, anodize.   D in code.
Thread: Class 2 NC.
Size: Machine screw size or diameter is given by first dash number
according to Table 2, page 195   Sizes are 2 through ⅜ dia.   Length
in 16ths of an inch are given by second dash number according to
Table 3, page 195 .
Examples: AN505–10–16 is flathead (82 deg countersunk) machine
screw, size 10–24, 1 in. long, made of steel.   AN505B10–16 is same
screw made of brass.   AN505D10–16 is same screw made of aluminum
alloy. **Add C for corrosion resistant steel. Add R between dash
numbers for recessed head.**

—— AN509 ——

100° FLUSH HEAD SCREW

(Same as above except for head angle.)

—— AN510 ——

SCREW, FLAT HEAD (FINE THREAD)

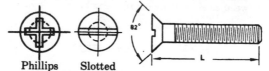

Phillips   Slotted

Material: Steel (S.A.E. 1120).   Process: cadmium-plate.
Corrosion-resistant steel, passivated.   C in code.
Brass.   B in code.
Aluminum alloy, "Inactive for design."   D in code.
Thread: Class 2 NF.
Sizes: No. 0 through ¼ in. dia. coded same as AN505
Example: AN510C10–16 is corrosion-resistant steel.
Add R between dash numbers for recessed head.

—— AN515 ——

SCREW, ROUND HEAD (COARSE THREAD)

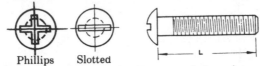

Phillips Slotted

Material: Steel (S.A.E. 1120). Process: cadmium plate.
Brass.
Aluminum alloy. Process: heat-treat harden and anodize.
Thread: Class 2 NC.
Size: Machine screw size or diameter of larger sizes are given by first dash number according to Table 2, page 195. Sizes are No. 2 through ⅜ dia. Length in 16ths of an inch in given by second dash number according to Table 3, page 195.
Example: AN515D10–16.
Add R between dash numbers for recessed head.

—— AN520 ——

SCREW, ROUND HEAD (FINE THREAD)

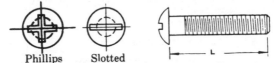

Phillips Slotted

Material: Steel (S.A.E. 1120). Process: cadmium plate.
Brass.
Aluminum alloy, "Inactive for design."
Corrosion-resistant steel, passivated.
Thread: Class 2 NF.
Sizes: No. 0 through ¼ dia., coded same as AN515.
Example: AN520B10–16.
Add R between dash numbers for recessed head.

—— AN525 ——

SCREW, WASHER HEAD

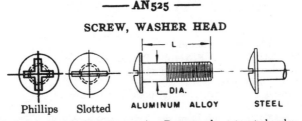

Phillips Slotted ALUMINUM ALLOY STEEL

Material: Steel (S.A.E. 2330). Process: heat-treat harden and cadmium plate.

Aluminum alloy. Process: heat-treat harden and anodize. D in code.

Thread: Class 3 NF.

Size: 8–36, 1032, and ½–28 coded according to Table 2, page 195 in first dash number. Length, given in second dash number, is in 16ths of an inch according to Table 3, page 195.

Examples: AN525–8–8 is washer-head screw, of steel, size 8–36, ½ in. long. AN525D8–8 is same screw made of aluminum alloy.

Add R between dash numbers for recessed head.

--- **AN526** ---

SCREW, TRUSS HEAD

Material: Steel (low carbon—S.A.E. 1120). Process: cadmium plate.

Corrosion-resistant steel, passivated, indicated by C.

Aluminum alloy. Process: heat-treat harden and anodize. DD in code.

Thread: Class 2 NF and Class 2 NC.

Size: No. 6, No. 8, No. 10, and ¼ in. dia. indicated by first dash number according to Table 1, page 195. Length in 16ths of an inch given by second dash number according to Table 3, page 195.

Examples: AN526–640–10 is button-head screw, made of low-carbon steel, size 6–40, ⅝ in. long. AN526C640–10 is same screw made of corrosion-resistant steel. AN526DD640–10 is same screw made of aluminum alloy.

Add R between dash numbers for recessed head.

--- **AN530** ---

SCREW, SHEET METAL—ROUND HEAD—PARKER KALON (PK)—TYPE Z

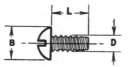

Material: Steel. Process: harden and cadmium plate (Spec. AN–QQ–P–421).

Description: Thread starts and makes its own threads in sheet metal owing to the reduced and grooved first two threads.

Size: First dash number gives screw size (−2, −4, −6, −8, −10, and −14) according to Table 2, page 195, of nominal diameter D, while second dash number gives L in 16ths of an inch.

Metal thickness	Hole sizes for screws					
	−2	−4	−6	−8	−10	−14 (¼ D.)
.015 to .028	.063	.086	.104	.116	.128	
.031 to .051	.073	.093	.110	.120	.136	.189
.063 to .081	.076	.101	.120	.140	.152	.201

Example: AN530–6–6 is sheet-metal screw, size 6 and ⅜ in. long.

—— AN531 ——

SCREW, SHEET METAL—FLAT HEAD—PARKER KALON (PK)—TYPE Z

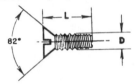

Material: Same as given with AN530, except that first dash numbers range from −4 to −14 only.

Example: AN531–6–6 is sheet-metal screw, size 6 and ⅜ in. long.

—— AN490 ——

ROD END, THREADED

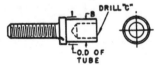

Material: Steel (Spec. AN–QQ–S–646). **Finish:** Cadmium plate indicated by P following dash number. Unfinished parts to be finished at assembly.

Thread: ¼–28 NF3 external.

SIZE

Dash No.	A, in.	B, in.	C, in.
−5	⁵⁄₁₆	.2425	⅛
−6	⅜	.305	³⁄₁₆
−8	½	.430	⁹⁄₃₂

Examples: AN490–6 is threaded rod end for a ⅜ tube. AN490–6P is cadmium-plated.

——— AN666 ———
MS21259
TERMINAL, THREADED CABLE (FOR SWAGING)

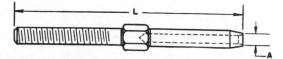

Sizes: See table under AN669.
Threads: Bolt R and L.
Example: AN666–8R is terminal, ¼ dia. cable, right-hand threads.

——— AN667 ———
MS20667
TERMINAL, FORK END CABLE (FOR SWAGING)

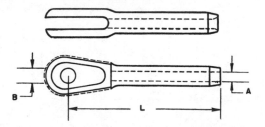

Sizes: See table under AN669.
Example: AN667–4 is terminal, ⅛ in. dia. cable, fork end.

——— AN668 ———
MS20668
TERMINAL, EYE END CABLE (FOR SWAGING)

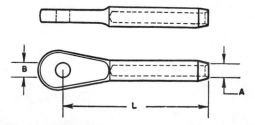

Sizes: See table under AN669.
Example: AN668–6 is terminal, ³⁄₁₆ dia. cable, eye end.

——— AN669 ———
Superseded by MS21260
TERMINAL, TURNBUCKLE CABLE (FOR SWAGING)

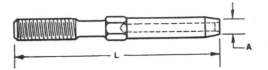

Sizes: See table.   Dash numbers −3, −4, −5, −6 are both long and short sizes.

Threads: Both R and L.

Dash No.	Cable dia., in.	Thread NF-3 AN666 and AN669	A, in.	B, in.	Length before swaging, in.				
					AN666	AN667	AN668	AN669	AN669-S
−2	1/16	6–40	.078	.188	2.473	1.572	1.631	2.616	
−3	3/32	10–32	.109	.188	2.879	1.945	2.043	3.738	2.863
−4	1/8	1/4–28	.141	.188	3.333	2.352	2.337	4.020	3.145
−5	5/32	1/4–28	.172	.250	3.627	2.655	2.684	4.314	3.429
−6	3/16	5/16–24	.203	.313	4.002	3.071	3.019	4.612	3.737
−7	7/32	3/8–24	.234	.313	4.516	3.440	3.382	4.914	
−8	1/4	3/8–24	.265	.375	4.937	3.806	3.763	5.218	
−9	9/32	7/16–20	.297	.438	5.391	4.120	4.153	5.542	
−10	5/16	1/2–20	.328	.438	5.844	4.438	4.546	5.875	

Examples: AN669–L6LH is terminal, long, 3/16 dia. cable, left-hand threads.   AN669–S6RH is terminal, short, 3/16 dia. cable, right-hand threads.

MS TURNBUCKLES
(CLIP-LOCKING)

Clip-Locking Turnbuckles utilize two locking clips instead of lockwire for safetying. The turnbuckle barrel and terminals are slotted lengthwise to accommodate the locking clips. After the proper cable tension is reached the barrel slots are aligned with the terminal slots and the clips are inserted. The curved end of the locking clips expand and latch in the vertical slot in the center of the barrel.

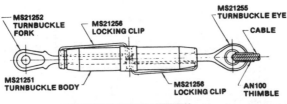

TYPICAL TURNBUCKLE ASSEMBLY

MS Standard Drawings for clip-locking turnbuckles supersede various AN Drawings for conventional (lockwire type) turnbuckle parts and NAS Drawings for clip-locking turnbuckle parts. Refer to the following cross reference tables for AN and NAS equivalents.

MS21251 TURNBUCKLE BARREL

Supersedes AN155 and NAS649 barrels. MS21251 items can replace AN155 items of like material and thread, but the AN155 items cannot replace the MS21251 items. MS21251 items are interchangeable with the NAS649 items of like material and thread. MS21251 barrels are available in brass (QQ-B-637, composition 2 or MIL-T-6945), steel (cadmium plated to QQ-P-416, type 2, class 3) or aluminum alloy (anodized to MIL-A-8725). The cross reference table shows equivalent items made of brass.

MS21251 DASH NO.	ROPE DIA.	THREAD SIZE	AN155 DASH NO	NAS649 DASH NO.	USES MS21256 CLIP DASH NO.
B2S	1/16	6-40	B8S	B8S	-1
B2L	1/16	6-40	B8L	B8L	-2
B3S	3/32	10-32	B16S	B16S	-1
B3L	3/32	10-32	B16L	B16L	-2
B5S	5/32	1/4-28	B32S	B32S	-1
B5L	5/32	1/4-28	B32L	B32L	-2
B6S	3/16	5/16-24	B46S	B46S	-1
B6L	3/16	5/16-24	B46L	B46L	-2
B8L	1/4	3/8-24	B80L	B80L	-2
B9L	9/32	7/16-20	B125L	B125L	-3
B10L	5/16	1/2-20	B175L	B175L	-3

TERMINALS
MS items can replace AN items of like thread except for the -22 and -61 sizes, but the AN items cannot replace the MS items. MS items are interchangeable with the NAS items of like thread except for the -22 and -61 sizes. These MS terminals are available only in steel cadmium plated to QQ-P-416, type 2, class 3. Available with right-hand (R) or left-hand (L) threads.

MS21252 TURNBUCKLE FORK supersedes AN161 and NAS645 forks.

MS21254 PIN EYE supersedes AN165 and NAS648 eyes.

MS21255 CABLE EYE supersedes AN170 and NAS 647 eyes.

MS21260 SWAGED STUD END supersedes AN669 studs.

MS21252 MS21254 MS21255 DASH NOS.		WIRE ROPE DIA.	THREAD SIZE	AN 161 AN165 AN170 DASH NOS.		NAS645 NAS648 NAS647 DASH NOS.	
RH THD	LH THD			RH THD	LH THD	RH THD	LH THD
-2RS	-2LS	1/16	6-40	-8RS	-8LS	-8RS	-8LS
-2RL*	-2LL*	1/16	6-40	—	—	—	—
-3RS	-3LS	3/32	10-32	-16RS	-16LS	-16RS	-16LS
-3RL	-3LL	3/32	10-32	-16RL	-16LL	-16RL	-16LL
-5RS	-5LS	5/32	1/4-28	-32RS	-32LS	-32RS	-32LS
-5RL	-5LL	5/32	1/4-28	-32RL	-32LL	-32RL	-32LL
-6RS	-6LS	3/16	5/16-24	-46RS	-46LS	-46RS	-46LS
-6RL	-6LL	3/16	5/16-24	-46RL	-46LL	-46RL	-46LL
-8RL	-8LL	1/4	3/8-24	-80RL	-80LL	-80RL	-80LL
-9RL	-9LL	9/32	7/16-20	-125RL	-125LL	-125RL	-125LL
-10RL	-10LL	5/16	1/2-20	-175RL	-175LL	-175RL	-175LL

*MS21254 and MS21255 eyes only; MS21252 fork not made in this size.

MS21256 TURNBUCKLE CLIP

Made of corrosion resistant steel wire, QQ-W-423, composition FS302, condition B. These are NOT interchangeable with the NAS651 clips. Available in 3 sizes: MS21256-1, -2 and -3. For applications, see the MS21251 Turnbuckle Barrel Cross Reference Chart.

PART NUMBER	THREAD	CABLE DIA.	DESCRIPTION
MS21251-B2S	6-40	1/16	
-B3S	10-32	3/32	
-B3L	10-32	3/32	Barrel (Body), Brass
-B5S	1/4-28	5/32	
-B5L	1/4-28	5/32	
MS21252-3LS	10-32	3/32	
-3RS	10-32	3/32	Fork (Clevis End)
-5RS	1/4-28	5/32	
MS21254-2RS	6-40	1/16	
-3LS	10-32	3/32	
-3RS	10-32	3/32	Eye End (for pin)
-5LS	1/4-28	5/32	
-5RS	1/4-28	5/32	

PART NUMBER	THREAD	CABLE DIA.	DESCRIPTION
MS21255-3LS	10-32	3/32	Eye End (for cable)
-3RS	10-32	3/32	
MS21256-1	—	—	Clip (for short barrels)
-2	—	—	Clip (for long barrels)
MS21260-S2LH	6-40	1/16	
-S2RH	6-40	1/16	
-S3LH	10-32	3/32	
-S3RH	10-32	3/32	
-L3LH	10-32	3/32	End (for cable)
-L3RH	10-32	3/32	
-S4LH	¼-28	1/8	
-S4RH	¼-28	1/8	
-L4LH	¼-28	1/8	
-L4RH	¼-28	1/8	

MS21260 SWAGED STUD END

These clip-locking terminals are available in corrosion resistant steel and in cadmium plated carbon steel. MS21260 items can replace AN669 items of the same dash numbers, but the AN669 items cannot always replace the MS21260 items.

Example: The AN "equivalent" (the AN equivalent would not be clip-locking) for MS21260 L3RH would be AN669-L3RH. There would be no AN equivalent for a MS21260FL3RH, since AN669 terminals are not available in carbon steel.

——— AN774 to AN932 ———
PLUMBING FITTINGS

Material:

Aluminum alloy............................(code D)
Steel...(code, absence of letter)
Brass..(code B)
Aluminum bronze.........................(code Z—for AN819 sleeve)

Size: The dash number following the AN number indicates the size of the tubing (or hose) for which the fitting is made, in 16ths of an inch. This size measures the O. D. of tubing and the I. D. of hose. Fittings having pipe threads are coded by a dash number, indicating the pipe size in 8ths of an inch. The material code letter, as noted above. follows the dash number.

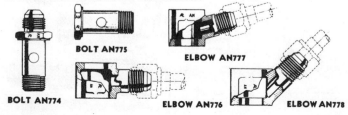

BOLT AN775

ELBOW AN777

BOLT AN774

ELBOW AN776

ELBOW AN778

PLUMBING FITTINGS   *(Cont.)*

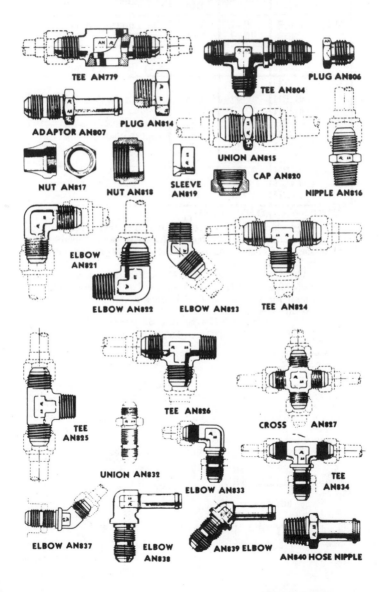

TEE AN779

PLUG AN806

TEE AN804

ADAPTOR AN807

PLUG AN814

UNION AN815

CAP AN820

NUT AN817

NUT AN818

SLEEVE AN819

NIPPLE AN816

ELBOW AN821

ELBOW AN822

ELBOW AN823

TEE AN824

TEE AN825

TEE AN826

CROSS AN827

UNION AN832

ELBOW AN833

TEE AN834

ELBOW AN837

ELBOW AN838

AN839 ELBOW

AN840 HOSE NIPPLE

PLUMBING FITTINGS *(Cont.)*

★ Inactive for new design.

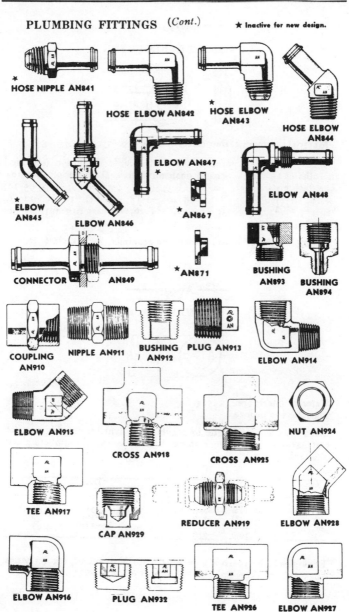

★
HOSE NIPPLE AN841

HOSE ELBOW AN842

★ HOSE ELBOW
AN843

HOSE ELBOW
AN844

ELBOW AN847
★

★ AN867

ELBOW AN848

★
ELBOW
AN845

ELBOW AN846

★ AN871

BUSHING
AN893

BUSHING
AN894

CONNECTOR AN849

COUPLING
AN910

NIPPLE AN911

BUSHING
AN912

PLUG AN913

ELBOW AN914

ELBOW AN915

CROSS AN918

CROSS AN925

NUT AN924

TEE AN917

CAP AN929

REDUCER AN919

ELBOW AN928

ELBOW AN916

PLUG AN932

TEE AN926

ELBOW AN927

—— AN931 ——

GROMMET, NEOPRENE

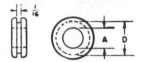

Material: Neoprene, durometer hardness 50–55.

Sizes: First dash number is size of hole, A dimension (see Fig.) in 16ths of an inch. Second dash number is D dimension in 16ths. The dash numbers are −2–16; −3–5; −3–9; −4–7; −4–16; −5–9; −5–12; −6–10; −6–16; −7–11; −8–13; −8–20; −9–13; −10–14; −10–20; −11–16; −12–17; −12–20; −12–23; −14–20; −14–26; −16–22; −16–30; −20–38; −24–28.

Example: AN931–6–10 is Neoprene grommet, ⅜ I.D., ⅝ O.D.

—— AN935 ——

WASHER, LOCK

Material: Steel, Spec. 25523.
Phospherous bronze.

Sizes: Washers are made in regular and light series. Light series are of narrower and thinner stock; L in code. Dash numbers given in the table.

Dash No.	Bolt size	Dash No.	Bolt size	Dash No.	Bolt size
−2	No. 2(.086)	−12	No. 12(.216)	−816	½
−4	No. 4(.112)	−416	¼	−916	%16
−6	No. 6(.138)	−516	%16	−1016	⅝
−8	No. 8(.164)	−616	⅜	−1216	¾
−10	No. 10(.190)	−716	%16		

Examples: AN935–10 is lock washer for No. 10 bolt, regular series. AN935–10L indicates light series. Add B for bronze.

—— AN936 ——

WASHER, LOCK—SHAKEPROOF

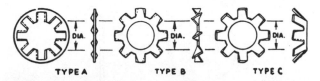

TYPE A   **TYPE B**   **TYPE C**

Material: Steel or bronze.

Finish: Steel. Process: cadmium plate, Spec. AN–QQ–P–421. Bronze. Process: tinned.

Sizes: Letters A, B, or C before dash number indicate type (see drawing). Letter B after dash number indicates bronze.

Type A: Dash numbers are –2 to –10 and –416 to –716 incl. (Refer to table under AN935 for bolt sizes.)

Type B: Dash numbers are –4 to –10 and –416 to –716 incl.

Type C: Dash numbers are –6 to –10 and –416 to –716 incl.

Examples: AN936A416B is washer, type A, for $\frac{1}{4}$ bolt, bronze. AN936B416 is type B, steel. AN936C416 is type C, steel.

—— AC940 ——
OBSOLETE
WASHER, BURR

Material: Tinned steel, brass, copper, aluminum, or aluminum alloy.

Sizes: Taken from United Screw & Bolt Corp. catalogue.

Dash No.	Screw, bolt or rivet size	Dash No.	Screw, bolt or rivet size	Dash No.	Screw, bolt or rivet size
–14	$\frac{1}{16}$(.083 dia.)	–9	No. 6(.148 dia.)	–5	.220 dia.
–13	$\frac{3}{32}$ dia.	–8	No. 8($\frac{5}{32}$ dia.)	–416	$\frac{1}{4}$ dia.
–12	No. 4(.109)	–7	.180 dia.	–516	$\frac{5}{16}$ dia.
–11	No. 5($\frac{1}{8}$)	–316	No. 10($\frac{3}{16}$ dia.)	–616	$\frac{3}{8}$ dia.

Examples: AC940–14 is washer, steel, for $\frac{1}{16}$ rivet. AC940B14 indicates brass. AC940C14 indicates copper. AC940A14 indicates aluminum. AC940D14 indicates aluminum alloy.

——— AC945 ———
OBSOLETE
WASHER, PLAIN—COMMERCIAL, STANDARD

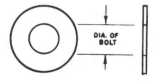

Material: Wrought iron or steel.

Sizes: Dash numbers are –4 to –24 incl.   They indicate bolt size in 16ths of an inch.

Example: AC945–18 is washer, wrought iron or steel, for 1⅛ bolt.

——— AN960 ———

WASHER, PLAIN

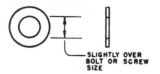

Materials: Carbon steel, Spec. AN–QQ–S–651 or S.A.E.–1010 hard finished.

Corrosion-resistant (stainless) steel, Spec. AN–QQ–S–757; C in code.

Aluminum, Spec. QQ–A–561; A in code.

Aluminum alloy, Spec. QQ–A–353; D in code.

Brass, Spec. QQ–B–611; B in code.

Carbon steel, aluminum, and stainless are made in both regular and light series.   Light series are made of thinner stock and are indicated by L following the dash number.

Finish: Carbon steel.   Process: cadmium plate, Spec. AN–QQ–P–421.

Aluminum alloy.   Process: anodize, Spec. AN–QQ–A–696.

Sizes: Dash numbers –3, –4, –6, –8, and –10 are machine screw sizes.   –416 to –4016 are bolt sizes in 16ths.

Examples: AN960–4 is carbon steel washer for No. 4 screw. AN960C416 is stainless steel washer for ¼ bolt.   AN960A4016L is aluminum washer, 2½-in. bolt, light series.   AN960B1716 is brass washer, 1¹⁄₁₆ bolt.   AN960D1716 indicates aluminum alloy.

—— AN970 ——

WASHER, FLAT—FOR WOOD

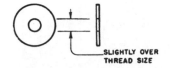

SLIGHTLY OVER
THREAD SIZE

Material: Steel.   Finish: cadmium plate, Spec. AN–QQ–P–421.
Sizes: Dash numbers –3 to –10 incl. are bolt sizes in 16ths.
Example: AN970–6 is washer for ⅜ bolt.

—— AN975 ——

WASHER, TAPER PIN

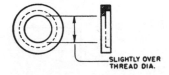

SLIGHTLY OVER
THREAD DIA.

Used with AC386 taper pins.
Material: Steel, Spec. AN–QQ–S–646 or AN–QQ–S–651.   Finish:
cadmium plate, Spec. AN–QQ–P–421.

Sizes: Dash numbers –3 to –14 incl. are bolt sizes in 16ths.
Example: AC975–5 is washer for taper pin with ⁵⁄₁₆ bolt thread.

—— AN995 ——
Superseded by MS20995
WIRE, FOR LOCKING

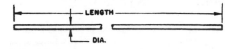

LENGTH

DIA.

Material: Copper, Spec. 57–222–1; C in code.
Galvanized steel, Spec. 48–19.

Sizes: Wire diameters are .032, .040, .051, .072, and .090, indicated
by first dash number.   Standard lengths are 1, 2, 3, 4, 6, 8, 10, 14, 18,
24, 36, 48, 60, 72, 84, and 100 in., indicated by second dash number.

——— NAS143 ———
Superseded by MS20002
WASHER, HIGH STRENGTH BOLT

Material: Steel.

Code: A dash number is added to the part number, indicating the diameter of the bolt it fits in 16ths of an inch.

——— NAS144 to NAS158 ———

BOLT-INTERNAL HEX HEAD

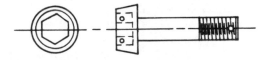

Material: Steel, heat treated to 160,000 - 180,000 p.s.i.   Finish: Cadmium plate.

Code: Diameter, from 1/4 inch to 1-1/8 inch, indicated by the last digit of the NAS number in 16ths of an inch.

Length, to 8 inches, is indicated by the dash number in 16ths of an inch. (-16 is one inch long; -32 is two inches long, and -38 is 2-3/8 inches long).

Add D. H. after the part number to indicate drilled head.

——— NAS334 to NAS340 ———
OBSOLETE
BOLT—100° INTERNAL HEX HEAD

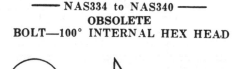

Material and **Code** like NAS144 to NAS158

Table 1. Dash No. (Size) Chart, Screw Parts
Fine Thread (NF)

Size and thread	Dash No.	Dia. and thread	Dash No.	Dia. and thread	Dash No.	Dia. and thread	Dash No.
4–48	–448	1/4–28	–428	1/2–20	–820	7/8–14	–1414
6–40	–640	5/16–24	–524	9/16–18	–918	1–14	–1614
8–36	–836	3/8–24	–624	5/8–18	–1018		
10–32	–1032	7/16–20	–720	3/4–16	–1216		

Coarse Thread (NC)

Size and thread	Dash No.	Size and thread	Dash No.	Size and thread	Dash No.
4–40	–440	10–24	–1024	3/8–16	–616
6–32	–632	1/4–20	–420	7/16–14	–714
8–32	–832	5/16–18	–518	1/2–13	–813

Table 2. Dash No. (Size) Chart—Parts Made in One Thread Only (NF or NC)

Size	Dash No.	Size	Dash No.	Size (dia.), in.	Dash No.	Dia., in.	Dash No.
0	–0	5	–5	1/4	–416	1/2	–816
1	–1	6	–6	5/16	–516	9/16	–916
2	–2	8	–8	3/8	–616	5/8	–1016
3	–3	10	–10	7/16	–716		
4	–4						

Table 3. Dash No. (Length) Chart—Part Lengths in 16ths of an Inch

Length, in.	Dash No.	Length, in.	Dash No.	Length, in.	Dash No.	Length, in.	Dash No.
1/4	–4	5/8	–10	1 3/8	–22	2 1/4	–36
5/16	–5	3/4	–12	1 1/2	–24	2 1/2	–40
3/8	–6	7/8	–14	1 5/8	–26	2 3/4	–44
7/16	–7	1	–16	1 3/4	–28	3	–48
1/2	–8	1 1/8	–18	1 7/8	–30		
9/16	–9	1 1/4	–20	2	–32		

Table 4. Dash No. (Size) Chart—Rivets
Diameter—First Dash No.

Dia., in.	Dash No.	Dia., in.	Dash No.	Dia., in.	Dash No.	Dia., in.	Dash No.	Dia., in.	Dash No.
1/16	–2	1/8	–4	3/16	–6	5/16	–10	7/16	–14
3/32	–3	5/32	–5	1/4	–8	3/8	–12		

Length—Second Dash No.

L, in.	Dash No.	L, in.	Dash No.	L, in.	Dash No.	L, in.	Dash No.
3/16	–3	9/16	–9	1 1/8	–18	2	–32
1/4	–4	5/8	–10	1 1/4	–20	2 1/2	–40
5/16	–5	3/4	–12	1 3/8	–22	3	–48
3/8	–6	7/8	–14	1 1/2	–24	3 1/2	–56
7/16	–7	1	–16	1 3/4	–28	4	–64
1/2	–8						

ADDITIONAL STANDARD PARTS (PATENTED)

The following pages illustrate a few fastener types widely used on high-performance aircraft. These fasteners are designed and manufactured by various companies, are patented, and are generally known by their trade names.

It is emphasized that the following pages are in no way a complete list of patented fasteners available. Representative examples only are shown for illustrative purposes. All these fasteners require special installation tools and procedures. Installation manuals are available from the manufacturers.

CONVERSION TABLE

NAS NUMBERS TO CHERRY RIVET NUMBERS
(A COMPLETE CONVERSION TABLE OF CHERRY RIVET NUMBERS IS AVAILABLE UPON REQUEST)

BULBED CHERRYLOCK® RIVETS

HEAD STYLE	NAS NUMBER	CHERRY NUMBER	RIVET MATERIAL	STEM MATERIAL
UNIVERSAL HEAD	NAS 1738B	CR2249	5056 Aluminum	Alloy Steel, Cad. Plt'd.
	1738E	2239	5056 Aluminum	Inconel 600
	1738M	2539	Monel	Inconel 600
	1738MW	2539P	Monel, Cad. Plt'd.	Inconel 600
	1738C	2839	Inconel 600	A286 CRES
	1738CW	2839CW	Inconel 600, Cad. Plt'd.	A286 CRES
COUNTERSUNK HEAD (MS20426)	NAS 1739B	CR2248	5056 Aluminum	Alloy Steel, Cad. Plt'd.
	1739E	2238	5056 Aluminum	Inconel 600
	1739M	2538	Monel	Inconel 600
	1739MW	2538P	Monel, Cad. Plt'd.	Inconel 600
	1739C	2838	Inconel 600	A286 CRES
	1739CW	2838CW	Inconel 600, Cad. Plt'd.	A286 CRES
UNISINK HEAD	–	CR2235	5056 Aluminum	Inconel 600
	–	2245	5056 Aluminum	Alloy Steel, Cad. Plt'd.
	–	2545	Monel	Inconel 600
	–	2845	Inconel 600	A286 CRES
COUNTERSUNK HEAD (156°)	–	CR2540	Monel	Inconel 600
	–	2840	Inconel 600	A286 CRES

BULBED CHERRYLOCK® RIVETS

NAS 1738 UNIVERSAL HEAD

PROCUREMENT SPECIFICATION NAS 1740 IS APPLICABLE TO NAS 1738 RIVETS.

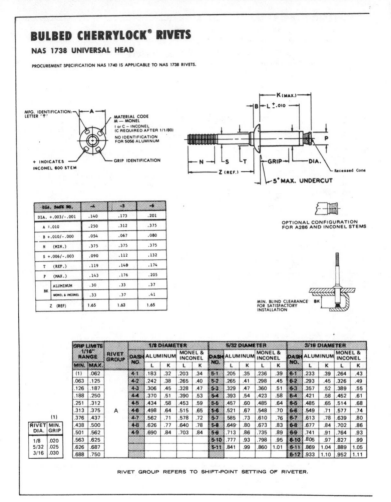

DIA. PART NO.	-4	-5	-6
DIA. +.003/-.001	.140	.173	.201
A ±.010	.250	.312	.375
B +.010/-.000	.054	.067	.080
N (MIN.)	.375	.375	.375
S +.006/-.003	.090	.112	.132
T (REF.)	.119	.148	.174
P (MAX.)	.143	.176	.205
BK ALUMINUM	.30	.33	.37
BK MONEL & INCONEL	.33	.37	.41
Z (REF)	1.65	1.63	1.65

OPTIONAL CONFIGURATION
FOR A286 AND INCONEL STEMS

MIN. BLIND CLEARANCE BK
FOR SATISFACTORY
INSTALLATION

GRIP LIMITS 1/16" RANGE MIN.	MAX.	RIVET GROUP	1/8 DIAMETER DASH NO.	ALUMINUM L	K	MONEL & INCONEL L	K	5/32 DIAMETER DASH NO.	ALUMINUM L	K	MONEL & INCONEL L	K	3/16 DIAMETER DASH NO.	ALUMINUM L	K	MONEL & INCONEL L	K
(1)	.062		4-1	.183	.32	.203	.34	5-1	.205	.35	.236	.39	6-1	.233	.39	.264	.43
.063	.125		4-2	.242	.38	.265	.40	5-2	.265	.41	.298	.45	6-2	.293	.45	.326	.49
.126	.187		4-3	.306	.45	.328	.47	5-3	.329	.47	.360	.51	6-3	.357	.52	.389	.55
.188	.250		4-4	.370	.51	.390	.53	5-4	.393	.54	.423	.58	6-4	.421	.58	.452	.61
.251	.312		4-5	.434	.58	.453	.59	5-5	.457	.60	.485	.64	6-5	.485	.65	.514	.68
.313	.375	A	4-6	.498	.64	.515	.65	5-6	.521	.67	.548	.70	6-6	.549	.71	.577	.74
.376	.437		4-7	.562	.71	.578	.72	5-7	.585	.73	.610	.76	6-7	.613	.78	.639	.80
.438	.500		4-8	.626	.77	.640	.78	5-8	.649	.80	.673	.83	6-8	.677	.84	.702	.86
.501	.562		4-9	.690	.84	.703	.84	5-9	.713	.86	.735	.89	6-9	.741	.91	.764	.93
.563	.625							5-10	.777	.93	.798	.95	6-10	.805	.97	.827	.99
.626	.687							5-11	.841	.99	.860	1.01	6-11	.869	1.04	.889	1.05
.688	.750												6-12	.933	1.10	.952	1.11

RIVET DIA.	MIN. GRIP
1/8	.020
5/32	.025
3/16	.030

RIVET GROUP REFERS TO SHIFT-POINT SETTING OF RIVETER.

hi-shear **RIVET IDENTIFICATION CHART**

PART NUMBER	IDENTIFICATION (HI-SHEAR CORPORATION) HEAD MARKING OR COLOR CODE	MATERIAL	PHYSICAL PROPERTIES ROOM TEMP.	HEAD TYPE	TOLERANCES MINIMUM C'SK HEAD HEIGHT	TOLERANCES MINIMUM SHANK DIAMETER	HI-SHEAR COLLAR TO ORDER	SUGGESTED MAXIMUM TEMP. FOR USE	CHARACTERISTICS	NAS OR CUSTOMER PART NUMBER
NAS177	⊕	Alloy Steel	125,000-150,000 psi Tensile	Csk			NAS179		Inactive. See H547, H547PB and H548, or NAS1054 and NAS1055.	
NAS178		Steel		Flat						
NAS179	Grey	2117-T4 Aluminum Alloy							Inactive. See HS15 or NAS528.	
NAS 528	Red	2024-T4 Aluminum Alloy							Hi-Shear Collar used in combination with 160,000-180,000 psi tensile Hi-Shear Rivet Pins. Same as HS15.	
NAS1806 thru NAS1816	NAS 1810 HV	6A1-4V Titanium Alloy	95,000 psi Shear Minimum	Flat		.0005	HS15		Chamfered lead style. Used in high performance aircraft where weight, shank and hole tolerances are critical.	
NAS1906 thru NAS1916	NAS 1910 HV	6A1-4V Titanium Alloy	95,000 psi Shear Minimum	Csk		.0005	HS15		Chamfered lead style. Used in high performance aircraft where weight, shank and hole tolerances are critical.	
H510	⊙	Alloy Steel	160,000-180,000 psi Tensile	Csk		.0025	HS15		Stud Rivet Pin — fastens primary structure and provides for a means of attaching removable elements.	NAS528
H515	Red	2024-T4 Aluminum Alloy					HS24	200°F	Hi-Shear Collar used in combination with 160,000-180,000 psi tensile Hi-Shear Rivet Pins.	
H523 H523A	*	7075-T6 Aluminum Alloy		Csk	.002	.001			Hi-Shear 100° head. Higher shear and tension allowables than DD Rivets. Small head permits countersinking in thin materials. "A" signifies sodium dichromate seal. For oversize, use HS39P or HS41P.	
H524	Blue	2117-T4 Aluminum Alloy						200°F	Hi-Shear Collar used in combination with 7075-T6 aluminum alloy Hi-Shear Rivet Pins.	
H525 H525A	*	7075-T6 Aluminum Alloy		Csk	.002	.001	HS24		MS20426 style head. Higher shear and tension allowables than DD Rivets. "A" signifies sodium dichromate seal. For oversize, use HS25, 32 or HS25, 64.	

PART NUMBER	IDENTIFICATION (HI-SHEAR CORPORATION) HEAD MARKING OR COLOR CODE	MATERIAL	PHYSICAL PROPERTIES ROOM TEMP.	HEAD TYPE	TOLERANCES MINIMUM C'SK HEAD HEIGHT	TOLERANCES MINIMUM SHANK DIAMETER	HI-SHEAR COLLAR TO ORDER	SUGGESTED MAXIMUM TEMP FOR USE	CHARACTERISTICS	NAS OR CUSTOMER PART NUMBER
HS25.32 HS25.64	No Head Marking 1/32 - Red 1/64 - Blue	7075-T6 Aluminum Alloy		Csk	.002	.001	HS24		Oversizes for HS25.	
HS26 HS26A	H	7075-T6 Aluminum Alloy		Flat		.001	HS24		Higher shear and tension allowables than DD Rivets. "A" signifies sodium dichromate seal. For oversize, use HS26.32 or HS26.64.	
HS26.32 HS26.64	No Head Marking 1/32 - Red 1/64 - Blue	7075-T6 Aluminum Alloy		Flat		.001	HS24		Oversizes for HS26.	
HS30	No Marking	Alloy Steel	160,000 - 180,000 psi Tensile	No Head		.0025	HS15 HS24 HS32		Dowel Pin grooved for collar on both ends. Lighter and stronger than Taper Pin. Precision fit molds to irregular surfaces (both sides). HS30 ground after plating; HS30 P plated after grind.	
HS32	Silver (Cadmium Plate)	Low Carbon Steel							Hi-Shear Collar used in combination with 160,000-180,000 psi tensile Hi-Shear Rivets. Ferrous material applications.	
HS39P HS40P	• 64	Alloy Steel	160,000 - 180,000 psi Tensile	Csk Flat	.002	.0011	HS15		1/64 oversize Rivet Pin for HS23, HS26, HS47, HS48, HS51P, and HS52P. HS39PB and HS40PB — Type II plating.	
HS41P HS42P	• 32	Alloy Steel	160,000 - 180,000 psi Tensile	Csk Flat	.002	.0011	HS15 or HS46		1/32 oversize Rivet Pin for HS23, HS26, HS47, HS48, HS51P, and HS52P. HS41PB and HS42PB — Type II plating.	
HS47 HS48	Ⓗ	Alloy Steel	160,000 - 180,000 psi Tensile	Csk Flat	.002	.0025	HS15		Chamfered lead style used in design where shank commercial tolerances are acceptable. For oversize use HS39P, HS40P, HS41P, or HS42P. HS47PB — Type II plating.	NAS1055 NAS1054
HS51P HS52P	H	Alloy Steel	160,000 - 180,000 psi Tensile	Csk Flat	.002	.0011	HS15		Chamfered lead style — plated after grind. Used in design where shank and hole tolerances are critical. For oversize use HS39P, HS40P, HS41P, or HS42P. HS51PB — Type II plating.	NAS825 NAS829
HS53	Red	2024-T4 Aluminum Alloy							Countersunk flanged Hi-Shear Collar used in double dimple applications. Used in combination with 160,000—180,000 psi tensile Hi-Shear Rivet Pins.	

PART NUMBER	IDENTIFICATION (HI-SHEAR CORPORATION) HEAD MARKING OR COLOR CODE	MATERIAL	PHYSICAL PROPERTIES ROOM TEMP.	HEAD TYPE	TOLERANCES MINIMUM C'SK HEAD HEIGHT	TOLERANCES MINIMUM SHANK DIAMETER	HI-SHEAR COLLAR TO ORDER	SUGGESTED MAXIMUM TEMP. FOR USE	CHARACTERISTICS	NAS OR CUSTOMER PART NUMBER
H554	Blue	2117-T4 Aluminum Alloy							Countersunk flanged Hi-Shear Collar used in double dimple applications. Used in combination with 7075-T6 aluminum alloy Hi-Shear Rivet Pins.	
H560	Natural	321 Stainless Steel						1600°F	Hi-Shear Collar for use in high temperature applications. Maximum temperature governed by conditions of application or use.	
H560M	Black	"R" Monel or 400 Monel	Rb 96 (Max.)					1000°F	Hi-Shear Collar used in high temperature applications to 900°F.	
H561	61	Type 431 Stainless Steel	125,000 psi Shear Minimum	Csk	.002		H560 or H560M	450°F	Used in high strength or temperature applications where shank and hole tolerances are critical. For oversize, use HS139, HS140, HS141, or HS142.	
H562	62			Flat		.0005				
H565	65	Type 305 Stainless Steel	125,000 psi Tensile	Csk	.002		H560 or H560M*		*Use H560 Collars for non-magnetic applications; H560M for other applications.	
H566	66			Flat		.0025				
H567	67	Type 431 Stainless Steel	125,000 psi Shear Minimum	Csk	.002		H560 or H560M	450°F	Used in high strength or temperature applications where shank commercial tolerances are acceptable. For oversize, use HS139, HS140, HS141, or HS142.	
H568	68			Flat		.0025				
H590	Natural	A-286 High Temp. Alloy						1200°F	Hi-Shear Collar used in non-magnetic and high temperature applications.	
H591	91	A-286 High Temp. Alloy	95,000 psi Shear Minimum	Csk	.002		H560M or HS90	1200°F (See Note)	Used in strength and temperature applications where shank and hole tolerances are critical. NOTE: For use in non-magnetic applications.	
H592	92			Flat		.0005				
H5104	Natural	Inconel 600 per AMS5665						1500°F	Used in combination with HS131 and HS132 Pins. For use at high temperature applications.	
H5106	No Head Marking	Alloy Steel	160,000-180,000 psi Tensile	Flat		Knurled Shank	HS24		Rivet Pin with threaded stud. Fastens primary structure and provides threaded stud to attach removal items.	

PART NUMBER	IDENTIFICATION (HI-SHEAR CORPORATION) HEAD MARKING OR COLOR CODE	MATERIAL	PHYSICAL PROPERTIES ROOM TEMP.	HEAD TYPE	TOLERANCES MINIMUM C'SK HEAD HEIGHT	TOLERANCES MINIMUM SHANK DIAMETER	HI-SHEAR COLLAR TO ORDER	SUGGESTED MAXIMUM TEMP. FOR USE	CHARACTERISTICS	NAS OR CUSTOMER PART NUMBER
HS108	⦿ HS	Alloy Steel	160,000-180,000 psi Tensile	Protruding		.0025	HS15		Stud Rivet Pin. Fastens primary structure and provides stud to attach removable items.	
HS131	131	Inconel X-750	160,000 psi Tensile	Csk	.002	.0025	HS104	1500°F	Used at high temperature applications where shank commercial tolerances are acceptable.	
HS132	132	Inconel X-750	160,000 psi Tensile	Flat		.0025	HS104	1500°F	Used at high temperature applications where shank commercial tolerances are acceptable.	
HS139	139	Type 431 Stainless Steel	125,000 psi Shear Minimum	Csk	.002	.0005	HS60M	450°F	1/64 oversize for HS61, HS62, HS67 and HS68.	
HS140	140	Type 431 Stainless Steel	125,000 psi Shear Minimum	Flat		.0005	HS60M	450°F	1/64 oversize for HS61, HS62, HS67 and HS68.	
HS141	141	Type 431 Stainless Steel	125,000 psi Shear Minimum	Csk	.002	.0005	HS60M	450°F	1/32 oversize for HS61, HS62, HS67 and HS68.	
HS142	142	Type 431 Stainless Steel	125,000 psi Shear Minimum	Flat		.0005	HS60M	450°F	1/32 oversize for HS61, HS62, HS67 and HS68.	
HS149	H 149	6-4 Ti Alloy	160,000-180,000 psi Tensile	Csk	.002	.0005	HS15 HS167 HS234		Used in high performance aircraft where weight, material fatigue, shank and hole tolerances are critical.	NAS1806 NAS1906
HS150	H 150	6-4 Ti Alloy	160,000-180,000 psi Tensile	Flat		.0005	HS15 HS167 HS234		Used in high performance aircraft where weight, material fatigue, shank and hole tolerances are critical.	NAS1806 NAS1906
HS154	155 P	Type H-11 Steel per AMS6485	156,000 psi Shear Min. RC 50-55	Flat		.0025	HS90		Used in high temperature applications. "P" code — cadmium plate. "N" code — diffused nickel.	
HS155	134 P	Type H-11 Steel per AMS6485	156,000 psi Shear Min. RC 50-55	Csk	.002	.0025	HS90		Used in high temperature applications. "P" code — cadmium plate. "N" code — diffused nickel.	
HS159	H 159	A-286 High Temp. Alloy	160,000-180,000 psi Tensile	Csk	.002	.001	HS60M		1/64 oversize for HS91 and HS92.	
HS160	H 160	A-286 High Temp. Alloy	160,000-180,000 psi Tensile	Flat		.001	HS60M		1/64 oversize for HS91 and HS92.	
HS161	H 161	A-286 High Temp. Alloy	160,000-180,000 psi Tensile	Csk	.002	.0015	HS60M		1/32 oversize for HS91 and HS92.	
HS162	H 162	A-286 High Temp. Alloy	160,000-180,000 psi Tensile	Flat		.0015	HS60M		1/32 oversize for HS91 and HS92.	
HS167	Natural	Ti-50A Com. Pure Titanium						700°F	Hi-Shear Collar used in combination with HS149 and HS150 Pins and in non-magnetic applications.	
HS234	Violet	2219-T6 Aluminum Alloy						425°F	Hi-Shear Collar used at elevated temperatures.	

TRI-WING®

1. NAS STANDARDS AND SPECIFICATIONS
2. AIRLINE AND MANUFACTURERS APPROVAL
3. THREE-WING RECESSED DESIGN PERMITS EASY IDENTIFICATION
4. REDUCED WORK EFFORT BY THE OPERATOR RESULTS FROM LESS END THRUST
5. CLOSE-TOLERANCE CONTROL OF THE RECESS AND THE DRIVER BIT ACHIEVE OPTIMUM PERFORMANCE
6. IMPROVED DRIVER BIT LIFE
7. PART NUMBERS ARE STAMPED ON THE FASTENER HEADS
8. DRIVER NUMBERS ARE STAMPED ON THE FASTENER HEADS
9. DRIVER BITS ARE NUMBERED WITH RECESS SIZE TO ELIMINATE MISMATCH PROBLEMS
10. POWER DRIVER OPERATIONS OF THE TRI-WING INSURE POSITIVE ENGAGEMENT — REDUCING THE CHANCE OF SURFACE DAMAGE TO THE ADJACENT STRUCTURE

TRI-WING® STANDARDS

NAS NUMBER	DIAMETER	HEAD STYLE	THREAD TYPE	MATERIAL	CLASSIFICATION	
NAS 4104-4116 NAS 4204-4216 NAS 4304-4316	.250 — 1.000"	100°	Long	Alloy Steel Cres Titanium	Bolt	
NAS 4400-4416 NAS 4500-4516 NAS 4600-4616	.112 — 1.000"	100°	Short	Alloy Steel Cres Titanium	Bolt	
NAS 4703-4716 NAS 4803-4816 NAS 4903-4916	.190 — 1.000"	100° Reduced	Short	Alloy Steel Cres Titanium	Bolt	
NAS 5000-5006 NAS 5100-5106 NAS 5200-5206	.112 — .375"	Pan	Short	Alloy Steel Cres Titanium	Screw	
NAS 5300-5306 NAS 5400-5406 NAS 5500-5506	.112 — .375"	Fillister	Full	Alloy Steel Cres Titanium	Screw	
NAS 5600-5606 NAS 5700-5706 NAS 5800-5806	.112 — .375"	100°	Full	Alloy Steel Cres Titanium	Screw	
NAS 5900-5903 NAS 6000-6003 NAS 6100-6103	.112 — .190"	Hex	Full	Alloy Steel Cres Titanium	Screw	

APPLICABLE SPECIFICATIONS

TRI-WING recess specification — NAS 4000   TRI-WING driver specification — NAS 4001
Alloy Steel process specification — NAS 4002   Cres process specification — NAS 4003
Titanium process specification — NAS 4004

TRI-WING® is a registered trademark of PHILLIPS SCREW COMPANY

STANDARDS COMMITTEE FOR HI-LOK® PRODUCTS
2600 SKYPARK DRIVE, TORRANCE, CALIFORNIA 90509

HI-LOK PIN

HI-LOK PIN PART NO.	PIN HEAD STYLE APPLICATION	MATERIAL	HEAT TREAT	SHANK DIA. TOL.	SUGGESTED MAXIMUM TEMP. FOR USE	GRIP VARIATION
HL10	Protruding ——— Shear	6Al-4V Titanium	95,000 psi Shear Minimum	.0005 or .0010	750° F or Sub. to Finish	1/16"
HL11	100° Flush ——— Shear	6Al-4V Titanium	95,000 psi Shear Minimum	.0005 or .0010	750° F or Sub. to Finish	1/16"
HL12	Protruding ——— Tension	6Al-4V Titanium	160,000 psi Tensile Minimum	.0005 or .0010	750° F or Sub. to Finish	1/16"
HL13	100° Flush MS24694 Tension	6Al-4V Titanium	160,000 psi Tensile Minimum	.0005 or .0010	750° F or Sub. to Finish	1/16"
HL14	Protruding ——— Shear	H-11 Steel Alloy	156,000 psi Shear Minimum	.001	900° F or Sub. to Finish	1/16"
HL15	100° Flush ——— Shear	H-11 Steel Alloy	156,000 psi Shear Minimum	.001	900° F or Sub. to Finish	1/16"
HL16	Protruding ——— Tension	H-11 Steel Alloy	260,000– 280,000 psi Tensile	.001	900° F or Sub. to Finish	1/16"
HL17	100° Flush MS24694 Tension	H-11 Steel Alloy	260,000– 280,000 psi Tensile	.001	900° F or Sub. to Finish	1/16"
HL18	Protruding ——— Shear	Alloy Steel	95,000 psi Shear Minimum	.001	450° F	1/16"
HL19	100° Flush ——— Shear	Alloy Steel	95,000 psi Shear Minimum	.001	450° F	1/16"
HL20	Protruding ——— Tension	Alloy Steel	160,000– 180,000 psi Tensile	.001	450° F	1/16"
HL21	100° Flush MS24694 Tension	Alloy Steel	160,000– 180,000 psi Tensile	.001	450° F	1/16"

HI-SHEAR CORPORATION (Patent Holder) — Federal Code Ident. No. 73197
VOI-SHAN DIV., VSI CORP. (Licensee) — Federal Code Ident. No. 92215
STANDARD PRESSED STEEL CO. (Licensee) — Federal Code Ident. No. 56878

IDENTIFICATION CHART

Issued: 3-20-68
Revised: October 1972

RECOMMENDED COMPANION HI-LOK COLLARS	NEXT OVERSIZE	CHARACTERISTICS
HL70 HL94 HL79 HL97 HL82 HL379	HL110	Used when weight conservation is essential and where pin shank and hole tolerances are critical. Anti-galling finish available for use with all types of Hi-Lok collar materials.
HL70 HL94 HL79 HL97 HL82 HL379	HL111	Used when weight conservation is essential and where pin shank and hole tolerances are critical. Anti-galling finish available for use with all types of Hi-Lok collar materials.
HL75 HL198 HL86 HL280	HL112	Used when weight conservation is essential and where pin shank and hole tolerances are critical. Anti-galling finish available for use with all types of Hi-Lok collar materials.
HL75 HL198 HL86 HL280	HL113	Used when weight conservation is essential and where pin shank and hole tolerances are critical. Anti-galling finish available for use with all types of Hi-Lok collar materials.
HL288 HL574	HL214	Used in high temperature applications where pin shank and hole close tolerances are required.
HL288 HL574	HL215	Used in high temperature applications where pin shank and hole close tolerances are required.
HL89 HL273	HL216	Used in high temperature applications where pin shank and hole close tolerances are required.
HL89 HL273	HL217	Used in high temperature applications where pin shank and hole close tolerances are required.
HL70 HL94 HL79 HL97 HL82 HL175	HL62	Used where pin shank and hole close tolerances are required.
HL70 HL94 HL79 HL97 HL82 HL175	HL63	Used where pin shank and hole close tolerances are required.
HL75 HL86 HL87	HL64	Used where pin shank and hole close tolerances are required.
HL75 HL86 HL87	HL65	Used where pin shank and hole close tolerances are required.

STANDARDS COMMITTEE
FOR HI-LOK® PRODUCTS
2600 SKYPARK DRIVE, TORRANCE, CALIFORNIA 90509

HI-LOK PIN

HI-LOK PIN PART NO.	PIN HEAD STYLE APPLICATION	MATERIAL	HEAT TREAT	SHANK DIA. TOL.	SUGGESTED MAXIMUM TEMP. FOR USE	GRIP VARIATION
HL22	Protruding ——— Shear	7075-T6 Aluminum Alloy	Spec. MIL-H-6088	.001	250°F	1/16"
HL23	100° Flush MS20426 Shear	7075-T6 Aluminum Alloy	Spec. MIL-H-6088	.001	250°F	1/16"
HL24	100° Flush ——— Sealing	6Al-4V Titanium	95,000 psi Shear Minimum	.0005	Subject to O-ring Limits	1/16"
HL25	100° Flush ——— Sealing	431 Stainless Steel	125,000 psi Shear Minimum	.0005	Subject to O-ring Limits	1/16"
HL26	Protruding ——— Shear	Inconel X-750	95,000 psi Shear Minimum	.0005	1200°F	1/16"
HL27	100° Flush ——— Shear	Inconel X-750	95,000 psi Shear Minimum	.0005	1200°F	1/16"
HL28	100° Flush ——— Shear	305 Stainless Steel	Annealed	.001	700°F	1/16"
HL29	100° Flush MS24694 Tension	7075-T6 Aluminum Alloy	Spec. MIL-H-6088	.001	250°F	1/16"
HL30	Protruding ——— Shear	431 Stainless Steel	125,000 psi Shear Minimum	.0005 or .0010	400°F	1/16"
HL31	100° Flush ——— Shear	431 Stainless Steel	125,000 psi Shear Minimum	.0005 or .0010	400°F	1/16"
HL32	Protruding ——— Tension	431 Stainless Steel	125,000 psi Shear Minimum	.0005 or .0010	400°F	1/16"
HL33	100° Flush MS24694 Tension	431 Stainless Steel	125,000 psi Shear Minimum	.0005 or .0010	400°F	1/16"

HI-SHEAR CORPORATION (Patent Holder) — Federal Code Ident. No. 73197
VOI-SHAN DIV., VSI CORP. (Licensee) — Federal Code Ident. No. 92215
STANDARD PRESSED STEEL CO. (Licensee) — Federal Code Ident. No. 56878

IDENTIFICATION CHART

RECOMMENDED COMPANION HI-LOK COLLARS		NEXT OVERSIZE	CHARACTERISTICS
HL77 HL182 HL277		HL122	Has higher shear and tension allowables than DD rivets. Interchangeable with MS20470 rivets.
HL77 HL182 HL277		HL123	Has higher shear and tension allowables than DD rivets. Interchangeable with MS20426 rivets.
HL70 HL79 HL82		HL124	Sealing Hi-Lok with silicone or synthetic rubber O-ring. Used when weight conservation is critical and pin shank and hole tolerances are critical.
HL70 HL79 HL86		HL125	Sealing Hi-Lok with general purpose Aromatic Fuel Resistant O-ring. Used in high strength applications where shank and hole tolerances are critical.
HL70 HL79 HL82	HL88 HL94 HL97	——	Used in high temperature shear applications where pin shank and hole close tolerances are required.
HL70 HL79 HL82	HL88 HL94 HL97	——	Used in high temperature shear applications where pin shank and hole close tolerances are required.
HL70 HL79 HL82		——	Stud pin, non-magnetic.
HL77 HL182 HL277		HL129	Has higher tension allowables than HL23.
HL70 HL79 HL82	HL94 HL97 HL175	HL66	Used in high strength applications where shank and hole tolerances are critical.
HL70 HL79 HL82	HL94 HL97 HL175	HL67	Used in high strength applications where shank and hole tolerances are critical
HL73 HL75 HL86	HL87 HL89 HL273	HL36	Used in high strength applications where shank and hole tolerances are critical.
HL73 HL75 HL86	HL87 HL89 HL273	HL37	Used in high strength applications where shank and hole tolerances are critical.

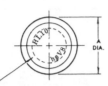

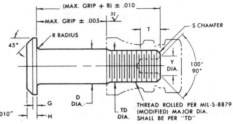

INDENTED HEAD MARKING MAXIMUM DEPTH .010"
"hs" indicates HI-SHEAR trademark.
"VS" indicates VOI-SHAN trademark.
"SPS" indicates STANDARD PRESSED STEEL trademark.
"V" after trademark indicates 6AL-4V Titanium alloy
material. The number or numbers following the "V"
indicate first dash number. Arrangement optional. ③

HI-LOK PIN

	FIRST DASH NO.	NOM. DIA.	A DIA.	B REF.	D DIA. 6		TD DIA.	G REF.	H	
					WITHOUT COATING OR SOLID FILM LUBE	WITH COATING OR SOLID FILM LUBE				
**	−5	5/32	.262 .242	.312	.1635 .1630	.1635 .1625	.1595 .1570	.020	.047 .037	
	−6	3/16	.315 .295	.325	.1895 .1890	.1895 .1885	.1840 .1810	.025	.055 .045	
	−8	1/4	.412 .387	.395	.2495 .2490	.2495 .2485	.2440 .2410	.030	.069 .059	
	−10	5/16	.505 .475	.500	.3120 .3115	.3120 .3110	.3060 .3020	.035	.078 .068	
	−12	3/8	.600 .565	.545	.3745 .3740	.3745 .3735	.3680 .3640	.040	.088 .078	
	−14	7/16	.676 .641	.635	.4370 .4365	.4370 .4360	.4310 .4260	.045	.105 .093	
	−16	1/2	.770 .735	.685	.4995 .4990	.4995 .4985	.4930 .4880	.050	.115 .103	
	−18	9/16	.864 .829	.770	.5615 .5610	.5615 .5605	.5550 .5500	.055	.127 .112	
	−20	5/8	.953 .918	.825	.6240 .6235	.6240 .6230	.6180 .6120	.060	.137 .122	
	−24	3/4	1.108 1.066	1.050	.7490 .7485	.7490 .7480	.7430 .7370	.070	.151 .136	
	−28	7/8	1.285 1.241	1.210	.8740 .8735	.8740 .8730	.8680 .8610	.090	.187 .172	
	−32	1	1.468 1.424	1.390	.9990 .9985	.9990 .9980	.9930 .9860	.110	.218 .203	

** −5 SIZE MUST BE INSTALLED USING A TORQUE CONTROLLED HEX KEY.

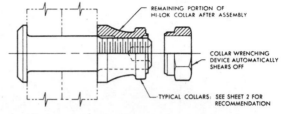

REMAINING PORTION OF
HI-LOK COLLAR AFTER ASSEMBLY

COLLAR WRENCHING
DEVICE AUTOMATICALLY
SHEARS OFF

TYPICAL COLLARS: SEE SHEET 2 FOR
RECOMMENDATION

HI-LOK PIN AND COLLAR AFTER ASSEMBLY

R RAD.	S CHAMFER REF.	THREAD	SOCKET			DOUBLE SHEAR POUNDS MINIMUM	TENSION POUNDS MINIMUM
			W HEX.	T DEPTH	Y DIA.		
.025 .015	1/32" x 37°	8-32UNJC-3A Modified	.0645 .0635	.135 .115	.090 .075	4,010	1,940
.025 .015	1/32" x 37°	10-32UNJF-3A Modified	.0806 .0791	.135 .115	.119 .104	5,380	2,500
.025 .015	1/32" x 37°	1/4-28UNJF-3A Modified	.0967 .0947	.150 .130	.142 .122	9,300	4,300
.030 .020	3/64" x 37°	5/16-24UNJF-3A Modified	.1295 .1270	.170 .150	.180 .160	14,600	6,300
.030 .020	3/64" x 37°	3/8-24UNJF-3A Modified	.1617 .1582	.200 .180	.217 .197	21,000	8,700
.030 .020	3/64" x 37°	7/16-20UNJF-3A Modified	.1930 .1895	.230 .210	.253 .233	28,600	12,100
.030 .020	3/64" x 37°	1/2-20UNJF-3A Modified	.2242 .2207	.260 .240	.289 .269	37,300	15,300
.040 .025	1/16" x 37°	9/16-18UNJF-3A Modified	.2555 .2520	.290 .270	.326 .306	47,200	19,000
.040 .025	1/16" x 37°	5/8-18UNJF-3A Modified	.2555 .2520	.330 .305	.326 .306	58,300	23,000
.045 .030	1/16" x 37°	3/4-16UNJF-3A Modified	.3185 .3150	.395 .365	.398 .378	83,900	30,700
.050 .035	5/64" x 37°	7/8-14UNJF-3A Modified	.3820 .3780	.455 .425	.471 .451	114,000	45,000
.060 .045	5/64" x 37°	1-12UNJF-3A Modified	.5100 .5040	.580 .550	.618 .598	149,000	60,900

**SEE COLLAR STANDARDS FOR
COLLAR STRENGTHS. LOWER STRENGTH
(PIN OR COLLAR) DETERMINES
SYSTEM STRENGTH.**

U.S. patents 2,882,773; 2,927,491; 2,940,495; 3,027,789; 3,138,987; design patent 191,883; other U.S. and Foreign patents granted and pending; property of Hi-Shear Corporation. "Hi-Lok" and "HL" are Registered Trademarks of Hi-Shear Corporation.

DRAWN	DATE	**hi-Lok® PIN**
Brlej	11-26-62	
APPROVED	**DATE**	PROTRUDING SHEAR HEAD
Cessna	11-26-62	TITANIUM 1/16" GRIP VARIATION
REVISION	**DATE**	**DRAWING NUMBER**
㉛	D. P. S. 3-22-76	**HL10** SHEET 1 OF 2

GENERAL NOTES:
1. Concentricity: "A" to "D" diameter within .010 FIR.
2. Dimensions to be met after finish.
3. Surface texture per ANSI-46.1.
4. Hole preparation per NAS618.
5. Use HL110 for oversize replacement.
6. Maximum "D" diameter may be increased by .0002 to allow for solid film or aluminum coating application.
7. Dimensions to be met before finish for "VY" code only.

CODE:
First dash number indicates nominal diameter in 1/32nds.
Second dash number indicates maximum grip in 1/16ths.
See "Finish" note for explanation of code letters.

MATERIAL: 6AL-4V titanium alloy per Spec. AMS4928 or AMS4967.

HEAT TREAT: 95,000 psi shear minimum.

To prevent seizing and galling, the following combinations are recommended.

FINISH:

RECOMMENDED COLLARS

HL10V-( )-( ) = Cetyl alcohol lube per Hi-Shear Spec. 305. ⎯ HL70, HL79, HL82, HL94K, HL94V, HL97K, HL97V, HL379V, HL379Y

HL10VAP-( )-( ) = Hi-Kote I aluminum coating per Hi-Shear Spec. 294 and cetyl alcohol lube per Hi-Shear Spec. 305. ⎯ HL70, HL79, HL82, HL94, HL97

HL10VAZ-( )-( ) = Hi-Kote I aluminum coating per Hi-Shear Spec. 294 with color code black on thread end, and cetyl alcohol lube per Hi-Shear Spec. 305. ⎯ HL70, HL79, HL82, HL94, HL97

HL10VF-( )-( ) = Surface coating per Hi-Shear Spec. 306, Type I, color blue, and cetyl alcohol lube per Hi-Shear Spec. 305. ⎯ HL70, HL79, HL82, HL94K, HL94V, HL97K, HL97V, HL379V, HL379Y

HL10VLJ-( )-( ) = Surface coating per Hi-Shear Spec. 306, Type II, and solid film lube per MIL-L-8937. ⎯ HL70, HL79, HL82, HL94, HL97

HL10VLV-( )-( ) = Phosphate fluoride treat and Esna-Lube No. 382 (Everlube Corp.). ⎯ HL70, HL79, HL82, HL379, HL379V, HL379Y

®

HL10VR-( )-( ) = Surface coating per Hi-Shear Spec. 306, Type II, and solid film lube per "Electrofilm" 4396. ⎯ HL70, HL79, HL82, HL94, HL97

HL10VRA-( )-( ) = Phosphate fluoride treat with color code red on thread end and cetyl alcohol lube per Hi-Shear Spec. 305. ⎯ HL70, HL79, HL82, HL94K, HL94V, HL97K, HL97V, HL379V, HL379Y

HL10VSY-( )-( ) = Phosphate fluoride treat, solid film lube per MIL-L-8937 and color code red on thread end. ⎯ HL70, HL79, HL82, HL94, HL97, HL379, HL379V, HL379Y

HL10VT-( )-( ) = Surface coating per Hi-Shear Spec. 306, Type I, color pink, and cetyl alcohol lube per Hi-Shear Spec. 305. ⎯ HL70, HL79, HL82, HL94V, HL94K, HL97K, HL97V, HL379V, HL379Y

HL10VTA-( )-( ) = Anodize Ti-Shield III and Hi-Kote II solid film lube per Hi-Shear Spec. 292 plus cetyl alcohol lube per Hi-Shear Spec. 305. ⎯ HL70, HL79, HL82, HL94, HL97

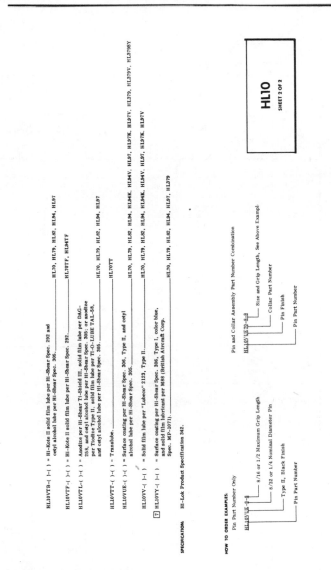

HL10VTB-( )-( ) = Hi-Kote II solid film lube per Hi-Shear Spec. 292 and
cetyl alcohol lube per Hi-Shear Spec. 305. _____ HL70, HL79, HL82, HL94, HL97

HL10VTF-( )-( ) = Hi-Kote II solid film lube per Hi-Shear Spec. 292. _____ HL70TF, HL94TF

HL10VTL-( )-( ) = Anodize per Hi-Shear Ti-Shield III, solid film lube per DAG-
258, and cetyl alcohol lube per Hi-Shear Spec. 305; or anodize
per Tiodize Type II, solid film lube per Ti-O-LUBE TAL-58,
and cetyl alcohol lube per Hi-Shear Spec. 305. _____ HL70, HL79, HL82, HL94, HL97

HL10VTT-( )-( ) = Translube. _____ HL70TT

HL10VUE-( )-( ) = Surface coating per Hi-Shear Spec. 306, Type II, and cetyl
alcohol lube per Hi-Shear Spec. 305. _____ HL70, HL79, HL82, HL94, HL94K, HL94V, HL97, HL97K, HL97V, HL379, HL379V, HL379SY

HL10VV-( )-( ) = Solid film lube per "Lubeco" 2123, Type II. _____ HL70, HL79, HL82, HL94, HL94K, HL94V, HL97, HL97K, HL97V

[T] HL10VV-( )-( ) = Surface coating per Hi-Shear Spec. 306, Type I, color blue,
and solid film lubricant per M86 (British Aircraft Corp.
Spec. MF-1071). _____ HL70, HL79, HL82, HL94, HL97, HL379

SPECIFICATION: Hi-Lok Product Specification 342.

HOW TO ORDER EXAMPLES:

Pin Part Number Only

HL10VUE-8-8
  │   │ └─ 8/16 or 1/2 Maximum Grip Length
  │   └─ 8/32 or 1/4 Nominal Diameter Pin
  └─ Type II, Black Finish
  └─ Pin Part Number

Pin and Collar Assembly Part Number Combination

HL10VUE70-8-8
  │   │ └─ Size and Grip Length, See Above Example
  │   └─ Collar Part Number
  │ └─ Pin Finish
  └─ Pin Part Number

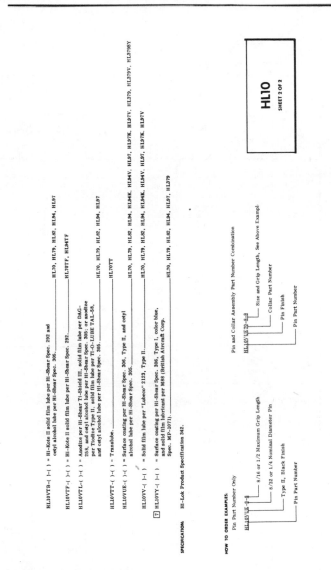

HL10

SHEET 2 OF 2

hi-lok® hi-tigue® PRODUCTS

2600 SKYPARK DRIVE, TORRANCE, CALIFORNIA 90509

						HI-LOK® HI-TIGUE®
HI-LOK HI-TIGUE PIN PART NO.	PIN HEAD STYLE APPLICATION	MATERIAL	HEAT TREAT	SHANK DIA. TOL.	SUGGESTED MAXIMUM TEMP. FOR USE	GRIP VARIATION
HLT10	Protruding —— Shear	6Al–4V Titanium Alloy	95,000 psi Shear Minimum	.001	600°	1/16"
HLT11	100° Flush Crown Shear	6Al–4V Titanium Alloy	95,000 psi Shear Minimum	.001	600°	1/16"
HLT12	Protruding —— Tension	6Al–4V Titanium Alloy	160,000 psi Tensile Minimum	.001	600°	1/16"
HLT13	100° Flush MS24694 Tension	6Al–4V Titanium Alloy	160,000 psi Tensile Minimum	.001	600°	1/16"
HLT18	Protruding —— Shear	Alloy Steel	95,000 psi Shear Minimum	.001	450°	1/16"
HLT19	100° Flush Crown Shear	Alloy Steel	95,000 psi Shear Minimum	.001	450°	1/16"
HLT22	Protruding —— Shear	6Al–6V–2Sn Titanium Alloy	108,000 psi Shear Minimum	.001	600°	1/16"
HLT23	100° Flush Crown Shear	6Al–6V–2Sn Titanium Alloy	108,000 psi Shear Minimum	.001	600°	1/16"
HLT24	Protruding —— Tension	6Al–6V–2Sn Titanium Alloy	180,000–200,000 psi Tensile	.001	600°	1/16"
HLT25	100° Flush MS24694 Tension	6Al–6V–2Sn Titanium Alloy	180,000–200,000 psi Tensile	.001	600°	1/16"
HLT314	Protruding —— Shear	H–11 Steel Alloy	132,000 psi Shear Minimum	.0010	900°	1/16"
HLT315	100° Flush —— Shear	H–11 Steel Alloy	132,000 psi Shear Minimum	.0010	900°	1/16"

PIN IDENTIFICATION CHART

RECOMMENDED COMPANION HI-LOK HI-TIGUE COLLARS		NEXT OVERSIZE	CHARACTERISTICS
HLT70 HLT71	HLT94 HLT97	HLT110	Used where weight conservation and high fatigue life is critical. Pins are designed for easy installation in interference fit holes. Anti-galling finish available for use with all types of Hi-Lok Hi-Tigue collar materials.
HLT70 HLT71	HLT94 HLT97	HLT111	Used where weight conservation and high fatigue life is critical. Pins are designed for easy installation in interference fit holes. Anti-galling finish available for use with all types of Hi-Lok Hi-Tigue collar materials.
HLT78 HLT87		HLT112	Used where weight conservation and high fatigue life is critical. Pins are designed for easy installation in interference fit holes. Anti-galling finish available for use with all types of Hi-Lok Hi-Tigue collar materials.
HLT78 HLT87		HLT113	Used where weight conservation and high fatigue life is critical. Pins are designed for each installation in interference fit holes. Anti-galling finish available for use with all types of Hi-Lok Hi-Tigue collar materials.
HLT70 HLT71	HLT94 HLT97	HLT118	Pins are designed for easy installation in interference fit holes.
HLT70 HLT71	HLT94 HLT97	HLT119	Pins are designed for easy installation in interference fit holes.
HLT70 HLT71	HLT94 HLT97	HLT122	Same as HLT10 except for material and heat treat.
HLT70 HLT71	HLT94 HLT97	HLT123	Same as HLT11 except for material and heat treat.
HLT78 HLT87		HLT124	Same as HLT12 except for material and heat treat.
HLT78 HLT87		HLT125	Same as HLT13 except for material and heat treat.
HLT73		HLT414	Used where very high shear and high fatigue life is critical. Pins are designed for easy installation in interference fit holes.
HLT73		HLT415	Used where very high shear and high fatigue life is critical. Pins are designed for easy installation in interference fit holes.

hi-lok® hi-tigue® PRODUCTS

2600 SKYPARK DRIVE, TORRANCE, CALIFORNIA 90509

							HI-LOK® HI-TIGUE® PIN
HI-LOK HI-TIGUE PIN PART NO.	PIN HEAD STYLE APPLICATION	MATERIAL	HEAT TREAT	SHANK DIA. TOL.	SUGGESTED MAXIMUM TEMP. FOR USE	GRIP VARIATION	
HLT318	Protruding ——— Shear	Alloy Steel	95,000 psi Shear Minimum	.0010	450°	1/16"	
HLT319	100° Flush ——— Shear	Alloy Steel	95,000 psi Shear Minimum	.0010	450°	1/16"	
HLT410	Protruding ——— Shear	6Al-4V Titanium Alloy	95,000 psi Shear Minimum	.0005	600°	1/16"	
HLT411	100° Flush ——— Shear	6Al-4V Titanium Alloy	95,000 psi Shear Minimum	.0005	600°	1/16"	
HLT412	Protruding ——— Tension	6Al-4V Titanium Alloy	160,000 psi Tensile Minimum	.0005	600°	1/16"	
HLT413	100° Flush ——— Tension	6Al-4V Titanium Alloy	160,000 psi Tensile Minimum	.0005	600°	1/16"	
HLT510	Protruding ——— Shear	6Al-4V Titanium Alloy	95,000 psi Shear Minimum	.001	450°	1/16"	
HLT511	100° Flush Crown Shear	6Al-4V Titanium Alloy	95,000 psi Shear Minimum	.001	450°	1/16"	
HLT512	Protruding ——— Tension	6Al-4V Titanium Alloy	160,000 psi Shear Minimum	.001	450°	1/16"	
HLT513	100° Flush MS24694 Tension	6Al-4V Titanium Alloy	160,000 psi Tensile Minimum	.001	450°	1/16"	
HLT803	70° Flush Crown Shear	6Al-4V Titanium Alloy	95,000 psi Shear Minimum	.0010	600°	1/16"	

STANDARDS
MANUAL

IDENTIFICATION CHART

RECOMMENDED COMPANION HI-LOK HI-TIGUE COLLARS	NEXT OVERSIZE	CHARACTERISTICS
HLT70 HLT94 HLT71 HLT97	————	Used where high fatigue life is critical. Pins are designed for easy installation in interference fit holes.
HLT70 HLT94 HLT71 HLT97	————	Used where high fatigue life is critical. Pins are designed for easy installation in interference fit holes.
HLT70 HLT94 HLT71 HLT97	HLT110	Same as HLT10 except diameter tolerance.
HLT70 HLT94 HLT71 HLT97	HLT109	Same as HLT11 except diameter tolerance.
HLT78 HLT86	HLT112	Same as HLT12 except diameter tolerance.
HLT78 HLT86	HLT113	Same as HLT13 except diameter tolerance.
HLT70 HLT94 HLT71 HLT97	————	Same as HLT10 except finish with cadmium plate.
HLT70 HLT94 HLT71 HLT97	————	Same as HLT11 except finish with cadmium plate.
HLT78 HLT87	————	Same as HLT13 except finish with cadmium plate.
HLT78 HLT87	————	Same as HLT13 except finish with cadmium plate.
HLT1070	HLT807	Used where weight conservation and high fatigue life is critical. Designed for easy installation in interference fit holes with 82° countersinks for head interference also.

STANDARDS COMMITTEE FOR
HI-LOK® HI-TIGUE® PRODUCTS
2600 SKYPARK DRIVE, TORRANCE, CALIFORNIA 90509

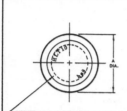

INDENTED HEAD MARKING MAXIMUM DEPTH .010"
"hs" indicates HI-SHEAR trademark.
"VS" indicates VOI-SHAN trademark.
"SPS" indicates STANDARD PRESSED STEEL trademark.
The number or numbers following the trademark indicate
first dash number.

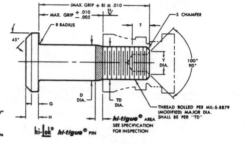

hi-lok® hi-tigue® PIN

FIRST DASH NO.	NOM. DIA.	A DIA.	B REF.	D DIA. WITHOUT SOLID FILM LUBE	D DIA. WITH SOLID FILM LUBE	TD DIA.	G REF.	H	R RAD.	
– 5	5/32	.262 .242	.312	.1695 .1690	.1695 .1685	.1595 .1570	.020	.047 .037	.025 .015	
– 6	3/16	.315 .295	.325	.1955 .1950	.1965 .1945	.1840 .1810	.025	.055 .045	.025 .015	
– 8	1/4	.412 .387	.395	.2555 .2550	.2555 .2545	.2440 .2410	.030	.069 .059	.025 .015	
– 10	5/16	.505 .475	.500	.3180 .3175	.3180 .3170	.3060 .3020	.035	.078 .068	.030 .020	
– 12	3/8	.600 .565	.545	.3805 .3800	.3805 .3795	.3680 .3640	.040	.088 .078	.030 .020	
– 14	7/16	.676 .641	.635	.4430 .4425	.4430 .4420	.4310 .4260	.045	.105 .093	.030 .020	
– 16	1/2	.770 .735	.685	.5055 .5050	.5055 .5045	.4930 .4880	.050	.115 .103	.030 .020	

① **GENERAL NOTES:**
1. Concentricity: "A" to "D" diameter within .010 FIR.
2. Dimensions to be met after finish.
3. Surface texture per ANSI B46.1.
4. Hole preparation per NAS618 (Column "B") for interference application.
5. Use HLT110 for oversize replacement.
6. Install per Hi-Shear Spec. 299.
7. Minimum required for head and Hi-Tigue feature.

MATERIAL: 6Al-4V titanium alloy per Spec. AMS4928 or AMS4967.

HEAT TREAT: 95,000 psi shear minimum.

FINISH: HLT10-( )-( )   = Cetyl alcohol lube per Hi-Shear Spec. 305.
HLT10AP-( )-( ) = Hi-Kote 1 per Hi-Shear Spec. 294, and cetyl alcohol
                lube per Hi-Shear Spec. 305.
HLT10TB-( )-( ) = Hi-Kote 2 and cetyl alcohol lube per Hi-Shear Spec.
                305.

SPECIFICATION: Hi-Lok Hi-Tigue Product Specification 342.

① **HI-SHEAR CORPORATION, U.S.A.** (Patent Holder) U.S. Federal Code I.D. No. 73187
Division of Hi-Shear Industries Inc.
VOI-SHAN, Division of VSI Corp., U.S.A. (Licensee) U.S. Federal Code I.D. No. 92215
SPS TECHNOLOGIES, U.S.A. (Licensee) U.S. Federal Code I.D. No. 56878
LITTON FASTENING SYSTEMS, U.S.A.
Division of Litton Systems, Inc. (Licensee) U.S. Federal Code I.D. No. 97928

KAMAX-WERKE, Germany (Licensee)
Rudolph Kellerman GmbH & Co.
ST. CHAMOND-GRANAT, S.A. France (Licensee)
TOKYO SCREW COMPANY, Japan (Licensee)

REMAINING PORTION OF HI-LOK
HI-TIGUE COLLAR AFTER ASSEMBLY

COLLAR WRENCHING
DEVICE AUTOMATICALLY
SHEARS OFF

TYPICAL COLLARS: HLT70, HLT71,
HLT94, HLT97

hi-lok® hi-tigue® PIN AND COLLAR AFTER ASSEMBLY

SEE COLLAR STANDARDS FOR
COLLAR STRENGTHS. LOWER STRENGTH
(PIN OR COLLAR) DETERMINES
SYSTEM STRENGTH.

S CHAMFER REF.	THREAD	SOCKET			DOUBLE SHEAR POUNDS MINIMUM	TENSION POUNDS MINIMUM	⑦ MIN. GRIP LENGTH
		W HEX.	T DEPTH	Y DIA.			
1/32" x 37°	8–32UNJC–3A Modified	.0645 .0635	.100 ①.080	.090 .075	4,210	1,940	–2
1/32" x 37°	10–32UNJF–3A Modified	.0806 .0791	.100 .080	.119 .104	5,550	2,500	–2
1/32" x 37°	1/4–28UNJF–3A Modified	.0967 .0947	.110 .090	.142 .122	9,620	4,300	–2
3/64" x 37°	5/16–24UNJF–3A Modified	.1295 .1270	.130 .110	.160 .160	14,890	6,300	–2
3/64" x 37°	3/8–24UNJF–3A Modified	.1617 .1582	.160 .140	.217 .197	21,430	8,700	–3
3/64" x 37°	7/16–20UNJF–3A Modified	.1930 .1895	.190 .170	.253 .233	29,000	12,100	–4
3/64" x 37°	1/2–20UNJF–3A Modified	.2242 .2207	.220 .200	.289 .269	37,900	15,300	–4

CODE: First dash number indicates nominal diameter in 32nds.
Second dash number indicates maximum grip in 16ths.
See "Finish" note for explanation of code letters.

HOW TO ORDER EXAMPLES:

Pin Part Number Only
HLT10–8–8
└── 8/16 or 1/2 Maximum Grip Length
└── 8/32 or 1/4 Nominal Diameter Pin
└── Pin Part Number

Pin and Collar Assembly Part Number Combination
HLT1070–8–8
└── Size and Grip Length, See Above Example
└── Collar Part Number
└── Pin Part Number

U.S. patents 3,138,987; 3,390,906; 3,578,367; and
foreign patents. "Hi-Lok," "HL," "Hi-Tigue," and "HLT"
are Registered Trademarks of Hi-Shear Corporation.

DRAWN VAN	DATE 6-28-68
APPROVED R. TING	DATE 7-25-68
REVISION ⑨	DATE D. P. S. 10-29-81

hi-lok® hi-tigue® PIN
PROTRUDING SHEAR HEAD
TITANIUM
1/16" GRIP VARIATION

DRAWING NUMBER
HLT10

STANDARDS COMMITTEE
FOR HI-LOK® PRODUCTS
2600 SKYPARK DRIVE, TORRANCE, CALIFORNIA 90509

HI-LOK COLLAR

HI-LOK COLLAR PART NO.	COLLAR MATERIAL	COLLAR FINISH COLOR OR PLATING	WASHER MATERIAL	WASHER FINISH COLOR OR PLATING	SUGGESTED MAXIMUM TEMP. FOR USE	GRIP VARIATION
HL70	2024-T6 Aluminum Alloy	See Drawing	2024 or 5052 Aluminum Alloy	Blue or Grey	300°F	1/16"
HL75	303 Series Stainless Steel	See Drawing	17-4PH, 17-7PH or PH15-7Mo Stainless Steel	See Drawing	700°F or Sub. to Finish	1/16"
HL77	2024-T6 Aluminum Alloy	See Drawing	2024 or 5052 Aluminum Alloy	Black	300°F	1/16"
HL78	A-286 Hi-Temp. Alloy	See Drawing	300 Series Stainless Steel	See Drawing	1200°F or Sub. to Finish	1/16"
HL79	2024-T6 Aluminum Alloy	Red	N/A	N/A	300°F	1/16"
HL82	2024-T6 Aluminum Alloy	See Drawing	17-4PH, 17-7PH or PH15-7Mo Stainless Steel	See Drawing	300°F	1/16"
HL87	303 Series Stainless Steel	See Drawing	300 Series Stainless Steel	Cadmium Plate	700°F or Sub. to Finish	1/16"
HL89	17-4PH Stainless Steel	See Drawing	17-4PH, 17-7PH or PH15-7Mo Stainless Steel	See Drawing	700°F or Sub. to Finish	1/16"
HL182	2024-T6 Aluminum Alloy	See Drawing	17-4PH, 17-7PH or PH15-7Mo Stainless Steel	See Drawing	300°F	1/16"
HL198	6Al-4V Titanium Alloy	See Drawing	300 Series Stainless Steel	See Drawing	750°F or Sub. to Finish	1/16"
HL199	6Al-4V Titanium Alloy	See Drawing	300 Series Stainless Steel	See Drawing	750°F or Sub. to Finish	1/16"
HL273	17-4PH Stainless Steel	See Drawing	N/A	N/A	700°F or Sub. to Finish	1/16"
HL379	6Al-4V Titanium Alloy	See Drawing	300 Series Stainless Steel	See Drawing	750°F or Sub. to Finish	1/16"

HI-SHEAR CORPORATION (Patent Holder) — Federal Code Ident. No. 73197
VOI-SHAN DIV., VSI CORP. (Licensee) — Federal Code Ident. No. 92215
STANDARD PRESSED STEEL CO. (Licensee) — Federal Code Ident. No. 56878

IDENTIFICATION CHART   Issue Date: November 1972

APPLICATION	NEXT OVERSIZE	CHARACTERISTICS
Shear	HL79 or HL80	For use with shear head pins except those made of aluminum alloy. Optional washer.
Tension	HL375	Self-aligning collar assembly. For use on sloped surfaces up to 7° maximum. Fits standard and 1/64" oversize tension head pins.
Shear	HL377	For use with aluminum alloy pins in shear applications. Optional washer.
Tension	HL278	Used in high temperature applications. Anti-galling lubricant available for use in titanium pins. Optional washer.
Shear	HL84	For standard and 1/64" oversize for HL70. For use with Hi-Lok Automatic Feed Driver Tools and shear head pins except those made of aluminum alloy.
Shear	HL382	Self-aligning collar assembly. For use on sloped surfaces up to 7° maximum. Fits standard and 1/64" oversize pins. Use with shear head pins except those made of aluminum alloy.
Tension	HL93	For standard and 1/64" oversize for HL86. Optional washer.
Tension	HL289	Self-aligning collar assembly. For use on sloped surfaces up to 7° maximum. Fits standard and 1/64" oversize tension head pins.
Shear	—	Self-aligning collar assembly. For use on sloped surfaces up to 7° maximum. Fits standard and 1/64" oversize aluminum alloy pins.
Tension	—	For use on standard and 1/64" oversize tension head pins. Optional washer.
Special	—	Special application.
Tension	HL373	For standard and 1/64" oversize for HL73.
Shear	—	For use on standard and 1/64" oversize shear head pins.

STANDARDS COMMITTEE
FOR HI-LOK® PRODUCTS
2800 SKYPARK DRIVE, TORRANCE, CALIFORNIA 90509

HI-SHEAR CORPORATION (Patent Holder) — Federal Code Ident. No. 73197
VOI-SHAN DIV., VSI CORP. (Licensee) — Federal Code Ident. No. 92215
STANDARD PRESSED STEEL CO. (Licensee) — Federal Code Ident. No. 56878

STANDARDS
MANUAL

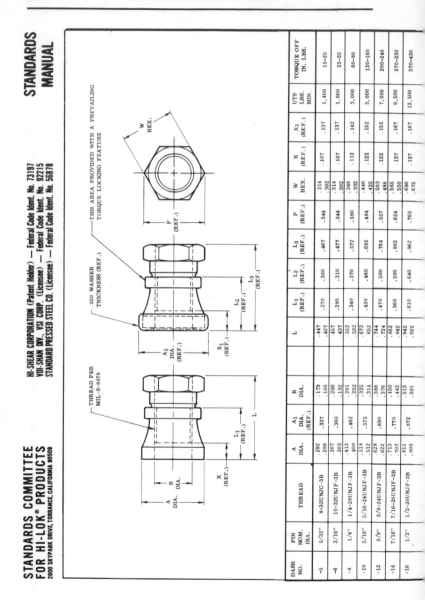

DASH NO.	PIN NOM. DIA.	THREAD	A DIA.	A_1 DIA. (REF.)	B DIA.	L	L_1 (REF.)	L_2 (REF.)	L_3 (REF.)	P (REF.)	W HEX.	X (REF.)	X_1 (REF.)	UTS LBS. MIN.	TORQUE OFF IN. LBS.
-5	5/32"	8-32UNJC-3B	.292 .288	.337	.173 .166	.447 .427	.270	.300	.467	.344	.314 .302	.107	.137	1,400	15-25
-6	3/16"	10-32UNJF-3B	.307 .303	.360	.200 .192	.457 .437	.280	.310	.477	.344	.314 .302	.107	.137	1,600	25-35
-8	1/4"	1/4-28UNJF-3B	.412 .408	.462	.261 .252	.552 .532	.340	.370	.572	.380	.346 .332	.112	.142	3,000	60-80
-10	5/16"	5/16-24UNJF-3B	.518 .512	.575	.325 .314	.672 .652	.430	.460	.692	.484	.440 .425	.122	.152	5,000	130-160
-12	3/8"	3/8-24UNJF-3B	.628 .622	.690	.388 .376	.744 .724	.470	.500	.764	.557	.503 .488	.122	.152	7,000	200-240
-14	7/16"	7/16-20UNJF-3B	.713 .707	.770	.450 .442	.862 .842	.560	.590	.882	.624	.565 .550	.137	.167	9,500	270-330
-16	1/2"	1/2-20UNJF-3B	.815 .809	.872	.513 .501	.942 .922	.610	.640	.962	.763	.690 .675	.137	.167	12,500	370-430

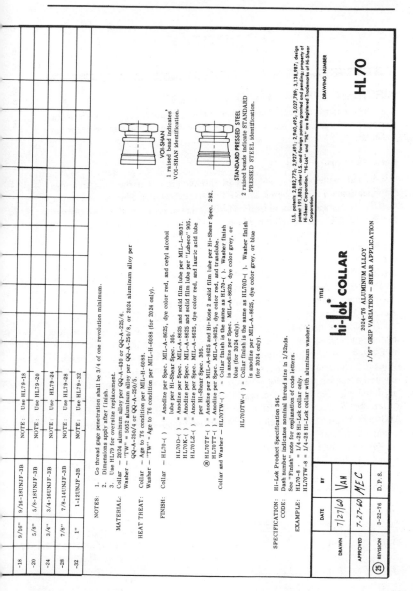

–18	9/16"	9/16–18UNJF-3B	NOTE: Use HL79-18
–20	5/8"	5/8–18UNJF-3B	NOTE: Use HL79-20
–24	3/4"	3/4–16UNJF-3B	NOTE: Use HL79-24
–28	7/8"	7/8–14UNJF-3B	NOTE: Use HL79-28
–32	1"	1–12UNJF-3B	NOTE: Use HL79-32

NOTES:
1. Go thread gage penetration shall be 3/4 of one revolution minimum.
2. Dimensions apply after finish.
3. Use HL79 for oversize replacement.

MATERIAL: Collar — 2024 aluminum alloy per QQ-A-430 or QQ-A-225/6.
Washer — "TW" = 5052 aluminum alloy per QQ-A-250/8, or 2024 aluminum alloy per QQ-A-250/4 or QQ-A-250/5.

HEAT TREAT: Collar — Age to T6 condition per MIL-H-6088.
Washer — "TW" = Age to T6 condition per MIL-H-6088 (for 2024 only).

FINISH: Collar — HL70-( ) = Anodize per Spec. MIL-A-8625, dye color red, and cetyl alcohol lube per Hi-Shear Spec. 305.
HL70LD-( ) = Anodize per Spec. MIL-A-8625 and solid film lube per MIL-L-8937.
HL70K-( ) = Anodize per Spec. MIL-A-8625 and solid film lube per "Lubeco" 905.
HL70LZ-( ) = Anodize per Spec. MIL-A-8625, dye color red, and lauric acid lube per Hi-Shear Spec. 305.
HL70TF-( ) = Anodize per MIL-A-8625 and Hi-Kote 2 solid film lube per Hi-Shear Spec. 292.
HL70TT-( ) = Anodize per Spec. MIL-A-8625, dye color red, and translube.
Collar and Washer — HL70TW-( ) = Collar finish is the same as HL70-( ). Washer finish is anodize per Spec. MIL-A-8625, dye color grey, or blue (for 2024 only).
HL70DTW-( ) = Collar finish is the same as HL70D-( ). Washer finish is anodize per MIL-A-8625, dye color grey, or blue (for 2024 only).

SPECIFICATION: Hi-Lok Product Specification 345.
CODE: Dash number indicates nominal thread size in 1/32nds.
See "Finish" note for explanation of code letters.
EXAMPLE: HL70-8 . = 1/4-28 Hi-Lok collar only.
HL70TW-8 = 1/4-28 Hi-Lok collar with aluminum washer.

VOI-SHAN
1 raised bead indicates
VOI-SHAN identification.

STANDARD PRESSED STEEL
2 raised beads indicate STANDARD
PRESSED STEEL identification.

hi-Lok® COLLAR

TITLE

2024-T6 ALUMINUM ALLOY
1/16" GRIP VARIATION — SHEAR APPLICATION

U.S. patents 2,883,773; 2,927,491; 2,940,495; 3,027,789; 3,138,987, design patent 191,883; other U.S. and foreign patents granted and pending; property of Hi-Shear Corporation. "Hi-Lok" and "HK" are Registered Trademarks of Hi-Shear Corporation.

DRAWING NUMBER

HL70

	DATE	BY
DRAWN	7/27/60	VAN
APPROVED	7-27-60	MEC
㉕ REVISION	3-22-76	D. P. S.

Appendix

AIRCRAFT THREAD AND DRILL SIZES

The screw and nut combination is probably the most used of machine elements. Certain thread series have, through their extensive use, come to be known as "standard."

Classification of Threads

Aircraft bolts, screws, and nuts are threaded in either the NC (American National Coarse) thread series, the NF (American National Fine) thread series, the UNC (American Standard Unified Coarse) thread series, or the UNF (American Standard Unified Fine) thread series. Although they are interchangeable there is one difference between the American national series and the American Standard Unified series that should be pointed out. In the 1-inch diameter size, the NF thread specified 14 threads per inch (1-14NF), while the UNF thread specifies 12 threads per inch (1-12UNF). Both type threads are designated by the number of times the incline (threads) rotates around a 1-inch length of a given diameter bolt or screw. For example, a 4-28 thread indicates that a 1/4-inch diameter bolt has 28 threads in 1 inch of its threaded length (Fig. A-1).

Threads are also designated by Class of fit. The Class of a thread indicates the tolerance allowed in manufacturing. Class 1 is a loose fit, Class 2 is a free fit, Class 3 is a medium fit, and Class 4 is a close fit. **Aircraft bolts are almost always manufactured in the Class 3, medium fit.** A Class 4 fit requires a wrench to turn the nut onto a bolt whereas a Class 1 fit can easily be turned with the fingers. Generally aircraft screws are manufactured with a Class 2 thread fit for ease of assembly. The general purpose aircraft bolt, AN3 thru AN20 has UNF-3 threads (American Standard Unified Fine, Class 3, medium fit).

Bolts and nuts are also produced with right-hand and left-hand threads. A right-hand thread tightens when turned clockwise; a left-hand thread tightens when turned counterclockwise. Except in special cases, all aircraft bolts have right hand threads.

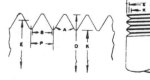 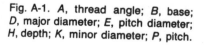

Fig. A-1. *A*, thread angle; *B*, base; *D*, major diameter; *E*, pitch diameter; *H*, depth; *K*, minor diameter; *P*, pitch.

TAP DRILL SIZES

NATIONAL COARSE THREAD SERIES MEDIUM FIT, CLASS 3 (NC)

Size and threads	Dia. of body	Body drill	Preferred dia. of hole	Tap drill
1–64	.073	47	.0575	No. 53
2–56	.086	42	.0682	No. 51
3–48	.099	37	.078	5⁄64 in.
4–40	.112	31	.0866	No. 44
5–40	.125	29	.0995	No. 39
6–32	.138	27	.1063	No. 36
8–32	.164	18	.1324	No. 29
10–24	.190	10	.1476	No. 26
12–24	.216	2	.1732	No. 17
1⁄4–20	.250	1⁄4	.1990	No. 8
5⁄16–18	.3125	5⁄16	.2559	F
3⁄8–16	.375	3⁄8	.3110	5⁄16 in.
7⁄16–14	.4375	7⁄16	.3642	U
1⁄2–13	.500	1⁄2	.4219	27⁄64 in.
9⁄16–12	.5625	9⁄16	.4776	31⁄64
5⁄8–11	.625	5⁄8	.5315	17⁄32 in.
3⁄4–10	.750	3⁄4	.6480	41⁄64 in.
7⁄8–9	.875	7⁄8	.7307	49⁄64 in.
1–8	1.000	1	.8376	7⁄8 in.

NATIONAL FINE THREAD SERIES MEDIUM FIT, CLASS 3 (NF)

Size and threads	Dia. of body	Body drill	Preferred dia. of hole	Tap drill
0–80	.060	52	.0472	3⁄64 in.
1–72	.073	47	.0591	No. 53
2–64	.086	42	.0700	No. 50
3–56	.099	37	.0810	No. 46
4–48	.112	31	.0911	No. 42
5–44	.125	29	.1024	No. 38
6–40	.138	27	.113	No. 33
8–36	.164	18	.136	No. 29
10–32	.190	10	.159	No. 21
12–28	.216	2	.180	No. 15
1⁄4–28	.250	F	.213	No. 3
5⁄16–24	.3125	5⁄16	.2703	I
3⁄8–24	.375	3⁄8	.332	Q
7⁄16–20	.4375	7⁄16	.386	W
1⁄2–20	.500	1⁄2	.449	7⁄16 in.
9⁄16–18	.5625	9⁄16	.506	1⁄2 in.
5⁄8–18	.625	5⁄8	.568	9⁄16 in.
3⁄4–16	.750	3⁄4	.6688	11⁄16 in.
7⁄8–14	.875	7⁄8	.7822	51⁄64 in.
1–14	1.000	1	.9072	59⁄64 in.

NATIONAL TAPER PIPE THREAD

Size pipe thread, in.	No. of threads per inch	Outside dia. of pipe for threading		Size pipe reamer, in.	Size tap drill, in.
		Decimal inch	Nearest fraction of inch		
1⁄8	27	.405	13⁄32	1⁄8	21⁄64
1⁄4	18	.540	35⁄64	1⁄4	7⁄16
3⁄8	18	.675	43⁄64	3⁄8	9⁄16
1⁄2	14	.840	27⁄32	1⁄2	45⁄64
3⁄4	14	1.050	13⁄64	3⁄4	29⁄32

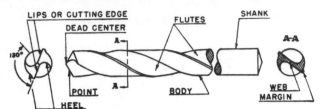

LIPS OR CUTTING EDGE — DEAD CENTER — FLUTES — SHANK — A-A — POINT — HEEL — BODY — WEB — MARGIN

TWIST DRILL SIZES

Decimal equivalent	Fraction	Number or letter	Decimal equivalent	Fraction	Number or letter	Decimal equivalent	Fraction	Number or letter
.0135	...	80	.096	....	41	.2187	7/32	
.0145	...	79	.098	....	40	.221	....	2
.0156	...	78	.0995	....	39	.228	....	1
.016	1/64		.1015	....	38	.234	....	A
.018	...	77	.104	....	37	.2343	15/64	
.020	...	76	.1065	....	36	.238	....	B
.021	...	75	.1093	7/64		.242	....	C
.0225	...	74	.110	....	35	.246	....	D
.024	...	73	.111	....	34	.250	1/4	E
.025	...	72	.113	....	33	.257	....	F
.026	...	71	.116	....	32	.261	....	G
.028	...	70	.120	....	31	.2656	17/64	
.029	...	69	.125	1/8		.266	....	H
.031	...	68	.1285	....	30	.272	....	I
.0313	...	67	.136	....	29	.277	....	J
.032	1/32		.1405	....	28	.281	....	K
.033	...	66	.1406	9/64		.2812	9/32	
.035	...	65	.144	....	27	.290	....	L
.036	...	64	.147	....	26	.295	....	M
.037	...	63	.1495	....	25	.2968	19/64	
.038	...	62	.152	....	24	.302	....	N
.039	...	61	.154	....	23	.3125	5/16	
.040	...	60	.1562	5/32		.316	....	O
.041	...	59	.157	....	22	.323	....	P
.042	...	58	.159	....	21	.3281	21/64	
.043	...	57	.161	....	20	.332	....	Q
.0465	...	56	.166	....	19	.339	....	R
.0468	3/64		.1695	....	18	.3437	11/32	
.052	...	55	.1718	11/64		.348	....	S
.055	...	54	.173	....	17	.358	....	T
.0595	...	53	.177	....	16	.3594	23/64	
.0625	1/16		.180	....	15	.368	....	U
.0635	...	52	.182	....	14	.375	3/8	
.067	...	51	.185	....	13	.377	....	V
.070	...	50	.1875	3/16		.386	....	W
.073	...	49	.189	....	12	.3906	25/64	
.076	...	48	.191	....	11	.397	....	X
.0781	5/64		.1935	....	10	.404	....	Y
.0785	...	47	.196	....	9	.4062	13/32	
.081	...	46	.199	....	8	.413	....	Z
.082	...	45	.201	....	7	.4218	27/64	
.086	...	44	.2031	13/64		.4375	7/16	
.089	...	43	.204	....	6	.4531	29/64	
.0935	...	42	.2055	....	5	.4687	15/32	
.0937	3/32		.209	....	4	.4843	31/64	
			.213	....	3	.500	1/2	

TYPICAL* MECHANICAL PROPERTIES OF WROUGHT ALUMINUM ALLOYS

| Alloy and temper | Tension | | | | Hardness | Shear | Fatigue |
| | Yield strength (set = 0.2 %), psi | Ultimate strength, psi | Elongation, per cent in 2 in. | | Brinell, 500-kg. load 10-mm. ball | Shearing strength, psi | Endurance limit, psi |
			Sheet specimen ($\frac{1}{16}$ in. thick)	Round specimen ($\frac{1}{2}$ in. dia.)			
1100-0	5,000	13,000	35	45	23	9,500	5,000
1100-H12	13,000	15,000	12	25	28	10,000	6,000
1100-H14	14,000	17,000	9	20	32	11,000	7,000
1100-H16	17,000	20,000	6	17	38	12,000	8,500
1100-H18	21,000	24,000	5	15	44	13,000	8,500
3003-0	6,000	16,000	30	40	28	11,000	7,000
3003-H12	15,000	18,000	10	20	35	12,000	8,000
3003-H14	18,000	21,000	8	16	40	14,000	9,000
3003-H16	21,000	25,000	5	14	47	15,000	9,500
3003-H18	25,000	29,000	4	10	55	16,000	.0,000
2017-0	10,000	26,000	20	22	45	18,000	11,000
2017-T4	40,000	62,000	20	22	100	36,000	15,000
Alclad 2017-T4	33,000	56,000	18	..	...	32,000	
2117-T4	24,000	43,000	..	27	70	26,000	13,500
2024-0	10,000	26,000	20	22	42	18,000	12,000
2024-T4	45,000	68,000	19	22	105	41,000	18,000
2024-T36	55,000	70,000	13	..	116	42,000	
Alclad 2024-T	41,000	62,000	18	..	...	40,000	
Alclad 2024-T36	50,000	66,000	11	..	...	41,000	
5052-0	14,000	29,000	25	30	45	18,000	17,000
5052-H12	26,000	34,000	12	18	62	20,000	18,000
5052-H14	29,000	37,000	10	14	67	21,000	19,000
5052-H16	34,000	39,000	8	10	74	23,000	20,000
5052-H18	36,000	41,000	7	8	85	24,000	20,500
6053-0	7,000	16,000	25	35	26	11,000	7,500
6053-T4	20,000	33,000	22	30	65	20,000	10,000
6053-T6	33,000	39,000	14	20	80	24,000	11,000
6061-0	8,000	18,000	22	..	30	12,500	8,000
6061-T4	21,000	35,000	22	..	65	24,000	12,500
6061-T6	39,000	45,000	12	..	95	30,000	12,500
7075-0	15,000	33,000	17	16	60	22,000	
7075-T6	72,000	82,000	11	11	150	49,000	
Alclad 7075-0	14,000	32,000	17	—	—	22,000	
7075-T6	67,000	76,000	11	—	—	46,000	

* These values are *not* guaranteed.

Copyrighted and furnished by courtesy of Aluminum Company of America.

WIRE AND SHEET METAL GAUGE TABLE

NUMBER OF GAUGE	AMERICAN OR BROWN & SHARPE A W G	WASHBURN & MOEN W & M G	BIRMINGHAM OR STUB'S IRON WIRE B W G	U. S. STANDARD FOR PLATE U S G
WIRE & SHEET METAL GAUGES				
7-0		.490		.500
6-0	.580	.461		.468
5-0	.516	.430	.500	.437
4-0	.460	.393	.454	.406
3-0	.409	.362	.425	.375
2-0	.364	.331	.380	.343
0	.324	.306	.340	.312
1	.289	.283	.300	.281
2	.257	.262	.284	.265
3	.229	.243	.259	.250
4	.204	.225	.238	.234
5	.181	.207	.220	.218
6	.162	.192	.203	.203
7	.144	.177	.180	.187
8	.128	.162	.165	.171
9	.114	.148	.148	.156
10	.101	.135	.134	.140
11	.090	.120	.120	.125
12	.080	.105	.109	.109
13	.072	.091	.095	.093
14	.064	.080	.083	.078
15	.057	.072	.072	.070
16	.050	.062	.065	.062
17	.045	.054	.058	.056

NUMBER OF GAUGE	AMERICAN OR BROWN & SHARPE A W G	WASHBURN & MOEN W & M G	BIRMINGHAM OR STUB'S IRON WIRE B W G	U. S. STANDARD FOR PLATE U S G
WIRE & SHEET METAL GAUGES				
18	.040	.047	.049	.050
19	.035	.041	.042	.043
20	.032	.034	.035	.037
21	.028	.031	.032	.034
22	.025	.028	.028	.031
23	.022	.025	.025	.028
24	.020	.023	.022	.025
25	.017	.020	.020	.021
26	.015	.018	.018	.018
27	.014	.017	.016	.017
28	.012	.016	.014	.015
29	.011	.015	.013	.014
30	.010	.014	.012	.012
31	.008	.013	.010	0.10
32	.008	.012	.009	.010
33	.007	.011	.008	.009
34	.006	.010	.007	.008
35	.005	.009	.005	.007
36	.005	.009	.004	.007
37	.004	.008		.006
38	.004	.008		.006
39	.003	.007		
40	.003	.007		

COLORS, FLUID LINES IDENTIFICATION

All bands shall be 1 in. wide and shall encircle the tube.

Bands shall be located near each end of the tube and at such intermediate points as may be necessary to follow through the system.

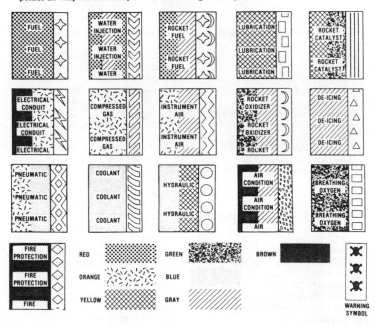

Index